Aryan Italy of the Etruscans

Sanskrit Affiliations of the Etruscan Language

by

ZORAN MASLIĆ

Ithaca Series – Book I

Published by Exile Kings Productions

Copyright © 2019 Zoran Maslić

All rights reserved.

ISBN-13:9780994855114

THE FRONT COVER PICTURE
is a cutout from a photograph that is in PUBLIC DOMAIN .
Title: Detail of two dancers from the Tomb of the Triclinium in the Necropolis of Monterozzi;
The photo shows a fresco from approximately 470 BCE, fresco artist unknown, exhibited in the National Etruscan Museum of Tarquinia, Italy
The work of art depicted in this image and the reproduction thereof are in the public domain worldwide. The reproduction is part of a collection of reproductions compiled by The Yorck Project. The compilation copyright is held by
Zenodot Verlagsgesellschaft mbH
and licensed under the GNU Free Documentation License.
Downloaded from
https://en.wikipedia.org/wiki/File:Etruskischer_Meister_002.jpg

THE BACK COVER PICTURE
is a cutout from a photograph that is in PUBLIC DOMAIN ..
Title:Ear-stud BM GR1980.2-1.42.jpg

Artist   Unknownwikidata:Q4233718

Description: Ear-stud decorated with a rosette surrounded by concentric bands, globules and flowers. Gold with vitreous glass paste insets, Etruscan artwork, 530–480 BC.

Current location: British Museum, Upper floor, room 71, Italy before the Roman Empire, case 27
Source/Photographer: **Marie-Lan Nguyen**, December 16, 2006

Licensing
PUBLIC DOMAIN, PD
https://commons.wikimedia.org/wiki/File:Ear-stud_BM_GR1980.2-1.42.jpg#filelinks
(Accessed on May 1, 2018)

DEDICATION

To my parents Milka and Dragoljub,

and to my son Rastko,

with owe and love!

CONTENTS

Acknowledgments   I

1   It All Started With Prosciutto   1

2   In the Waters of Sanskrit   10

3   Rivers of Tuscany   15

     3.1 First Attempts............16

     3.1.1 Bure..........................16

     3.1.2 Chiana.......................18

     3.1.3 Era.............................20

     3.1.4 Idice...........................20

     3.1.5 Limentra...................21

     3.1.6 Magra........................22

     3.1.7 Marecchia.................23

     3.1.8 Metauro....................25

     3.1.9 Savena.......................26

     3.1.10 Serchio....................27

- 3.1.11 Sieve..................30
- 3.1.12 Tora..................31

3.2. Major Rivers of the Etruscan World 34

- 3.2.1 Arno..................34
- 3.2.1 Marta..................35
- 3.2.1 Po..................38
- 3.2.1 Reno..................40
- 3.2.1 Tiber..................45

3.3 Italian Context, Conclusion..................49

4 Cities of Etruria 54

4.1 Test Reconstructions of City Names..................55

- 4.1.1 Statna..................55
- 4.1.2 Capeva..................58
- 4.1.3 Capena..................59
- 4.1.4 Nepete..................60

4.1.5 Saturnia...................60

4.1.6 Gravisca..................61

4.1.7 Mutina…................62

4.1.8 Narce 64

4.1.9 Parma.....................66

4.2 Dodecapoli.................69

4.2.1 Arretium..................70

4.2.2 Caere........................70

4.2.3 Clevsin.....................73

4.2.4 Curtun......................77

4.2.5 Perusia…................78

4.2.6 Pupluna...................79

4.2.7 Tarchuna.................81

4.2.8 Veia..........................82

4.2.9 Velathri....................82

4.2.10 Velch......................83

4.2.11 Velzna....................84

4.2.12 Vetluna...................90

4.3 Conclusions.............92

5   Etruscan Vocabulary: 95
Reconstructions

5.1 Testing the Waters.........97

5.2 Family Relations and
Social Terminology.............102

5.3 Some Random Etruscan
Words...................................111

5.4 Religious Terms...........128

5.5 Political Terms.............139

5.6 Culture and
Entertainment....................163

5.7 Funerary Customs......170

5.8 Animals........................184

5.9 Vessels, Ceramics.......188

5.10 Names of Months....198

5.11 Words Believed to be
Taken From Other
Languages...........................212

5.12 Words Believed to be of

　　　　Etruscan Origin..................218

　　　　5.13 Names of Famous
　　　　Persons................................230

　　　　5.14 The Name of the
　　　　Etruscans.............................241

6　　　The Conclusion　　　　　　252

7　　　It All Ends With　　　　　　261
　　　　Prosciutto

　　　　Notes　　　　　　　　　　　265

　　　　Index　　　　　　　　　　　351

　　　　Index of Discussed　　　　　365
　　　　Words

ACKNOWLEDGMENTS

While writing this book, I have consulted various scientific and non-scientific works that were available to
me, but one of them was my constant companion -
"The Etruscan Language: An Introduction"
by Giuliano and Larissa Bonfante. It was my teacher and my guide. Its authors became something like my intimate friends who I loved, respected, and frequently disagreed with. The short list of other scholars I admired would be too long to present, but it would have to include Radivoje Pešić, Massimo Pallottino, Vladimir Georgiev, Nancy Thompson de Grummond, Erika Simon...

Since I started the research as an amateur with a journalistic background, Wikipedia provided me with quick essential information on any topic. I needed a snapshot of current opinions.

A huge help came from my mother tongue: all Serbian verbs look like Sanskrit verbs, they are often identical. In that aspect, somehow, we can say that no language is closer to Sanskrit than Serbian.

I extensively used online Sanskrit dictionaries at *sanskritdictionary.com* and *spokensanskrit.de*.

A very special thanks goes to my son Rastko who polished my immigrant English.

POLITICAL WARNING

I use the term Aryan in a manner of Indian or Iranian authors, to denote ancient users of Sanskrit, and their linguistic cousins. Since I reject all racial theories that contaminated this word, the question is why didn't I use the term Indo-European which is widely accepted and politically correct?

The reason for that is simple: the term Indo-European blurs the nature of my discovery.

1 IT ALL STARTED WITH PROSCIUTTO

I was searching the Internet to get inspiration for a science fiction novel I wanted to write. It was supposed to be a sequel to my book, *Northern Guard*, where the only surviving humans are now on a distant planet that was once a penal colony of the mother planet. They live like gods and all the labour is done by the Dogs, a genetically engineered species that is inferior to humans. My main characters are three "Dogs" who are members of a terrorist cell embedded in an official military squad. A bloody war follows and the Dogs lose. The story of the second book was to take place 600 years later. There are no Dogs on that planet, only humans, but my main character gradually discovers that the Dogs killed all humans 500 years earlier. Since the general culture they were born into was human, they continued it with some modifications. They thought of themselves as humans and acted accordingly, thoroughly erasing their uncomfortable past. They even changed their DNA, humanizing themselves more.

All of this was forgotten at the time when my story happened...

So, I searched the Net to get some inspiration from real history and somehow I ended up reading an article about prosciutto. The very word reminds me of my grandfather Risto Tabaković, who passed away when I was six and a half. When it happened, I lost almost all memories of our moments together and felt guilty for the emptiness I had in me. It wasn't until I was twenty-eight when I wept over his death. I can still see prosciuttos hanging from a ceiling in the cellar of his stone house in the Mediterranean town of Bileća. The image is charged with sacred memories of my Yugoslav homeland.

And now, in this article I am reading, they are talking about Italian prosciutto, how many types there are, about measures from the European Union to protect the best types of it. They barely mentioned South-Slavic prosciutto, called 'pršut'. I know it sounds stupid, but I felt insulted, expelled from history. It was like someone dumped a truck of feces on me. "They" set my country on fire, their firefighters poured gasoline on it, "they" threw me across the ocean like in some bad joke and now they found me at the place of my last refuge, in my memories, in the cellar of my grandfather's house.

And they are laughing.

"You know what? It is we who invented prosciutto and it then spread all over the Mediterranean!" I said.

My son said nothing, but I saw in his eyes that he was asking for an additional explanation.

"OK, we were under Rome for hundreds of years, so there is a chance we got it from them, but what if it was us who brought it to Italy in prehistoric times?!"

Then I realized that things are complicated, so I added, "Even if I am not right I will show that they cannot prove their claim!" That sounded good for the moment. I was embarrassed by all the anger I displayed and I went back to the article.

"The word prosciutto is derived from Latin pro (before) + exsuctus (past participle of exsugere "to suck out [the moisture]"); the Portuguese presunto has the same etymology. It is similar to the modern Italian verb prosciugare "to dry thoroughly" (from Latin pro + exsucare "to extract the juices from")." [1]

Damn! It looked convincing. I lost my Sunday searching for proof of an "Eastern origin of prosciutto", but I found nothing. The next day, I decided to examine Tuscany as an eventual place that might offer some evidence of prehistoric prosciutto production. That brought me to the Etruscans, a people who inhabited Tuscany in ancient times. For some reason unknown to me, it was love at first sight. But prosciutto was still my main focus. Then I had a "great idea", inspired by an article I read in a Serbian newspaper long ago. Somebody claimed that the ancient Etruscans were Serbs and they spoke an ancient form of Serbian language! [2] I laughed like a devil! There it is!!! Here is a path to victory! I will avenge our *pršut!* I will walk over western histories like King-Kong, smashing "their houses of styrofoam".

I started reading more about the Etruscans. The names of their cities sounded like names of villages from the Mediterranean part of the former Yugoslavia (Dalmatia, Herzegovina, and Montenegro).

"This will be easy!" I thought.

But when I looked at the Etruscan language, I was not sure it was an ancient form of Serbian but there was something strangely familiar in it. I learned that parts of prehistoric Italy were settled by people from the Balkans.

Etruscan toponyms and language sounded to me closer to my heritage than Latin or contemporary Italian. I read anything I could find about the Etruscans. And the more I read, the more I loved them. And the more I loved them, the more I got obsessed. I forgot about prosciutto. Anger melted and something surprisingly big appeared out of it.

Pain.

Herodotus wrote that the Etruscans came to the Italian Peninsula from Lydia in Asia Minor and settled in the land of Umbrians. But even his account contained anti-Lydian or anti-Etruscan propaganda. According to him, the Lydians had almost the same customs as the Hellenes except that they prostituted their female children![3]

Some others thought that they were natives of Italy. The Etruscans developed from an indigenous culture called Villanovan, which possibly fell under the influence of some mysterious newcomers. They built a chain of cities, they were great in hydraulics, draining nearby marshlands, turning them into agricultural fields, thereby reducing malaria.

Massimo Pallottino wrote that Etruscan thalassocracy or their supremacy at the western Mediterranean Sea stretched from the seventh (possibly the eighth) to the sixth century BC.[4] Their pirate ships scared Greeks, who were also pirates at the time. The Etruscans became wealthy by developing mining and metallurgy, exporting their goods and ore. It is usually thought that their civilization started around the ninth century BC. Etruria proper included Tuscany, western Umbria and northern and central Latium (Lazio), but Etruscans later expanded into the Po valley and the eastern Alps as well as to Campania. After several centuries of the good life, they fell victim to the much smaller Rome.

Rome swallowed the Etruscans and erased their identity, but Rome itself was built on Etruscan foundations. I knew I was idealizing the Etruscans, but I could not help it. I hated the imperial concepts of Rome and loved the Etruscans for everything they did, even for their failure to form a unified state.

Easterners or not, the Etruscans looked lonely to me, misunderstood, in a shadow of our admiration for Greeks and Romans. When I looked at objects of their art, the artifacts from the Villanovan period felt like they were an extension of Vincha (Vinča) culture and generally of the Balkans. Another stage looked Near-Eastern, then you can clearly see "Greek influences". But what won my heart were tomb paintings of dancers - vivid colours, lots of motion, and happiness! That dynamism of composition you cannot find anywhere else in ancient Europe.

In the darkness of tomb chambers, my Etruscans danced! They were bathing in the sunshine. And that sunlight was as beautiful and painful as the sunlight in Mihalkov's film "Burnt by the Sun".

My sorrow for Etruria was profound. They took me like a storm and I felt I had to do something. Maybe, if I believe enough I can resurrect them, or at least give them back their honour, avenge them. I concluded that my best chances were in the field of language because I believed that scholars didn't know much about it. We are told that the Etruscan language is a language isolate, not like any other language known to us. As such, it is classified as non-Indo-European. I never believed that language isolates could even exist, thinking that it must be just about our failure to see connections.

When the book I ordered finally arrived, I discovered that the Etruscan language was well researched. In fact, it was an excellent book that I still hated because it didn't love the Etruscans as much as I did. *"The Etruscan Language: An Introduction"* earned its space at my bedside table and its authors Giuliano and Larissa Bonfante became something like my friends and teachers I frequently disagree with.

They reminded me that I am neither historian nor linguist, but just another amateur who hopes to discover a hidden treasure. Knowing how insufficient I was for the task made me turn to "unsuccessful" professional and amateur theories. None of them convinced me. The Etruscans were Serbs, Etruscans were Turks, Hungarians, Slovenians... Maybe they were all of it, but I did not see it proven, yet I felt that some things in those works must be right.

Since I was at "war", I had to evaluate my weapons. It was very little. As a young man, I was a journalist so I should not be trusting every story that prevails. I had training in techniques and the methodology of scientific research, and I am an artist, which means I might be able to "feel things". That was it. Not much.

But those amateurs kept bothering me. What do they have in common? Well, amateurs mostly compared it with Indo-European languages. So, that is the common thing? Then it crossed my mind that in most Indo-European languages you can find Sanskrit words. Could that be "the lead"? I checked some Etruscan toponyms with the website *spokensanskrit.de* and I didn't find anything. Somebody wrote that people tried to compare Etruscan language with all possible languages, even with Sanskrit! And they all failed! Giuliano and Larissa Bonfante stated:

"Yet Etruscans were pocket of non-Indo-European speakers in an area where almost everyone else spoke an Indo-European language. Like the Basques their language is different from any of their neighbours." [5]

Ellen Macnamara had no doubts, *"Etruscan language does not belong to the Indo-European family of languages, though it was influenced by them at an early date."* [6]

I was stuck, desperate. I decided that I would turn to

dreams and let dreams guide me! You will agree that it was not much of a strategy, but I thought "What the hell! If Mendeleev could do it, why not me?"

That very night I could not sleep, I kept thinking about Etruscans, especially about the picture that Graeme Barker and Tom Rasmussen put on the cover of their book.[7] It shows a relief of a mid-aged Etruscan couple. They lay next to each other, embraced. He looks away, like in some kind of pain. The face of the female is serious and compassionate. She is there for him. By their body language, you understand that there is an unbreakable bond between the two. They go through some kind of trouble where nothing can be done. Maybe he was dying, maybe they lost an adult son or daughter. The feeling of defeat hangs in the air. Maybe it was about dying, but what I saw was a melancholy of vast proportions, caused by the awareness that their world was slipping into a black hole of history.

I guess I did not know how to mourn for Yugoslavia, my homeland that fell apart a decade and a half before. All the sorrow I had in me was projected to the Etruscans. It became love and spread all over Italy. I would go on YouTube and find some Italian folk song, I'd listen to it and I would cry like I was born in Maremma or some Calabrian village, and not in Šamac, Bosnia.

It was already 3:30 AM and my mind raced on Etruscan chariots. When dawn was just about to announce itself, I started falling asleep. And it happened!

The face appeared from the darkness, just a face, no neck, no body. It came slowly and smoothly as if it were a digital effect from an opening sequence of a "reality" TV show. It was the face of a man. His skin was covered with dried mud that was full of cracks, like on frescoes. The image was dark but black and white. And I actually knew that face! It was the face of my friend and co-worker Vipin

Sharma from India, we both worked as video editors on David Cherniack's TV-series "Spiritual Literacy", for a company called Sleeping Giant. I haven't seen Vipin for ages and found out on the Internet that he left Toronto and went back to India where he continued his old career. He is an actor and you can see him in Bollywood movies playing the father of the bride or a similar role. But this Vipin was not really my friend Vipin, but rather some spirit that took Vipin's face to make me comfortable. And the voice was not Vipin's. It was a much deeper and raspier voice but with the same accent. What Vipin-Who-Was-Not-Vipin told me sounded like a joke.

"Sons are not older than fathers," he said slowly, stretching every word.

"What do you mean? Everybody knows that!"

"Sons are not older than fathers!" he repeated in his ceremonial voice.

"Yeah! OK! I know that!" said I. "You mean that the Etruscans are older than the Romans? That is what you mean?"

But Vipin-Who-Was-Not-Vipin had no intention to converse. He backed into the darkness and I woke up.

And that's it?! Oh, no!

But I kept thinking! Etruscan is older? Well, that has been already assumed. But why was it Vipin's face? He is pretty much the only Indian friend I have. To my mind came the writing from "Etruscan Places" by my favourite "etruscologist", English writer D.H. Lawrence. The book was on the floor, beside my bed. It belonged to the

Toronto Public Library. I opened it right on the page where somebody had underlined this:

"B., who has just come back from India, is so surprised to see the phallic stones by the doors of many tombs. Why, it's like Shiva lingam at Benares! It's exactly like the lingam stones in the Shiva caves and Shiva temples! And that is another curious thing. One can live one's life, and read all the books about India or Etruria, and never read a single word about the thing that impresses one in the very first five minutes, in Benares or in an Etruscan necropolis: that is, the phallic symbol." [8]

Reading this helped me "understand".

VIPIN SHARMA + D.H. LAWRENCE = I MUST GO BACK TO INDIA AND SANSKRIT

This didn't look like a good idea. Great scholars loudly warn you that you should never go in that direction because you will simply embarrass yourself. Experts like Giuliano and Larissa Bonfante wrote that

"The so-called 'etymological method', which involves a comparison of Etruscan with other languages, living or dead, was widely used until about 1885, but gave little or no results. Though now generally abandoned by scholars, a naive brand of it continues to flourish in amateur circles." [9]

2 IN THE WATERS OF SANSKRIT

To examine Etruscan with Sanskrit looked like a crazy enterprise. No university in Europe or North America would fund this type of research. They would prevent you from "wasting time and resources". The relation between European languages and Sanskrit is believed to be detected through Proto-Indo-European, that ancestral language which linguists reconstructed based on known languages. Nobody ever heard it being spoken nor saw a word of it written, but there is a strong assumption that it existed. That belief is based on evidence of similarities between Indo-European languages. Mother is 'moeder' in Dutch, 'madre' in Italian, 'mater' in Serbian and Latin, 'mitera' in Greek, 'mutter' in German, 'mAtR' in Sanskrit. These words belong to the same family. Linguists have done amazing work in reconstructing a common root for all of them and they produced lots of support for the idea that all Indo-European languages came out from the same source, but these proofs are speculative and soft. There is no material evidence for it, no smoking gun. In the end, it comes to this: we don't have a recording of a speaker of Proto-Indo-European that you could play in the court of linguistics, we don't have a single document written in that language. Even though this theory is very convincing, it still requires a leap of faith. We are told that both the Romans and the Greeks considered Etruscan to be an alien tongue.

When British chap George Dennis started exploring Etruria in 1842, he was just twenty eight years old. The result was a beautiful book called *"Cities and Cemeteries of Etruria"*; published in 1848 by the British Museum. His work sparked an interest in the Etruscans that never ceased to exist. The "mysterious Etruscans" are the best researched ancient nation after the Greeks and the Romans. The only puzzling things that remained are their origin and their language.

Naturally, I was reading a Sanskrit dictionary day and night. I would think that I discovered something only to understand that the lead was wrong. Then I remembered one feature of Sanskrit that also exists in German.

Dictionary.com stated, *"But in German, any speaker can put two unrelated words next to each other and create a novel compound word, so you don't have to be Shakespeare or Lewis Carroll to create new compounds."* [10]

The same situation is in Sanskrit. The fact that you cannot find many of the words in a dictionary does not mean that those words are wrong or not "Sanskrit words". As long as you find words or stems that could be used to make a compound similar to the word you are reconstructing, you might be onto something. Most European languages do not feature this elasticity, they prefer simple compounds.

I made some experiments with toponyms from Serbia and Bosnia. The first word I searched was Sava. I was born on the southern bank of Sava river. The Sava was the second biggest river in ex-Yugoslavia and it is the biggest tributary of the Dunav (Danube). My father Dragoljub Maslić, a TV-journalist, became nationally known while reporting about numerous floods this river caused in the 1970s.

Sava or Savo is a very common Slavic and South Slavic personal name. The meaning of it is unknown as much as the meaning of the name of the river is.

Romans called it Savus, but it is not likely that they named this river. In Romania, three rivers are named Sava and Romans conquer Dacia rather late, at the begging of the second century AD. Before Romans, it was Celts who extensively used this river as their trading route. Marjeta Šašel Kos thinks that this name is probably pre-Celtic[11] (Celts enter Pannonian plain in the fourth century BC). The name could be Illyrian or pre-Illyrian but it had to be local. Checking SanskritDictionary.com gave me an intriguing and meaningful result.

sava m.   pouring it out [12]

It made sense. The Sava floods. Since I already read a Sanskrit dictionary so much that I memorized many words, I was aware that one of the Sanskrit words for water was 'va'.

What if I reconstruct the Sava as a compound? It worked, too!

Sa   adj.   excellent, best [13]
va   m.   water [14]

Sa + va → Sava

So, Sava is THE BEST WATER, EXCELLENT WATER. In this context, the word 'water' should be understood as RIVER. Problem solved? Not really! Variations of SA and VA have other meanings in Sanskrit.

sA (the weak form of san-) giving, bestowing, granting[15]

Now, it means GIVING WATER or maybe WATER GIVER. But this is not all!

Sa   m.   heaven, paradise[13]

The region around the Sava, called Posavina, is extremely fertile. Besides, the Sava was probably a holy river in prehistoric times. Together with 'va' (water), this 'Sa' gives "HEAVEN-WATER" which we can read as PARADISE RIVER or even HOLY RIVER.

But there was also this...

Sa   m.   destruction [13]

Again, it could be about Sava's destructive floods. This meaning is not probable because the benefits that the Sava gives are much bigger than occasional troubles it makes.

Sa   n.   endurance [13]

Now, we can speculate that it is a 'water' or river that shows endurance, Sava river is wide and it is 900 km long.

This illustrates the "problem" we will often face: too many alternative translations. By the way, as a personal name, it has nothing to do with water (this is dedicated to my late uncle Savo Maslić and my cousin Sava Maslić).

sava m.   the sun (see savitṛ-) [12]

sava m.   (fr.2. sū-) offspring, progeny [12]

sava m.   setting in motion, vivification, instigation,

impulse, command, order (especially applied to the activity of savitṛ-; dative case sav/āya-, for "setting in motion") [12]

Some of these apply to the river, too. The results are so many! Simple logic suggests that some meanings are likelier than others to be behind Sava as a personal name (those would be 'sun'. 'offspring', 'vivification'). The same is with the name of the river. The Sava is formed by the confluence of two smaller rivers: Sava Bohinjka and Sava Dolinka. So, the meaning of the name has to be simple, generic.

sA   (weak form of san-), giving, bestowing, granting [15]
va   m.   water [14]

sA + va → sava

So, it is probably WATER GIVER or, as previously mentioned, EXCELLENT WATER. There is one more option, possibly the best of all.

zava n.   water [16]

This Harvard-Kyoto Z in *zava* is pronounced like SH in word 'shore' (it is *śava* in IAST transliteration). So, this etymology would assume a sound change, but the meaning is so strong that we cannot ignore it.

It could be that WATER or RIVER is the best translation of The Sava. Even though it is hard to decide about the exact etymology, we are now in a radically different situation.

Sanskrit gave us several options while without Sanskrit we had nothing.

Altogether, these results made me optimistic. I had to jump into Etruscan rivers, head first!

3 RIVERS OF TUSCANY

I made a very broad list of rivers in which I included not only Tuscan rivers but also some rivers from neighbouring regions. I hoped this would give me insight regarding the bigger picture. Reluctant to immediately face the most important names like Arno, Marta or Tiber, I started with some less important hydronyms.

The first results were encouraging and sometimes confusing.

3.1 FIRST ATTEMPTS: BURE, CHIANA, IDICE, LIMENTRA, MAGRA, MARECCHIA, METAURO, SAVENA, SIEVE, TORA

3.1.1 BURE (torrent)

The name Bure is very similar to the South Slavic word *bura*, used for a fast Northern wind in the region of the Adriatic Sea. The same wind is called *bora* by Greeks. It is believed that Greek and also Italian *bora* and South Slavic *bura* are not etymologically related.[17]

According to this view, *bura* is related to Slavic *burja*, meaning 'storm', which came out of verb **buriti*.

These "Slavic" words are definitely Sanskrit words. Remember that J in *burya* is equal to Y in *yolk!* Take a look!

bhurati { bhur } verb 1   move rapidly, quiver, stir, palpitate [18]

The stem that represents verb *bhurati* in compound words is *bhur*. We need to see if *ya* means something in Sanskrit.

ya   m.   wind [19]

So, we can actually easily explain Slavic *burya* (spelt as *burja*).

bhur + ya → bhurya → H is dropped → burya

It seems that Slavic word for storm means RAPID WIND or STIRRING WIND in Sanskrit! The connection between Slavic languages and Sanskrit is strong and real. Serbian verbs generally have the same form as Sanskrit verbs. Even the very word for wind is practically the same in these languages. It is VETAR (wind) in Serbian, while it is *vAtR* in Sanskrit.

vAtR   m.   wind [20]

It is more or less the same in other Slavic languages.

VATR (Sanskrit)
VETAR (Serbian)
VETER (Russian)
VETRA (Slovenian)
VITR (Czech)
WIATR (Polish)

Now, since Slavic words for wind and storm have an obvious and strong Sanskrit connection we have to ask ourselves why it would not be the case with Greek and Italian *bora*. The similarity of words from different languages does not guarantee they came from the same, common source. In their book "The Oxford Introduction to Proto-Indo-European and the Proto-Indo-European World", J.P. Mallory and D.Q. Adams hint a possibility that Greek word *boreas* (North Wind) could develop from root *$g^w orh_x$- meaning mountain.[21] Why not from the Sanskrit stem *bhur*?

bhurati { bhur } verb 1   move rapidly, quiver, palpitate, stir[18]

This stem can be behind the name of Tuscan torrent Bure. In the end, every torrent is a rapid and forceful flow of water!

Should we be sure about this etymology because it makes sense? Not really. One reconstruction alone doesn't prove much.

3.1.2 CHIANA

According to Encyclopedia Britannica, Chiana changed her course and behavior throughout history.[22] This makes her name hard to decode. In prehistoric times it was Arno River that was going through Chianna Valley, but Arno changed its course. Chiana River also changed her course, both naturally and by human intervention. In Middle Ages, Chiana formed a swamp and inhabitants of the valley had to leave because of malaria.[6]

Once we view Chiana from this angle, some other Sanskrit reconstructions that make sense. We need to be reminded that the Etruscans were famous for their river regulation. When Romans took over, they stopped regulating some rivers and some territories of Etruria turned back into malaria-infested swamps. This was probably a political decision.

The Latin name of Chiana River was Clanis. Switching between G and K is very common in early Latin, they sometimes wrote G, sometimes C (K).

glAna   adj.   languid, wearied, sick, torpid, sluggish [23]
glAna   n.   exhaustion, sickness [23]

So, Clanis most likely meant SICK (referring to malaria-infested surrounding), maybe EXHAUSTED or SLUGGISH. It fits the behaviour of this river. How about Chiana?

SanskritDictionary.com tells us that *khyA* means *tell*, but it can also mean *betray* and *denounce*.[24]

The second word is one of the most general Sanskrit words for water.

anna n.   water [25]

khyA + anna → khyana → H is dropped; no Y as in 'yolk' in Etruscan, it becomes I → kiana

KIANA (reconstructed)
CHIANA (Italian)

The literal translation would be "BETRAYING" WATER or BETRAYING RIVER, maybe BETRAYED RIVER. This also fits this river's "biography".

Another option would require the dropping of one vowel.

kheya	n.	ditch [26]
kheya	adj.	that can be dug, to be dug out[26]

The assumed dynamics would be

kheya + anna → kheyana

After H was dropped, we get *keyana*. There is no Y as in 'yolk' in written Etruscan or Latin, so it would now be KEIANA. We have three vowels in a row in *kEIAna*, two of them merge into one, which is a process identified in Etruscan but also common for many other languages. We end up with KIANA (spelt Chiana).

It would mean DITCHED WATER or DITCHED RIVER, this would point to river regulation.

We cannot be confident that these reconstructions are correct, but they do look possible.

If these are just accidental similarities we need to see how many accidents we can collect.

3.1.3 ERA

The Era is a tributary of Arno. It is 54 km long. Its name could be very generic, based on one of many Sanskrit words for water.

irA f.   water [27]

3.1.4 IDICE

This is a torrent and it pretty much dries out during the summer. It is pronounced close to "idiche". Sanskrit offers many options.

iDA f.   vital spirit [28]
+
cahati   { cah } verb   cheat [29]

Literally, this IDACA(h) is "CHEATING SPIRIT" and it might be connected to the unsteady flow of this torrent. By the way, there is an obvious connection between *cahati* and English verb *to cheat;* drop H and *cahati* becomes *caati* or *ca-at*. The character C in this Harvard-Kyoto *transliteration* is pronounced as CH in *cheat*.

We can use another ending word and get a better sound match.

icchA   f.   question or problem[30]

iDA + icchA → idiccha → H is dropped → idicca

IDICCA (reconstructed)
IDICE (the name of the river)

This gives QUESTIONABLE SPIRIT or PROBLEMATIC SPIRIT.

Still, it is hard to say if this is a valid etymology or just a case of projecting a Sanskrit meaning into an Italian name based on an accidental similarity of words.

The only solution to this is to keep reconstructing.

3.1.5 LIMENTRA

"Limentra is the name of two streams of the Bolognese and Pistoiese Apennines, both among the major tributaries of the Reno River." Wikipedia [31]

There are two Limentra streams: Eastern and Western Limentra.

lī	f.	adhering, clinging to [32]
ma	n.	water [33]
netra	n.	river [34]

lī + ma + netra → limanetra

The Etruscan language is known for corrupting word-endings by dropping vowels.

limanetra → limantra

LIMANTRA (reconstructed)
LIMENTRA (name of the river)

The translation is not completely clear, it would literally mean ADHERING-WATER-RIVER, therefore WATER THAT ADHERES TO (the) RIVER. This could be describing a TRIBUTARY.

Or, it could be...

lI	f.	adhering [32]
manA	f.	attachment[35]
netra	n.	river[34]

Now, it is tautological "ADHERING ATTACHMENT TO THE RIVER." Again, it might mean TRIBUTARY. The two Limentra streams are tributaries of the Reno river.

It could be that these reconstructions are just partially correct. Again, it looks possible, but it is hard to claim this was the exact way in which this name formed.

However, we are constantly getting optional translations from Sanskrit, which does feel like something when compared to the previous nothing.

3.1.6 MAGRA

Maybe the name of Magra can help.

ma   n.   water [36]

We now look for the -GRA part.

gRh   adj.   moving [20]
gṛh   mfn.   only in fine composition or 'at the end of a compound' "seizing"(the mind), moving [21]

ma + gRh + A (name ending) → magrha → H is dropped → magra (would be MACRA in Etruscan)

It is MOVING WATER or RUNNING WATER. This would mean FLOW or RIVER.

Again and again, what if this is an accident? Can accidents happen regularly?

But there is an encouragement that the Sanskrit connection is real. Look at the name of Magra's tributary Vara.

vArI   f.   water [38]

Now, it all looks easy. We should not claim that every name here is correctly reconstructed, but we should take Sanskrit very seriously.

3.1.7 MARECCHIA

The source of Marecchia River is in Arezzo Province of Tuscany, but it flows east from the Apennines and drains into the Adriatic Sea. The ancient name of Marecchia was Ariminus.[39]

What can we do for a river that flows through the birthplace of Italian film director Federico Fellini?

First, let's see what are the character traits of the Marecchia River. The Italian Wikipedia article says that the Marecchia regularly dries out in the summer, but only seemingly because it still keeps a significant flow under the surface of its dried-out bed.[40] So, this river appears to stop flowing.

ma   n.   water [36]
rAti { rA }   verb 2   give, grant, surrender [41]
khyAyate { khyA }   verb pass.   be known [42]

ma (water) + rA (surrender) + khyA → marakhya → marakia → Marecchia

It means WATER (RIVER) KNOWN (or TOLD) TO

SURRENDER.

On this line is another reconstruction.

maraka   m.   mortality [43]
yA   (in fine composition or 'at the end of a compound') going, moving [44]

maraka + yA → marakya → marakia → Marecchia

The literal meaning is MORTALITY-MOVING or MORTAL GOING, which we should understand as MORTAL FLOW or RIVER THAT DIES, RIVER THAT STOPS FLOWING.

Now, let's focus on its ancient name – ARIMINUS.

Aramati   { A- ram }   verb   finish, cease [45]
āramP.   -ramati- () , to pause, stop ; to leave off; to delight in [45]
ina   adj.   powerful, mighty, strong [47]

A- ram+ ina + OS → Ariminos

Meaning: CEASING STRENGTH, CEASING TO BE POWERFUL, LOSING POWER.

Both the Greek and the contemporary name can be translated with Sanskrit and both translations mean the same! They describe the behavior of this river. But some other reconstructions that look equally good. Here are words to play with. And remember, Greeks don't have V, they drop it or replace it with a vowel. In this case, they could have dropped it.

vArI   f.   water [48]

mInAti { mI }   verb   diminish, lessen, destroy, lose one's way [49]

vArI → Greeks don't have V, it is dropped → Ari

Ari + mI + ina → arimina + OS → ARIMINOS

The literal translation is" "WATER-DIMINISH-POWERFUL". Again, we get a RIVER THAT LOSES ITS POWER.

It looks like Marecchia and Ariminos have the same or similar meaning and we can treat these names as bilinguals! We could also employ some other Sanskrit words in reconstructions of both names and they would carry the same idea!

We cannot talk seriously about the names of Tuscan rivers if we ignore Sanskrit!

3.1.8 METAURO

Metauro is a river formed by the union of two torrents: Meta and Auro. Its name is a merger of these two names. In Latin, it was called Metaurus or Mataurus.[50]

madA   f.   river [51]

Etruscans don't have D, they always use T or TH instead of D. So, Sanskrit *madA* becomes *mata*, which matches one of the Latin versions of the name (*Mataurus*). It means RIVER.

Regarding Auro, we can consider words *ha* and *uru*.

ha   m.   water [52]
uru   adj.   excellent, wide, excessive [53]

ha + uru → hauru → H is dropped → auru → Auro

Meaning EXCESSIVE WATER applies if you think of torrent as a sudden release of water. But it could be about its force (people practice kayaking on Auro).

AvRhate   { AvRh }   verb   pull or tear out or off [54]

AvRh → H id dropped → AVR → V often becomes U both in Etruscan and in Latin → AUR → AURO

Certainly, there is a strong possibility that this is a "Sanskrit name".

3.1.9 SAVENA

This is the Italian rendering of the name. The real local name sounds so Etruscan – Savna, similar to Sava River.

On Italian Wikipedia page you can find that *"Savena literally means 'water vein'(...)"* [55]

Even when you have no intention to dispute the existing etymology, Sanskrit will still offer results that are impossible to ignore.

savana   n.   bathing, ablution, together with woods[56]

There could be other approaches to this hydronym.

sA   f.   giving[57]
vana   n.   water[58]

sA + vana → savana → Savena (WATER GIVER)

Or...

sava m.   pouring it out, order, stimulator [59]
sava m.   (fr.1. sū-) one who sets in motion or impels, an instigator, stimulator, commander [59]
+
enI f.   river [60]

sava + enI → saveni → Savena

The meanings could be ORDER-RIVER (proper river), STIMULATING RIVER and maybe RIVER THAT POURS OUT (the river that floods).

Finally, there is a word that is too similar to the name that it cannot be skipped.

sAvinI   f.   river [61]

So, even when we have an Italian etymology (water vein) that sounds good, Sanskrit is still very competitive. Why? It might be that a good Sanskrit etymology is sometimes better than a good Italian etymology.

3.1.10 SERCHIO

"Serchio (in antiquity the Auser) is the third longest river in the Italian region of Tuscany at 126 kilometres (78 mi) [...]" (Wikipedia) [62]

The name is pronounced as 's:erkio'. It looks like reconstructing Serchio with Sanskrit will be easy.

sAra   m.   water [63]
khyAti   { khyA }   verb   tell, say, declare,

betray, denonce [64]

sAra + khyA → sarkhya → H is dropped → sarkya

The sound Y always becomes I in Etruscan and Latin.

sarkya → sarkia

Literally, it is a "water that is talked about" which means FAMOUS WATER or WELL-KNOWN RIVER or FAMOUS RIVER. We should doubt this meaning. If you remember from the discussion about Chiana, *khyA* can also mean *betray* and *denounce*. So, Serchio might have the same or similar words included in its name, eventually meaning "WATER-BETRAY", BETRAYING RIVER.

Let's try another quiz.

sisarti { sR } verb 1   flow, move, run [65]
kheya   adj.   that can be dug, to be dug out [66]
kheya   n.   ditch [66]

sR + kheya → srkheya → H would be dropped → srkeya → srkeia

If we render it with Etruscan speech patterns, dropping a vowel in the second part of the word is something that would happen. 'Srkeia' would become 'Srkia'. Names of many Italian rivers are of male gender, so the ending A is turned into O. The result is SRKIO. But SRKIO has it's first three sounds as consonants and this is hard on Latin speakers, it falls out of Latin melody patterns.. Therefore a vowel is inserted to ease the word. The result is SERKIO or Serchio, as it is spelt in modern Italian.

The meaning would be DITCHED RIVER, "CHANNELED" RIVER or literally "WHOSE FLOW

WAS DUG OUT". This has a grounding in historical fact. Italian Wikipedia says that after the fall of the Western Roman Empire the maintenance of the river channels stopped. Serchio started making problems and people gradually retreated from its surrounding.[67]

So, the river was indeed regulated, the article mentions maintenance of the river channels!. Looking from that angle, "DITCHED" WATER or "DITCHED" RIVER feels right. At the same time, Sanskrit will offer a translation which looks like the other side of the same coin. After the fall of the Western Roman Empire, the river was abandoned. Now, look at this!

sargam.   stream, downpour [68]
ya m.   abandoning [69]

This gives SARGYA but because G always becomes K and Y turn into I it would end up es SARKIA or SARKIO.

SARKIO (reconstructed)
SERKIO (spelt as Serchio)

The literal translation is "STREAM-ABANDONING". We can read it as a RIVER THAT ABANDONS ITS BED or as ABANDONED RIVER (humans didn't live around anymore).

The previous name of Serchio, Auser, is not easy to reconstruct. But let's try it!

avati { av }   verb 1   guard [said of kings or princes], lead, govern [70]
+
sAra   m.   water [63]

av + sAra → avsara → V becomes U or W → ausara →

ending A is dropped to make a name of the male gender →
ausar → Auser

This would mean GUARDED WATER or RIVER, "GOVERNED" RIVER. More or less, it delivers the idea of a REGULATED or "DITCHED" RIVER.

3.1.11 SIEVE

Sieve is the biggest tributary of the Arno river. A local proverb says that the Arno cannot flood unless the Sieve grows. In Summer, the Sieve almost disappears, but during the rainy season of Autumn it might cause very damaging floods.[71]

The ending word in Sieve could be *va*, one of Sanskrit words for water.

va   m.   water, the ocean [72]

What would be IEVE in Sieve?

yA   going [73]

yA + va → yava

But both Etruscan and Latin, as well as Greek, either don't have Y as in 'yolk' or they pronounce it or write as the sound I, as in 'tin'. YAVA becomes IAVA. This should mean "GOING WATER", therefore it is FLOW or simply RIVER. Now, we only need SI-part at the beginning.

si   (See sāyaka-, senā-), to hurl, cast [74]

This would now offer SI + IAVA, resulting in SIAVA.

SIAVA (reconstructed)
SIEVE (Italian, Tuscan)

It would mean HURLING RIVER and would eventually apply to the Sieve's behaviour during rainy seasons. However, there is no way we can be sure if this exact reconstruction is correct. It could be completely deceiving, partially correct, or absolutely correct. Since linguists always warn us of the instability of vowels, the first syllable could be SU.

suvati   { sU }   impel, incite, urge. produce, set in motion [75]

Now, Sieve would mean URGING WATER FLOW or URGING RIVER. It certainly urges the Arno to make floods. It also might mean WHICH PRODUCES THE RIVER, because Sieve takes an important role in making of Arno River.

But, again, what if all of this is accidental and just my projection of Sanskrit lego blocks into the names of Italian rivers?

3.1.12 TORA

The river-name Tora could not exist as an Etruscan hydronym simply because their language didn't have the letter O. The same feature is displayed in the neighbouring Umbrian language. We have to look for words like 'tara', 'tura' etc. In addition, we have to take into account the absence of D in Etruscan. It is always substituted with T or TH. So, we also have to look for similar words that contain D.

dhArA   f.   current, stream [76]

D would become T or TH in Etruscan, H would be dropped. We get TARA.

TARA (reconstructed)
TORA (name of Tuscan stream)?

Tora is a stream and it might mean STREAM. Still, Tora and Tara don't feel like a match.

Is there any connection between Tora and the Italian word TORRENTE ('torrent' in English)? Here is one option.

dhorati { dhor }   verb   run, trot, be quick, be alert [77]
+
rantu   f.   river [78]

dhor → thor → H is dropped → tor

tor + rantu → torrantu → torrente

The translation is "TROTTING" RIVER, RUNNING RIVER, QUICK RIVER. It could be that I just explained both the name of Tora and the word 'torrent' (torrente). But what if I didn't?! There is another way.

dhara   m.   mountain [79]
andha   n.   water, turbid water [80]

dhara + andha → dharandha → H is dropped → daranda → D becomes T → taranta

The meaning of this would be MOUNTAIN WATER.

Certainly, we can still use *rantu* (river) as the second

word. That would give *dharrantu* → *tarrantu*, justifying double R in *torrente* (and *torrent*). The meaning would also fit – MOUNTAIN RIVER.

We do get "cleaner" reconstruction by employing stem *dhor*. It is also a better option for Tora.

All of these results ask for a deeper understanding of sound changes. But it looks obvious that Sanskrit talks to us here!

3.2 MAJOR RIVERS OF THE ETRUSCAN WORLD: ARNO, MARTA, PO, RENO AND TIBER

Some of these rivers are not exclusively Etruscan. Arno and Marta are iconic rivers of Etruria. The Tiber defined its southern border being also deeply rooted in Roman history. Po and Reno were in the zone of interactions even though they were part of the Etruscan world.

3.2.1 ARNO

Here is what is currently thought about the name of the Arno River.

"From Latin Arnus (Pliny, Natural History 3.50). The philologist Hans Krahe related this toponym on a paleo-European basis *Ar-n-, derived from Proto-Indo-European root *er-, 'flow, move'." [81]

Hans Krahe was a great linguist, but I am sure that he didn't check a Sanskrit dictionary.

arNA   f. river [82]

The Arno is also known for its floods.

arNa   n. flood stream, wave[83]

We can debate if the meaning of Arno is RIVER or FLOODER, but we cannot question Sanskrit relevance in the understanding of this name. It is undeniable.

However, Krahe was not entirely wrong. What is called "Proto-Indo-European root *er-*" has its own Sanskrit affiliation.

ArI P. (/ā-riṇanti-) to pour, let drop: A1. /A-rIyate-, to

trickle or flow upon ; to flow over [84]

Compare it!

ArI (Sanskrit)
er-" (assumed Proto-Indo-European)

This changes everything. Now, we can be confident that at least some of the reconstructions made so far are correct.

3.2.2 MARTA

The Italian Wikipedia page says that the Marta was once called Larthe. It is 50 km long and it flows into the Tyrrhenian Sea, near Tarquinia, at the location of the town called Martanum.[85]

At first glance, this name tells us that it must contain a word for water.

ma   n.   water [86]
Rta n.   water [87]

To translate it as WATER-WATER would be funny, but both 'ma' and 'Rta' have other meanings.

MA
ma   n.   welfare, happiness [86]
mAyate { mA }   verb   build, prepare, measure [88]

RTA

Rta n.   wealth[87]
Rta adj.   proper, respected, fit, true, able [87]

If we combine this with 'ma' we get WATER

RESPECTED or RESPECTED RIVER, TRUE RIVER, PROPER RIVER, RIVER OF WEALTH.

But there is more.

Rta n.   faith, divine truth, sacred or pious action or custom, divine law, law, rule [87]

Now, the optional meaning is WATER-FAITH or RIVER OF FAITH, which we can see as HOLY RIVER. We should not doubt that most major rivers were holy in prehistoric times; their waters were inhabited and ruled by gods and other divine beings. But the Marta river's ties with the Etruscan religion are even stronger than that. The Marta doesn't have a conventional spring, it is generated by surplus water from Lake Bolsena, she is a daughter of the lake. Likely, Lake Bolsena was sacred for the Etruscans because the major Etruscan religious sanctuary was located there. It was Fanum Voltumnae, where leaders of all twelve cities of the Etruscan League met every year. Fanum Voltumnae was for the Etruscans what Delphi was for the Greeks.

Marta also had another deep connection to the Etruscan faith. The mythical founder of Etruscan religion was Tages, a divine boy who one day sprung out of the furrow and initiated an Etruscan king into sacred knowledge. Then he disappeared as suddenly as he came, merging with the soil. That happened during agricultural works, in the field that was close to the banks of Marta River. But, that is not all...

Since the Etruscan language did not have the sound D and always used T or TH instead (see the Bonfantes), we have to consider words that sound like RD or RDA.

Rdhnoti { Rdh }   verb 5   succeed, prosper, increase [89]

ARYAN ITALY OF THE ETRUSCANS

Now, it suggests WATER-INCREASE (floods).

If you read these words again, it turns out that the meanings of Marta could be WATER (or RIVER) OF WELFARE, RIVER OF HAPPINESS, maybe even "BUILT" RIVER, "PREPARED" RIVER, MEASURED RIVER, PROMOTED RIVER. This makes sense, too. 'Built', 'prepared' and 'measured' might point to human work in the regulation of its flow.

The old name of Marta was Larthe. We can guess that RTHE-part represents 'rta' or water. How about LA?

lA	f.	act of taking or giving [90]
lAti { lA }	verb 2 Par	receive [90]

So, LARTHE could mean RECEIVING WATER or HAVING WATER GIVEN TO. As we know, Marta receives water from Lake Bolsena. It also can be just a simple WATER-GIVER or RIVER THAT GIVES etc.

Now, we are ready to examine the names of settlements that Etruscans had on this river. One of them was Martanum.

UM is a common ending of Latin city-names. However, we can find this word in Sanskrit dictionaries.

uma	m.	city, town [91]

But if you check Latin dictionaries you will not find *uma* as a word for *city*. It would be interesting to explore this relation. In any case, it works here.

We are missing a word that would explain N in MartaNum.

anu	prep.	along, near to, at [92]

The whole "formula" looks like this.

Marta + anu + uma → martanuma → Martanum

So, Martanum is TOWN ON MARTA (RIVER).

How about another Etruscan settlement at the banks of the Marta? Its name is La Cannara.

My idea was that this also meant CITY ON THE RIVER.

kha	n.	city [93]
nAra	m.(plural)	water [94]

kha + nAra → H is dropped → kanara

KANARA (reconstructed)
LA CANNARA (Italian)

3.2.3 PO

"The Po (Latin: Padus and Eridanus, Italian: Po Italian pronunciation: ['pɔ], ancient Ligurian: Bodincus or Bodencus, Greek: Πάδος and Ἠριδανός) 9...)
The Po is the longest river in Italy; at its widest point its width is 503 m (1,650 ft).[1]" [95]

I included the Po in Rivers of Tuscany because it was at some point the northern border of Etruscan lands. It is reasonable to think that Etruscans did not name it. There are many short P-words in Sanskrit and, since vowels are changeable each of them can be behind the name.

payate { pI }   verb 1   overflow [96]

ARYAN ITALY OF THE ETRUSCANS

pha   n.   flowing, swelling [97]

It might just mean FLOW or RIVER, even FLOODER. But if make a parallel with Latin name Padus, it actually could be FLOWS, DIVISIONS.

pada   n.   division, portion, part [98]

pada + US (name-ending) → Padus

This makes sense. The Po is divided into many smaller flows.

"Near the end of its course, it creates a wide delta (with hundreds of small channels and five main ones, called Po di Maestra, Po della Pila, Po delle Tolle, Po di Gnocca and Po di Goro) at the southern part of which is Comacchio, an area famous for eels." [95]

Another Latin name for the Po is Eridanus. It means the same as Padus.

ArIyate { ArI }   verb   flow over [99]
AriNanti { ArI }   verb   pour [99]
dAna   m.   dividing, splitting, dispenser, distributor, gift [100]

ArI (or 'Ari') + dAna → aridana + US (name-ending) → aridanus → Eridanus (FLOW THAT DIVIDES, or DIVIDED FLOWS)

Ligurians, who were North from the Po, called it Bodincus. The meaning is the same.

bhedin   adj.   splitting, dividing [101]
+
ka   n.   water [102]

bhedin + ka → bhedinka + US → bedinkus → Bodincus (RIVER THAT SPLITS)

BEDINKUS (reconstructed)
BODINCUS (Ligurian)

There is a river far away from the Po, that also branches out and has the same name meaning. It is the Visla (*Wisła*) in Poland. We just need to combine two Sanskrit stems.

viveSTi	{ viS } verb	flow [103]
lunIte	{ lU } verb	divide [104]

viS + lU → vislu → Visla or Wisła

Visla (Wisla) means DIVIDED FLOW(s)!

Another name used is Vistula (Sanskrit *tu* is 'going', 'moving') which has the literal meaning FLOW-GOING-DIVIDE).

3.2.4 RENO

"The name of the river has the same etymology as the name of the Rhine, as both derive from the same Celtic hydronym *Rēnos, the Reno basin being situated within Gallia Cisalpina, in what was the territory of Boii before the Roman conquest of 220 BC.

In Italian both rivers are called Reno, and in Latin both were called Rhenus." [105]

So far, even if you assume that I have made many mistakes, there are some serious results that we got from Sanskrit.

We don't have to dispute the existing etymology. Generally, I can accept the thesis about Celtic roots of this

ARYAN ITALY OF THE ETRUSCANS

name. It makes sense. Celts lived around those rivers. But I want to examine it with Sanskrit! Once you try that, you gain a very different vision.

Here are some examples of how you can view Reno or Rhenus from the Sanskrit angle.

    raNa   m.   motion, delight, joy, pleasure [106]

What if the names Reno and Rhenus are in connection with a word that is altogether a different word?

    RNa   n.   water [107]

If this would be the right etymology, then the sound E had to be inserted in RNA by a language that did not like "knotting" of consonants. But there is more.

    R   going, moving / gati [108]
    anna   n.   water [109]

R + anna → ranna → rana

RANA (reconstructed)
RENO (current name)

It would mean "MOVING WATER" or, interpreted, RIVER. The other option is very similar

Rcchati { R }   verb   rise [110]
enI f.   river [111]

R + enI → reni

RENI (reconstructed)
RENO (current name)
This means RISING RIVER. The Reno does have some

flooding "habits". Regarding the Reno's release of water, Wikipedia says that *"the typical value when the river is in flood is around 1,000 cubic metres per second (35,000 cu ft/s)."* [96]

There is a quite serious and complex theory about the origin of name Reno but we will simplify it to a short Wikipedia citation.

"The Gaulish name Rēnos (Proto-Celtic or pre-Celtic[note 5] *Reinos) belongs to a class of river names built from the PIE root *rei- "to move, flow, run", also found in other names such as the Reno in Italy." [112]

This **rei*-theory is applicable when it comes to the Rhine or Rayna, but I would not be that confident when it comes to Reno. Slavic Rayna and German Rhein (Rhine) might have a very different etymology than Reno.

raya m.   stream of a river, course [113]

Why this would be better than PIE root **rei-*? Because the PIE root is an assumed, guessed word, while *raya* is a real word from a real dictionary. Now, we need the ending that contains N.

na   adj.   unbroken [114]
na   m.   welfare [114]

So, we get this "formula':

raya + na → rayna (or 'raina')

Is it RIVER OF UNBROKEN STREAM or FLOW, or it is RIVER OF WELFARE? However, NA is a frequent ending of female gender nouns. If it is just an ending, the meaning would be FLOW or RIVER.

But why would we put that much faith in Sanskrit? The

simple answer to the question is: it works better.

Many other European hydronyms can be translated and explained with Sanskrit. Here is just one example – River Odra. Let's take a look at its name variations.

"The Oder is known by several names in different languages, but the modern ones are very similar: English and German: Oder; Czech, Polish, and Lower Sorbian: Odra, Upper Sorbian: Wódra; Kashubian: Òdra (pronounced ['wɛdra]); Medieval Latin: Od(d)era; Renaissance Latin: Viadrus (invented in 1534)." [115]

Now, look at this Sanskrit word and ask yourself if you see a similarity with the Slavic Odra.

udra   n.   water [116]

UDRA (Sanskrit)
ODRA (Slavic)

We can even go further and treat this 'udra' as a compound.

uda n.   water [117]
drAti { drA }   verb   run [118]

uda + dra → uddra → udra → Odra

This would mean RUNNING WATER and simply should be translated as RIVER. Let's examine the Germanic version – Oder.

uda n.   water [117]
dara m.   stream [119]

uda + dara → uddara → udar → Oder
UDAR (reconstructed)

ODER (German)

The meaning is now WATER-STREAM or RIVER!

It seems that most old river names meant WATER or RIVER.

It looks like our ancestors simply named some river after one of the many possible Sanskrit words or compounds that meant RIVER or WATER. People of prehistory did not use these words as 'names' in our sense of the word. They used them as nouns that were simply marking what it was. They became river names over time.

What if some of those compounds stayed in use as general words for *river*? I simply had to check words for *river* in two languages I actively use, English and Serbian. Let's examine the word RIVER from the Sanskrit perspective.

rI   f.   going, motion [120]
vAr n.   water (pl.) [121]

rI + vAr → rivar → river

So, RIVER is GOING WATER, MOVING WATER or RUNNING WATER. Sanskrit dictionary.com also offers some additional meanings of *rI*, one of them being FLOW. So, RIVER can also be WATER FLOW. How about the Serbian 'reka' (means 'river')?

rI   f.   going, motion [120]
ka n.   water [122]

rI + ka → rika → reka

It has the same Sanskrit translations as English word

RIVER!

Even though Sanskrit often offers many options, making it challenging to choose the one, chances are that the simplest and most generic translations are those that are correct.

3.2.5 TIBER

"The Tiber (Latin Tiberis, Italian Tevere, Italian pronunciation: ['te:vere]) is the third-longest river in Italy, rising in the Apennine Mountains in Emilia-Romagna and flowing 406 kilometres (252 mi) through Umbria and Lazio to the Tyrrhenian Sea." [123]

The Tiber or Tevere is the most important river in Italian history. It defined the southern border of Etruria and it flows through Rome. If the Latin name Tiberis does not spark too many Sanskrit associations, the Italian name Tevere does it easily. My first idea came through the Serbian word 'dever' which is almost identical in Sanskrit and has the same meaning - "brother in law'. This is a Sanskrit word.

| devara | m. | brother in law, lover, husband [124] |
| devR | m. | husband's brother [125] |

Etruscans do not have D, they use TH or T instead of it. Therefore, 'devara' easily becomes Thevara, becoming very close to Tevere. This explanation is satisfactory regarding the name's modern pronunciation, but the meaning is clearly problematic.

It is interesting that modern name Tevere looks more like an Etruscan than a Latin rendering. Let's check the existing thinking about the name of Tiber.

"It is probable that the genesis of the name Tiber was pre-Latin,

like the Roman name of Tibur (modern Tivoli), and may be specifically Italic in origin. The same root is found in the Latin praenomen Tiberius. There are also Etruscan variants of this praenomen in Thefarie (borrowed from Faliscan *Tiferios, lit. '(He) from the Tiber' < *Tiferis 'Tiber') and Teperie (via the Latin hydronym Tiber)." [123]

Well, that is one way of looking at it. We will use the Sanskrit approach. Many ancient river-names meant *river* or *water* in Sanskrit. Is it worth checking the same idea on Tevere?

dhI   f.   splendour, intellect, intention, prayer, mind, devotion, design, thought, wisdom [126]

Sanskrit dictionary.com presents dhI in this way.

dhī   f.   thought, (especially) religious thought, reflection, meditation, devotion, prayer (plural Holy Thoughts personified) [127]

The second word is well known.

vArI   f.   water

dhI + vAr → dhivar → Etruscans always use TH or T instead of D → thivar or tivar (or thevar)

The literal meaning would be SPLENDID WATER, "PRAYER-WATER", etc. How this THIVAR became Tiberius? The interchangeability of V (that sometimes also turns into F) with B is already accepted by scholars who equated Etruscan name Thevarie with Roman name Tiberius.

There might be something in the literal translation we got - "PRAYER WATER" because Tiber was probably a

HOLY RIVER in prehistoric time. Romans indeed associated this river with a god. That brings another possible clue.

    deva   m.   god [128]
    or
    deva adj   divine [128]
    +
    vAr n.   water

deva + vAr → devvar → D becomes T or TH in Etruscan → thevar → Tevere

The meaning is now: DIVINE WATER, DIVINE RIVER, HOLY RIVER! This looks like a good explanation, the river was believed to have a god living in it.

"The legendary king Tiberinus, ninth in the king-list of Alba Longa, was said to have drowned in the river Albula, which was afterward called Tiberis.[8]
[...]
According to the legend, Jupiter made him a god and guardian spirit of the river (also called Volturnus, 'rolling water'). This gave rise to the standard Roman depiction of the river as a powerfully built reclining god, also named Tiberinus, with streams of water flowing from his hair and beard." [129]

Let's make a little digression and check the name of god Volturnus, which is understood as ROLLING WATER.

    valate { val }   verb   turn [130]
    tauti { tu }   verb 2   be strong [131]
    RNa   n.   water [132]

val + tu + RNa → valturna → Volturnus
Literally, it is TURN-STRONG-WATER, therefore it is

ONE WHO TURNS WATER STRONGLY or WHO ROLLS WATER STRONGLY. It is as simple as that!

Let's repeat: Volturnus, thought to mean "rolling water" is translated with Sanskrit as WHO TURNS WATER STRONGLY!

There are at least to other ways to get a convincing Sanskrit reconstruction of Volturnus, but this is enough at the moment. In this context, it could be acceptable to translate Tiber as HOLY RIVER. It is possible that people at some point in history saw the Tiber as holy, but I am looking for more down to earth, generic meaning of it.

There are two attractive options.

datte { dA }   verb   give [133]
+
vAr n.   water

dA + vAr → davar → D changes to T or TH in Etruscan → THAVAR or TAVAR

TAVAR (reconstructed)
TEVERE (Italian name of Tiber)

It means WATER GIVER. Another option is also convincing.

dhAvati   { dhAv }   move, stream [134]
or
dhav cl.1 A1. dhavate-, to run, flow [119]
+
vAr n.   water

dhav (or dhAv) + vAr (or 'ArI', 'flow over') → dhavar → thavar

This means RUNNING WATER, STREAMING

WATER, FLOWING WATER. Therefore, it is a RIVER!

But then, there is an alternative option, where we can use the Sanskrit word *TA*, meaning 'earth'. This would give TAVAR with literal meaning EARTH-WATER, which we could read as MUDDY or SOIL COLOURED RIVER. This should be a serious proposal for Tevere because even today the Tiber is called Flavus (Blonde) because its water is of yellowish (muddy) colour.

The sedimentation of the Tiber was so big that Romans had to abandon their port of Ostia and build another port. The Tiber brought that much silt that ancient Ostia is now way inland. It is interesting how I came to the etymology of Ostia through Serbian. Ostia was placed at the mouth of the Tiber. The Serbian word for mouth is 'usta'. How about Sanskrit?

oSTha	m.	lip [136]
auSTha	adj.	lip-shaped [137]

Ostia, city placed at the mouth of the Tiber, means either LIPS or MOUTH.

Let's be modest and conclude that Tevere-Tiber is fully reconstructable with Sanskrit.

3.3 ITALIAN CONTEXT, CONCLUSION

Is the presence of Sanskrit in hydronyms of Tuscany something isolated, exclusive? Or we can find it in other Italian regions? This is a study about the Etruscan language and the answer will be brief, but convincing.

Here are just the most obvious examples of river-names from other regions of Italy that offer an effortless Sanskrit translation.

AVISIO
aviSI f.   river, earth [138]
havis   n.   water [139]

BORBERA
barbura   n.   water [140]

CAVONE
kavana   n.   water [141]

ENNA
anna   n.   water [142]
enI f.   river [143]

NERA (also the river in Serbia and Romania)
nAra   m. (plural)   water [144]
nIra n.   water [145]

RAM (ROM)
rAmA   f.   river [130]
(This also applies to Rama River in Bosnia-Herzegovina)

SELE
sala m.   water [146]

TAMMARO
tAmara   n.   water [148]
(The same applies to Tamar River in South-West England.)

VARA
vAr n.   water, stagnant water [149]

VERDURA

ARYAN ITALY OF THE ETRUSCANS

vArdara   n.   water [150]
(applies to Vardar River in Northern Macedonia.)

VERSA
vRSa   m.   water [151]

Generally, Tuscan and Italian river names are very responsive to Sanskrit. The percentage of river names translatable by Sanskrit would hardly be higher in the old Aryan lands (Pakistan, North-West India).

This is not just a Tuscan or an Etruscan phenomenon. It belongs to Italy as a whole.

Some of these reconstructions are undeniable (like Arno or various names of the Po) or almost undeniable (Marecchia). Some of them should be taken with caution, but not because those names have no connection to Sanskrit, rather because there are too many ways to translate them with Sanskrit, at least for now.

Some other Italian toponyms illustrate a lack of European belief in Sanskrit's relevance. Such an example is Lake Como. It is believed that it was named after the city of Como but it must be the opposite.

kUma   n.   lake, pond [152]

Huh! We can conclude that "Sanskrit based" Indo-European hydronyms are overwhelmingly present on the Italian Peninsula. There is nothing or very little in the names of Tuscan rivers that would point to the use of non-Indo-European languages.

Does this prove that Etruscan was an Indo-European language closely associated with Sanskrit?

No, it does not.

Most of these names could be formed before Etruscan

culture and language developed, though that triggers another question. What happened to all the people who named these rivers? Did they all just disappear?

Massimo Pallottino (1905-1999), who is often called the "father of Etruscology", wrote that *"Even toponymy (i.e. the collection and study of place names), although very rewarding, for place names stubbornly resist the ebb and flow of languages, is of little use as a source of knowledge for the study of prehistoric linguistic conditions and phases except in vague and limited way, owing to the difficulty in establishing the date of origin of names and, more particularly, their original meaning."* [153]

Pallottino was right in his time, toponymy was of little use because the Italian toponyms were approached from the wrong angle.

OK, we concluded that names of Tuscan rivers are Indo-European, but might not be Etruscan. Still, some of them should be at least suspected to be Etruscan. That applies to all those river-names that have translations that point to river regulation. The Etruscans are the first known people of Italy that extensively regulated rivers, so even some rough dating could be done. Having possible "river-bilinguals" might also be helpful. Chiana-Clanis, Serchio-Auser, Marecchia-Ariminus, Po-Padus-Bondinkus could be examples of those so-called bilinguals (even trilinguals) but there are also other optional translations of these.

Alright, the names of rivers do not prove that the Etruscan language was Indo-European, but they prove even less that it wasn't.

But there is lots of other new knowledge that this chapter has brought. We learned that toponymy searches and general Indo-European searches were consciously or subconsciously biased. They have shown no interest in what appears to be the Indo-part of Indo-European heritage.

Why?

It did not fit imperialistic and colonial goals of major European powers.

4 CITIES OF ETRURIA

During the time of their recognized history, the Etruscans built, took over or influenced many cities of Italy. Etruria was not a country in a sense in which Egypt and the Hittite empire were. Just like Greece, it was a collection of city-states bound by language and culture.

Etruria Proper stretched to the North-West side of the peninsula, from Arno River in the North to the Tiber in the South, while contained by the Apennines in the East and the Tyrrhenian Sea in the West.

Etruscans expanded their influence over all of Italy, almost succeeding in unifying it. As we know, the credit for finishing that job goes to the Romans.

The list of Etruscan cities is long, but it is an open question if every city name included in it was of the Etruscan origin or it was Umbrian, Pelasgian, Latin or else. We also need to be open to the idea that some names could be of shared cultural and linguistic heritage.

4.1. TEST RECONSTRUCTIONS OF CITY NAMES

Again, I decided to first check "smaller fish" before I encounter "big guys".As I looked at the list of the names of Etruscan cities it was clear that at least some of them are of Indo-European stock. To me, the most obvious Indo-European city name on that list was the name of Statna in southern Tuscany. It flourished in seventh century BC.

4.1.1 STATNA

Indo-European root STA we can find in various languages. i.e. Serbian verb STATI means 'to stand', Latin STATUS means 'manner of standing'. There is a big family of Indo-European words that come out of this 'sta': the Serbian 'stanica' or English 'station', Serbian 'stanje' or English 'state' (as in 'state of things'). Its core meaning is 'standing' but it also means PLACE (in Serbian it is 'meSTO') and it extends to mark regions and even countries (like AfghaniSTAN). You will find Stanley in England or Stanislav and Stanko in Slavic lands. My paternal grandmother's name was Stana Maslić. It means 'who will stand', 'who will stay', 'who will survive'.

Let me list some relevant Sanskrit words.

stha adj.   place, abiding, staying, standing, occupied with, existing in, being in [154]

Also, there is stem 'sthA'.

sthApayati { sthA }   verb caus.   place, lay, stop, found, institute, raise, erect, fix, set up [155]
sthAtR   adj.   immovable, which stands or stays[156]

sthAtR	m.	authority [156]
sthAtra	n.	station, place [157]
sthAna	n.	place, house, station, dwelling, province [158]

But even reconstructing Statna with Sanskrit gave me some problems. I considered Statna to be a compound name that was made from STAT + NA. Generally, interpreted, Statna with 'stha' or 'sthA' works. It would simply mean ABIDING, ABODE, dwelling or settlement. But the second T in STAT stayed unexplained by Sanskrit, but understandable from the angle of Latin or Serbian! Also, how to read NA at the end? Was it just some kind of noun ending or it was a word with a meaning?

What would happen if we examine the Latin name of Statna which was Statonia. Considering STAT already explained enough, we need to check -ONIA with Sanskrit.

oNi	m.	protection, shelter [159]

We find -ONIA in many Indo-European toponyms. It should generally be understood as PLACE, REGION OR even COUNTRY, but I liked what I found in Sanskrit.

STATONIA would mean PROTECTED PLACE OF STAYING or PROTECTED SETTLEMENT.

Latins lived close to Etruscans, and sometimes mixed with them, so their STATONIA might be pointing to the original Etruscan compound. If an Etruscan would pronounce STATONIA it would become STATUNIA or rather STATUNA (because Etruscans did not have the sound O and used U instead). But Etruscan language is also known for dropping vowels in the ending part of words and that is how we arrive from STATUNA to STATNA. We find a similar example in the name of an important Etruscan City – Tarchuna, which was also called Tarchna. A significant number of names of Etruscan cities end with

UNA or NA.

What if these names are some kind of generic terms for settlements, cities, or protected places of habitation? When I looked at Sanskrit words that meant 'protection', 'defence' and similar, my blood boiled from excitement because I just found the origin of two Serbian words that mean 'town'. Those words are PALANKA and VAROŠ.

There are two options for PALANKA. The first one looks simple and clean.

pAlana   n.   protection, defending [160]
kha n.   city [161]

pAlana + kha → palankha → palanka

The meaning is PROTECTED CITY.

Still, the cleanest reconstruction does not have to be the correct one.

pallI   f.   city [162]
aNaka   adj.   smal l[163]

This would end up as PALANAKA → PALANKA. Here, arriving at the Serbian noun requires that we drop a vowel, but the meaning is identical to the contemporary meaning of *palanka*. It does mean SMALL TOWN in Serbian. Regarding VAROŠ, I also found a direct Sanskrit explanation.

vAra { vR }   m.   gate, cover, anything which covers or surrounds or restrains[164]
vara   m.   enclosing [165]
Aste { As }   verb 2   abide, dwell, stay

vara + As → VARAS (compare with VAROŠ)

It suggests some kind of enclosing, gated community, maybe an oppidum or a fort. These particular ties between Sanskrit and Serbian, which are both Indo-European languages, are still undetected. What if Etruscan city names hide Sanskrit words and stems in the same manner in which 'palanka', 'reka', and 'river' hid it?.

If Etruscan toponyms were ever examined with Sanskrit, it was probably just a brief examination. Even if somebody checked it out, he or she searched for identical words, never thinking of viewing them as compounds. Just as I did with river names, I started breaking Etruscan city names into parts and had an instant suspicion that some of them might contain a Sanskrit word that means CITY.
So, I tried my lack with Capua.

4.1.2 CAPEVA (Capua)

According to Massimo Pallottino, Capeva was also known as Volturnum).[166] There is an existing etymology of Capeva.

"The name of Capua comes from the Etruscan Capeva.[1] The meaning is 'City of Marshes'." Wikipedia [167]

I don't know how exactly they came to this translation, but if you ask a Sanskrit dictionary it is absolutely correct.

kha	n.	city [168]
pava	m.	marsh [169]

kha + pava → kapava → kapeva → this would end up as Kapva

Kapva → V becomes U → Capua

This might be another moment of clarity! Why don't we check a very similar name – Capena?

4.1.3 CAPENA OR CAPNA

Capena was a city of Faliscan people who were culturally, politically and even linguistically close to the Etruscans. Could this one also hide in its name the main characteristics of the landscape it occupied? This is how one website describes the area.

"Capena has origins in ancient history – traces of habitation go back to prehistoric times, doubtless because of the plentiful supply of caves for shelter, sources of water and rich animal life." [170]

Again, it looked like a lucky find.

kha n.   cave, cavern, cavity of the body [171]
paNa   m.   house, dwelling [172]

kha + paNa → → khapana → kapana → Capena

Meaning: CAVE-HOUSE(S), CAVE DWELLINGS.

That is one option. Another path is to view this name as an expression of the security concept.

kha n.   city
pAna   n.   protection, defence [173]

This gives khapana → kapana → Capena!

My bet is on the second reconstruction, which offers translation, DEFENDED or PROTECTED CITY.

4.1.4 NEPETE or NEPET

The contemporary name of this town in Lazio is Nepi.

Wikipedia says that "*The town is known for its mineral springs, sold and bottled under the Acqua di Nepi brand throughout Italy.*" [174]

Good water of Nepete was equally important in Etruscan times. Its etymology is visibly Sanskritic.

nepa   n.   water [175]
+
edhate   { edh } verb   rise, swell, increase, go strong [176]

nepa + edh → nepedh → H is dropped → neped → no D in Etruscan, becomes T → nepet

This NEPET literally means WATER-RISE. We should read it as SPRING and Nepete might mean SPRINGS.

4.1.5 SATURNIA

Saturnia is a spa town in Tuscany, inhabited since ancient times. There is an existing etymology.

"*Saturnia takes its name from the Roman god Saturn(us). Legend has it that he grew tired of the constant wars of humans, and sent a thunderbolt to earth that created a magic spring of warm sulphurous water which would pacify mankind.*
Dionysius of Halicarnassus lists Saturnia as one of the towns first occupied by the Pelasgi and then by the Etruscan civilization." [177]

We will often find Pelasgians as the founders of places that are considered Etruscan. The name is indeed almost identical to the name of god Saturnus, but what if the village was named after springs and the legend came later.

sAta	adj.	given, granted, gained [178]
sAta	n.	gift, delight, pleasure [178]
RNa	n.	water [179]

This would give SATARNA or SATRNA, a GIFT-WATER or DELIGHTING WATER. Are there other ways?

sAdhu   adj.   pure, well-born, proper, good, powerful, noble, virtuous [180]

There is no doubt that Etruscans would turn D into T. The H would be dropped.
So, *sAdhu* becomes 'sAtu'. When we add 'Rna' to it, we get SATURNA or GOOD WATER, "VIRTUOUS" WATER, NOBLE WATER, etc.

4.1.6 GRAVISCA

It is called Porto Clementino now, but in Etruscan time it was Gravisca, the port of Tarchuna. The major Etruscan cities were never built directly on the seashore, which would expose them to pirate raids. They were a bit inland.

graha	m.	house [181]
+		
vAsam.		dwelling, residence, staying [182]
+		
ka	n.	water [183]

graha + vAsa + ka → grahvaska → H is dropped → gravaska

GRAVASKA (reconstructed)
GRAVISCA (ancient name)

The name could not be Gravisca because Etruscans had no G sound. It had to be CRAVISCA. The meanings of 'graha' and 'vAsa' overlap significantly, but let's translate Gravisca as HOUSE-STAYING-WATER, which we could view as SEA-SHORE SETTLEMENT.

Another reconstruction is quite possible and also convincing, but we first need to know that in ancient times, Gravisca was *"[...] in an unhealthy position on the coast (due to malaria from nearby marshes)".* [184]

jighrati   { ghrA }   verb 1 3 smell, perceive by smell [185]
viSa m.,n.   poison [186]
or
viSa n.   water [186]

ka   n.   water [183]

ghrA + viSa + ka → ghraviska → graviska

The literal layout is "PERCEIVE BY SMELL POISON WATER", which is easy to see as STINKY INFESTED WATER. Indeed, next to Gravisca was a malaria-infested marsh.

If we treat ending CA in Gravisca as if it came from Sanskrit *kha* (city) then translation could be SWAMP CITY or something similar.

4.1.7 MUTINA or MUTNA

"The territory around Modena (Latin: Mutina, Etruscan: Mutna) was inhabited by the Villanovans in the Iron Age, and later

by Ligurian tribes, Etruscans, and the Gaulish Boii (the settlement itself being Etruscan)." [187]

This time we can discuss and reconstruct both the Etruscan and the Roman name at the same time. Mutina might have a meaning that appears as an option in some other Etruscan city-names.

mud   f.   happiness, delight, gladness, joy, pleasure [188]
moda   m.   (2. mud-) joy, delight, gladness, pleasure [ZM: this word would be rendered by Etruscan as 'muta'] [189]
ina adj.   glorious, powerful, determined, energetic, strong [190]
ina m.   king, master, lord [190]

mud + ina → mudina → no D in Etruscan, becomes T → Mutina → Etruscans drop a vowel in the ending syllable of the name → Mutna

Is it a PLEASANT KINGDOM, HAPPY KINGDOM, GLORIOUS KINGDOM, DELIGHTFUL KINGDOM?

Well, that is just an option. We can look at Mutina differently.

mUta   adj.   bound [191]
ina m.   king, master, lord [190]

This would give us BOUND BY KING or BOUND KINGDOM. It might be bound by city walls or it could have the meaning of UNITED KINGDOM if we consider that different groups lived together here.

4.1.8 NARCE

This was a Faliscan city. The Faliscans were culturally similar to Etruscans and they also had good relations with them. Wrongly or not, the Faliscan language is considered to be close to Latin, not to Etruscan. Still, Sanskrit can translate the name of Narce. We already analyzed La Cannara, and proposed that its translation is CITY ON THE RIVER or by the river. Narce can easily have the very same etymology. It was also located on a river.

nAra   n.   water [192]
+
kha   n.   city, cavern, fields, sky [193]

The meaning would be CITY ON THE RIVER, or by the river. The same as La Cannara (seem to be just reversed word order).

But Narce might also have the literal meaning of "WATER FIELDS" or RIVER VALLEY. But then, another reconstruction would fit in what I call CAPITAL-pattern.

nRNAti { nRR }   verb   lead [194]
nr̩   leading / naya [195]

nRR + kha → nrrkha → vowel A is inserted instead of first R → narkha

H was dropped, we end up with 'narka' or LEADING CITY.

NARKA (reconstructed)
NARCE (Faliscan)

Pelasgians are often mentioned as part of the pre-Roman history of Italy. They were natives of Greece, the inhabitants of "Greece before the Greeks", they were one of the major ingredients in the mix out of which was born Greek identity. What would happen if we would run the ethnonym PELASGIANS through an Etruscan speech filter?

You see, the Roman word for Pelasgians was PELASGI. The Etruscans had no G, so they would use K. We now get PELASKI. But the Etruscan P often turns into F, which is the sound other Italians eventually got from them.

Now, it is FELASKI, which in Etruscan would be written FELASCI. The Latin word for Faliscans is FALISCI. Please, compare these names.

PELASGI (Latin name based on Greek name)
FELASCI (hypothetic "Etruscan" pronunciation)
FELUSKEŚ (from Etruscan inscription)
FALESCE (from Faliscan inscription)
FALISCI (Latin)

Falisci-Felasci-Pelasgi?

The similarity is worth noticing. Pelasgians settled at many shores and islands of the Mediterranean, but nobody ever explained what happened with the Pelasgians in Italy. Did they merge into the Etruscans but one group kept their old identity which is known to us as the Faliscans?

What happened with the Faliscans?

That is known. They disappeared. The cradle of our civilization, Rome, committed genocide against them.
Over time, the surviving Faliscans became Romans.

Pelasgi, Falisci...

4.1.9 PARMA

We find on Wikipedia some interesting guesses regarding the name of Parma.

"[...] The city was most probably founded and named by the Etruscans, for a parma (circular shield) was a Latin borrowing, as were many Roman terms for particular arms, and Parmeal, Parmni and Parmnial are names that appear in Etruscan inscriptions. (...) Whether the Etruscan encampment was so named because it was round, like a shield, or whether its situation was a shield against the Gauls to the north, is uncertain." [196]

So, Parma might be associated with a shield! If you take a look at an Etruscan shield exhibited in the Altes Museum in Berlin, you will see that the front of the round shield is decorated with many metal "dots" that form concentric circles. In the middle of it, we find an encircled solar cross. Those "dots" are mini-shields, a repetition of the design that dominates the whole shield. What does it mean? Is it some kind of expression of heavenly order? Visuals on that shield have religious meaning and the solar cross in the middle makes you think of Etruscan city-building rite or procedure. In fact, by that rite, the cross was scraped on the ground to mark the center point of a circle that would define future city walls. Is Parma's name connected with a broader religious motif? It could be. In the light of "shield parallel", one must notice the Sanskrit character of the name.

phara   n.   shield [197]
ma   n.   welfare, water, magic formula [198]

phara + ma → pharma → Parma

The literal meaning is SHIELD-MAGIC-FORMULA.

ARYAN ITALY OF THE ETRUSCANS

Still, there is more.

parama   n.   chief part or matter or object, highest point, extreme limit [199]

parama   adj.   primary, supreme, highest, remotest, best, superior or inferior to [199]

parama → Etruscans corrupt endings of words → Parma

Now, the meaning would be CHIEF, PRIMARY, SUPREME. This matches an idea of a city-state that ruled its region and which was the seat of power.

But there are other Sanskrit words we can employ here.

pAra   m.   town, guardian, keeper, crossing, boundary[200]

para   adj.   succeeding, greatest, highest, supreme, chief [201]

For example, if you combine *pAra* (town) with *ma* (water), the result is PARMA meaning TOWN WATER, (which suites the stream called Parma) or "TOWN PLACED NEAR WATER".

If you treat these names as compounds, Sanskrit is very responsive. But Sanskrit is also too responsive. One short Sanskrit word or stem sometimes has ten or twenty meanings. Not to mention that Etruscan language turns every B, D or G into P, T or K and the vowel O is always U for them. This increases the number of possibilities so much that it often becomes messy. But it doesn't mean that one of those options is not the right one.

Maybe some of these city-names were not really Etruscan names. Some of the cities were founded by other peoples. Statna and Saturnia are obviously Indo-European names. Saturnia is an interesting example because historical records mention that it was a Pelasgian town. If this name was Pelasgian, then Pelasgians were Indo-Europeans, but it is often speculated that they were not. It is also speculated and more or less accepted that Etruscans were not Indo-Europeans.

We have to check the names of the main cities of Etruria. If any city-names are supposed to be Etruscan, it is them.

4.2 TWELVE MAIN CITIES OF ETRURIA PROPER

The Twelve main cities of Etruria formed what historians call the Etruscan League, a loose confederation of autonomous city-states. The complete list of cities that constituted this Dodecapoli is still debated.

If one of them was captured by enemies, another one would be promoted as a member of the Dodecapoli. Possibly, some cities whose names we examine in this section were not part of the Etruscan Dodecapoli, but it doesn't change much regarding our goal, which is to examine their names with Sanskrit.

Those names are: *Arretium, Chaire, Clevsin, Curtun, Perusia (Perusna?), Pupluna, Tarchuna, Vatluna, Veia, Velathri, Velch and Velzna.*

All of these names responded to Sanskrit. But for almost all of them, we got multiple reconstructions that made sense in the context. However, some meanings tend to repeat. It was very similar to the examination of Tuscan and Italian hydronyms. Most of them seemed to have a generic meaning that marked a city, fort, a concept of defence, a seat of a king, state and power.

At this place, only reconstructions that gave "generic meanings" are being presented.

4.2.1 ARRETIUM

This is contemporary Arezzo. Here are words to use.

arhati { arh }　　　　verb 1　be able, be obliged or required to do anything, be entitled to, have a right to [202]

arhati + um

ARATIUM (reconstructed)
ARRETIUM (ancient name)

The meaning would be ENTITLED CITY. But if we insist that double R in Arretium has to be explained, we have to reconstruct it as a three-word compound. These would be words to use.

arhati { arh }　　　　verb 1　be obliged or required to do anything, be entitled to, have a right to [202]
rATi f.　　war, battle [203]
uma m.　　city, town [204]

arh + rATi + uma → arhratiuma → H is dropped → arratiuma

The literal translation is "OBLIGED-WAR-CITY" or ENTITLED TO BATTLE CITY. That would suggest a FORTIFIED CITY, which Arretium really was. It is positioned at the place that is hard to approach and protected by stone walls.

4.2.2 CAERE

At the location of modern town Cerveteri, once was a

big and prosperous city called Caere. However, Caere was likely a Latin version of the Etruscan name. Massimo Pallottino wrote that the *"original Etruscan form of the name was probably Chaisre, whence Cisra, and χaire"*.[205] So, the real name is still guessed and we can try to explore those guesses.

I will assume that what Pallottino wrote as χaire is equal to *Chaire* or *Khaire*.[49] There are interesting options here.

ka	m.	king [206]
kha	n.	city [207]
+		
irA	f.	earth [208]

So we get KAIRA or "KING-EARTH, meaning "KING-LAND" or KINGDOM.

Or, the result is KHAIRA, meaning "CITY-EARTH", therefore CITY-LAND. Remember, in many languages, i.e. Slavic languages, the same word might mark soil, earth, and country. Thus, the translation might even be CITY-STATE!

But there is another way!

kAya	m.	capital, principal, house [209]
+		
irya	mfn.	powerful, active, energetic [210]
irya	mfn.	a lord [210]
irya	mfn.	destroying enemies [210]

Since Etruscan does not have sound Y as in 'yolk" or simply represents it with the character I, Sanskrit 'kAya' would be KAIA and irya would be IRIA. Therefore, the formula goes like this.

kaia + iria → kairia

You already know that Etruscan language drops vowels

in ending sections of words.

kairia → kaira

The literal meaning is either POWERFUL CAPITAL or LORD'S HOUSE, maybe CAPITAL THAT DESTROYS ENEMIES, suggesting a city well equipped for war.

Now, let's take a look at another name that Pallottino mentioned - CHAISRE. Without going into an in-depth explanation, we need to know that Etruscans wrote K in several ways: as K, C and Q. This was well explained by Giuliano and Larissa Bonfante in "The Etruscan Language: An Introduction".[211] Here is how I reconstruct CHAISRIE.

kAya   m.   capital, principal, house [209]
+
zrI   f.   power, might, royal dignity [212]

We can also use another shape of ZRI.

zrIyate   { zri }   verb Pass.   be protected [213]

Well, I present Sanskrit words using Harvard-Kyoto transliteration, so 'zrI' and 'zri' are pronounced as SHRI, with SH as in the word 'shore'. Here is the reconstruction.

kaia + shri → kaishri → H is dropped → kaishri

KAISHRI (reconstructed)
CHAISRE (Etruscan)

Possible meanings are POWERFUL CAPITAL, MIGHTY PRINCIPAL, ROYAL HOUSE (or ROYAL CITY), PROTECTED HOUSE, PROTECTED CAPITAL, etc. They all express the SEAT OF POWER and/or FORTIFIED CITY.

Both Chaire and Chaisre appear to offer the same idea. Cisra should be just a short form of Chaisre.

It is interesting that the contemporary name Cerveteri can be translated by Sanskrit as CAPITAL.

karvaTa   m.n.   village, market-town, the capital of a district [214]

4.2.3 CLEVSIN

There are two approaches to the origin of the name Clevsin. One is connected to the Etruscan word *cleva (kleva)*, which is translated by the Bonfantes as *offering*. [216]

This would put the name in a religious context, eventually pointing to Clevsin as a place of an important temple.

But the word CLEVA could have other meanings, but its main meaning was probably GLORY, FAME. In that view, the Etruscan word CLEVA came from Sanskrit stem 'glev'.

glevate { glev }   verb   worship, serve [217]
glev serving, worshipping / sevan [218]
+
sinite { si }   verb 5 9   bind [219]
+
ina   m.   king, master, sun [220]

GLEV + si + ina → glevsina → G becomes K in Etruscan → klevsina → Klevsin (spelt as Clevsin)

The literal meaning is WORSHIP-BIND-KING. We can read it as KINGDOM BOUND BY FAITH. This would fit into a picture of the Etruscans as very religious people. But...

The Roman name Clusium is translated as ENCLOSURE, coming from Latin verb *cludo, cludere.*

cludo, cludere, clusi, clusus... (Latin verb) → enclose[221]
uma m.   a city, town [222]

clusi + uma → CLUSIUM ("ENCLOSED PLACE or ENCLOSED, FORTIFIED CITY).

Why do we have to take the Roman name of Clevsin seriously? Most often, Romans did not change city names, they either left them untouched or they just Latinized them. After Romans took over, Clevsin became Clusium, Tarchuna became Tarquinii, etc. Besides, its translation ENCLOSED CITY or FORTIFIED CITY belongs to a pattern that seems to exist in the names of the Dodecapoli cities. Let's compare Greek, Roman and Etruscan name of Clevsin.

Kloúsion (Greek)
Clusium (Roman)
Clevsin (Etruscan)

When you look at the Greek and Roman names they appear to be coming from the same root. Both of them are looking as they belong to the same family as the English verb *to close*. On the other hand, we get some other insight when we compare the Greek version with the Etruscan. Let's break both names into two parts.

Kloú-sion (Greek)
Clev-sin (Etruscan)

Now, we see something else. Because the Greeks did

not have the sound V, they replace it with U in this particular case. If we put back that V, we get KLOVSION.

KLOVSION (a hypothetical earlier form of Greek)
KLEVSIN (Etruscan)

Now, let's compare their ending parts.

SION (Greek)
SIN (Etruscan)

Etruscans drop vowels in ending parts of words quite regularly (just like the citizens of Sarajevo pronounce the name of their city as Saraj'vo, dropping E). Etruscan SIN is likely just shortened SION. What do we get if we reconstruct this SION with Sanskrit?

| Sinite | { si } | verb 5 9 | bind [219] |
| oNi | m. | protection, shelter [223] | |

si + oNi → sioni → SION

The literal layout is BIND-SHELTER, BIND-PROTECTION. But as a noun, Sanskrit *si* means 'service', so the translation might be "SERVICING AS SHELTER". We need to try again KLEV (or KLOV) part of the name. Few Sanskrit words start with K-L and those rare that could be considered have meanings that don't match at all.

But we can still try to explain it using Sanskrit.

Michael Coulson wrote, *"Classical Sanskrit is based on a more easterly dialect than the Rgveda, as is shown by the fact that it contributes the number of words which preserve an original Indo-European L, where the Rgvedic dialect (in common with Iranian) changes this sound to R: thus both Vedic raghú 'swift, light' and Classical Sanskrit laghu 'light, nimble' are cognate with Greek elakhús."* [224]

This means that what is sometimes R in Classical Sanskrit might be a transformed L from older Indo-European speech. Now, it makes sense to look for roots that contain K-R.

kirati{ kRR }   verb   cover with [225]

We can argue if meanings TO ENCLOSE and TO COVER WITH are similar or not, but to enclose something in many ways means to cover it. Clearly, what is KRR in Sanskrit can be an older Indo-European KLL or KL. We need the rest of KLEV or KLOV.

avi   m.   wall, enclosure [226]

KL + avi → klavi → klav

KLAVi (reconstructed)
KLOU (Greek)
CLEV (Etruscan)

Let's say that we translate it as COVERED WITH WALL or WALL-COVER.

The whole thing is now COVER-WITH-WALL-BIND-SHELTER. How should we read it? Maybe we can see in it THE SHELTER ENCIRCLED (bound) BY WALL COVER. It is not a very elegant translation, but it does suggest a FORT.

Any translation is an interpretation. Let's see an example: the Serbian verb ZAZIDATI means *to enclose with a wall*. The literal translation of it is TO FOR-BUILD or TO FOR-WALL!

At the end, which reconstruction of Clevsin is right, if

any? It is hard to give a definitive answer, but I do prefer a fort pattern.

4.2.4 CURTUN

Most major Etruscan cities were heavily fortified. Giuliano and Larissa Bonfante wrote that Curtun, which is modern Cortona, was placed *"on a high cliff, surrounded by powerful walls whose remains are still visible"*.[227]

As you know, Etruscans have no G, it is always K for them. Here are the candidates for the first word.

gurate	{ gur }	verb 6	raise [228]
guru		adj.	great [229]

In this proposal, the second word is not known as an Etruscan, Latin or Italic word. It would be DUN, the Celtic word for 'fort'. This should be doubted. If we would try to defend this option we would underline that Curtun was in the northern part of Etruria proper, where the influences of Gauls were possible.

For Etruscans, DUN would be TUN and *gur* and *guru* would be *kur* and *kuru*. The compound made of two would be KURTUN. The literal translations would be RAISED FORT, in the meaning of a fort on a hill, BIG FORT, CHIEF FORT, MASTER'S or MASTER FORT, etc.

But we can also offer a purely Sanskritic option.

gurdayati	{ gurd }	verb 10	dwell, inhabit [230]
oNi	m.		protection, shelter

gurd + oNi → gurdoni

By the rule, Etruscan speech would transform three

consonants here.

G → K
D → T
O → U

GURDONI → KURTUNI → KURTUN

The literal translation is DWELL-PROTECTION, INHABIT-SHELER. So, it is PROTECTED PLACE OF HABITATION.

It is a FORTIFIED CITY!

4.2.5 PERUSIA (PERUSNA?)

This is contemporary Perugia. Sometimes you can find a claim that the Etruscan name was Perusna, but the Bonfantes only mention Perugia and Perusia while Pallottino uses a contemporary name. We can attempt to reconstruct Perusia. Following the logic of river names, we look for a simple, straightforward meaning. In that context, some words look attractive.

pAra   m.   town [231]

para adj.   chief [232]

But it is hard to reconstruct the rest of the name (USIA) with Sanskrit.

If we try to see in it a noun that eventually expressed a security concept, we can find this.

peru adj.   rescuing [233]

We can even attempt to reconstruct it as a compound.

pA   f.   guarding, protecting [234]
+
rUSati   { rUS } verb   cover [235]

These two give PARUS which might mean PROTECTIVE COVER. Eventually, if we assume that IA is a name ending, we can end up with PARUSIA or PERUSIA. We can still combine the already mentioned *pAra* (town) and *rUS* and the meaning would be TOWN-COVER or COVERED CITY. Would *cover* present a concept of *walls*?

It is interesting that if Perusna was the real Etruscan name of Perugia, we would be able to reconstruct it in a way that would provide the same meaning. Here is how.

rUSaNa   n.   covering [236]

pA + rUSaNa

Since Etruscans corrupted word endings, PARUSANA would end up as PARUSNA (Perusna).

Certainly, there are Sanskrit options available, but it is not easy to claim they give us a real explanation of the name of Perusia. At the same time, they work better than any current explanation!

4.2.6 PUPLUNA or FUFLUNA or PUPULUNA

The Romans called it Populonia. What would happen if we approach the Roman name as their version, a bilingual one, a translation that used very similar Latin words?

In that case, we would reach to *populus, populi*, which is a noun that means PEOPLE, FOLLOWING, NATION,

STATE.[237]

The second word in this Latin compound you know very well.

oNi m protection, shelter

popul(i) + oNi + A (name ending) → POPULONIA

Translations go from PEOPLE'S SHELTER and NATIONAL SHELTER to STATE SHELTER.

However, in Indo-European toponyms, ending ONIA generally marks a PLACE, region, and even a CITY. So, Populonia could mean PEOPLE'S CITY, NATIONAL CITY (maybe a CITY-STATE)!

In Etruscan, this 'oNi' is transformed in UNA. We need the first word.

bhUpAla m. king [238]

bhUpAla + UNA → bhupaluna

As always, B becomes P.
H is dropped. The result is PUPALUNA.

PUPALUNA (reconstructed)
PUPULUNA (Etruscan)

We can read it as KING'S SHELTER, PROTECTED or FORTIFIED KINGDOM, even as KING-CITY.

Another way is to use a similar Sanskrit word.

bhUpAlana n. sovereignty, dominion, earth-protection [239]

The common belief is that this city was named after the god who was the Etruscan equivalent of Dionysus. The name of this god is Fufluns which is pretty much the same as Fufluna (Pupuluna, Pupluna). This is a logical interpretation.

The name of the god Fufluns is fully reconstructable with Sanskrit. The article about it you can find in my book "The Etruscans, Sanskrit, and Homer".

4.2.7 TARCHUNA

tAra adj.	high [240]
ku f.	earth [241]
oNi m.	protection, shelter

tAra + ku + oNi → tarkoni → since 'oNi' is always rendered as UNA → TARKUNA

TARKUNA (reconstructed)
TARCHUNA (Etruscan)

Don't forget, this CH is just one of three ways in which Etruscan writes the letter K.

The literal translation is HIGH-EARTH SHELTER. It suggests a FORT or a PROTECTED SETTLEMENT placed ON A HIGH GROUND, on elevated terrain. And that is how Tarchuna was positioned.

Wikipedia states, *"The city towered above the Marta valley and was about 6 km from the sea."* [242]

We also know that it was fortified.

"The large walls were built during the city's most prosperous period in the 6th century BC and measured about 8 km long,

enclosing 135 ha (...)." Wikipedia [243]

4.2.8 VEIA

Again, just as in the case of Pupluna, it is thought that the city was named after the goddess Vei or Veia, which was the Etruscan Demeter. We focus here on the concept of the city. The name of the goddess we discuss in the second book about Etruscan vocabulary, which explains the cultural and mythological terminology of the Etruscans.

va	m.	dwelling [244]
+		
yA	f.	support [245]
yA	f.	prosper [245]
ya	m.	fame [246]

This gives VAIA → VEIA.

It means DWELLING SUPPORT, PROSPEROUS DWELLING, FAMOUS DWELLING or GLORIOUS CITY. "Dwelling support" also works as a translation of Veia as Demetre because this fertility goddess, mother goddess, also protects the home and family.

We also should consider two other words.

vAya	m.	leader [247]
vayA	f.	power, strength [248]

4.2.9 VELATHRI

The Etruscan city Velathri is the contemporary tourist attraction Volterra.

valate   { val }   verb   cover, enclose, to

be covered [249]
    vala m.   enclosure [250]
    +
    adri m.   mountain, stone, rock [251]

val + adri → valadri

D, which Etruscans don't have, is changed to TH and we end up with VALATHRI.

VALATHRI (reconstructed)
VELATHRI (Etruscan)

Translations are MOUNTAIN ENCLOSURE or MOUNTAIN FORT, STONE ENCLOSURE or STONE FORTH.

Is this a correct etymology? Look at the first sentence in the Wikipedia article about Volterra.

"Volterra (Italian pronunciation: [volˈtɛrra]) is a walled mountaintop town in the Tuscany region of Italy." [252]

4.2.10 VELCH

Both Pallottino and the Bonfantes use Vulci, the Latin version of the name.
Eventually, the real Etruscan name was Velch (pronounced as Velk).

    valate   { val } verb   cover or enclose or to be covered [249]
    kha   n.   city

val + kha → valkha → H is dropped → valka → valk

VALK (reconstructed)
VELCH (Etruscan)

Again, CH in Velch is how Etruscans wrote the sound K.

The translation is ENCLOSED CITY, therefore it could be WALLED CITY or FORTIFIED CITY.

But we should be careful here! Velch was raised several centuries before its walls.

"The walls were built in the first half of the 4th c. BC before the wars with the Romans and are about 6.5 km in circumference." [253]

Still, ENCLOSED CITY doesn't have to assume stone or brick walls. It could be enclosed by earth-works and wooden walls. The fact that city walls of Velch were built two, three or more centuries after its foundation does not discard enclosure-etymology.

There are other Sanskrit options here. For example, Velch was a maritime city.

velA	f.	coast	[seashore] [253-B]
kha	n.	city	

This reconstructs Velkh(a) or Velch as SEASHORE CITY or MARITIME CITY. Velch was not exactly on the seashore, but it was close to it as much as security concepts of the era allowed. At the height of its might, Velch was a maritime power.

4.2.11 VELZNA

Velzna was the center of the Etruscan religion, placed on the shores of Lake Bolsena. It was known under Roman variant Volsinii, which is used by Pallottino who also gives us its Etruscan name as Velsna and Velzna.[254] The Bonfantes, use Volsinii but also mention it as Velsna.[255] Wikipedia page about Etruscan cities lists three variations: Velzna, Velsu, and Velznani.[256] Another Wikipedia page gives us Velusna as one of the variants.[257] In any case, we have a rough idea about its Etruscan name.

When Romans conquered Velzna they moved population out of the city. The location of Velzna is still unknown. It is believed that the city of Orvieto is at the place of ancient Velzna.

Wikipedia says that *"Excavations at Bolsena have uncovered huge double walls surrounding the group of small hills over which the city was built. A system of lateral walls within these enabled its defenders to cut off portions of the city and retreat behind further positions."* [257]

Let's give it a try.

vala	m.	enclosure [258]
senA	f.	army [259]

This VALSENA that eventually ended up as Velsna would mean ARMY ENCLOSURE, MILITARY ENCLOSURE, therefore FORT. There are reasons not to go with this etymology. Velzna was the center of Etruscan Religion and Fanum Voltumnae was their major sanctuary. It was the religious and political beacon of the Etruscans. The meaning of FORT might be too narrow, too ordinary.

We should look for other possibilities.

vala	m.	cavern, cave, enclosure [258]
+		
sanna	ppp.	sunken [260]

This would result in VALSANNA → VALSNA → VELZNA.

The literal translation is SUNKEN CAVERN. It might simply mean LAKE. But there is another, simpler way to arrive at the meaning of LAKE.

sunau   n.   water [261]

vala + sunau

Now, we get VALSUNAU, which is very close to VALSUNA → VALSNA → VELZNA.

Again, this can simply mean LAKE. There is a relevant analogy. In Lombardy, we find Lake Como and on its shores is a city called Como. Both names are identical and I think that both are coming from Sanskrit *kUma*, meaning 'lake'. But why would they use word CAVERN in the description of a lake? The reason could be in a simple fact that Lake Bolsena is a volcanic crater filled with water.

Another option might be more serious because variation Velznani should be an older shape of the city's name. Velzna or Velsna could be just a short form of it.

velA   f.   coast, shore [262]
snAna   n.   bathing in sacred waters, religious or ceremonial lustration, cleansing, ablution [263]

velA + snAna → velsnana

VELSNANA (reconstructed)
VELZNANI (Etruscan)

This would mean SHORE BATHING IN SACRED WATERS. It contains information about Velzna's placement, but also its religious significance.

An additional possible reconstruction includes a word that means 'grove'.

vela   n.   grove, garden [264]

Combined with 'snAna' this gives GROVE or GARDEN BATHED IN SACRED WATERS. If this was the meaning of the name, then this place had religious significance in pre-Etruscan times. All over Europe, from the Celts to the Slavs, rituals were practiced in sacred groves.

In the case of Velzna, the potential meaning of 'grove' is supported by history, which remembers the sacred grove of Fanum Voltumnae. This was a temple of god Voltumna or Voltumnus. Here, the leadership of twelve main cities of the Etruscan confederation met every year to strengthen or redefine their ties. Livy mentioned this in "The History of Rome". [265]

Pallottino wrote about fluidity and elasticity of the Etruscan religious story-line. According to him, *Voltumna or Veltha or Voltune* could be a local earth-spirit or deity that was promoted into "a superior divinity, the national god par excellence". [266]

Voltumna could be a version, an aspect or even an avatar of the chief god Tinia, the Etruscan Jupiter and the ruler of heaven. But here, he is an earth-god, a chthonic deity. At Velzna, you could occasionally feel his power coming from below, from the ground.

In ancient times, the volcanic complex at Lake Bolsena was still showing some activity.

Let's take a different approach!

valli   f.   earth [267]
+
uSNa   m. n.   heat [268]

uSNa   adj.   passionate, active, hot, pungent [268]

valli + uSNa → vallusna → valusna → Velusna

We get HOT EARTH, PASSIONATE EARTH, ACTIVE EARTH, pointing to an idea of a volcano or seismically active terrain. Sanskrit gives us a reconstruction even for that. But what is "seismical" to us, was a matter of religion to them. Needless to say, there are earthquakes in this region even in our time. That information is also included in the name.

velati { vel } verb   move, shake [269]
vellati { vell }   verb   tremble, be tossed or agitated[270]
+
uSNa   adj.   passionate, active, hot, pungent

vel (or 'vell) + uSNa → Velusna

This means SHAKING PASSIONATELY, TREMBLING ACTIVELY!

All of this looks confusing. Which of these translations is correct?

Instead of offering an answer, I will ask another question. What if this name was meant to puzzle you? And what if all of these reconstructions are correct?

"How could it be?" you might rightfully ask.

That is a concept that is completely foreign to our rationalistic time, but I invite you to think of religion as a story and to think of a story as an artistic creation. If you look from that angle, multiple answers come as natural, they are even desired. The deeper the story, the more complex answers to questions become. You don't have to accept this idea, but keep it in your mind. We will discuss this in the second book.

By the way, the Etruscans had a prophecy about how long their civilization would last and when it would die out. Most scholars agree that the Etruscan world faded away at the approximate time that was already predicted by their religion. The temple in Velzna had a famous wall in which a nail would be ritually driven with the passing of each year, as the Etruscan slowly but surely approached their doom. This gives me an idea for an additional reconstruction.

velayati { vel }   verb   count or declare the time [271]

uSNa   adj.   passionate, active, hot, pungent [268]

vel + uSNa → velusna (ACTIVE COUNTING OF TIME, PASSIONATE TIME-COUNT)

Let's leave it at this!

Interchangeability of B and V is something that we see frequently in Indo-European terminology, so let's take a look at the Italian name Bolsena. Could it have a Sanskrit meaning?

bala n.   power, might, strength, bulkiness [272]
bala n.   cavern [272]
sena   adj.   having a master or lord [273]
sana m.   acquisition [274]

bala + sena → balsena → Bolsena

First, notice that the Sanskrit words 'vala' and 'bala' mean 'cavern' and that B and V seem to be interchangeable in Sanskrit (at least occasionally). This would mean POWER THAT IS MASTERED, WHOSE POWER IS ACQUIRED or WHOSE POWER IS CONTROLLED.

Maybe CONTROLLING POWER? We can also decide to translate it as CAVERN or LAKE THAT IS CONTROLLED, LAKE THAT IS HARNESSED).

Since this was the leading city of the Etruscan League, this same reconstruction could be suggesting POWER-CONTROL. This fits, too. Velzna, scholars tell us, was a major center of the Etruscan religion and the seat of their confederation.

sana	adj.	lasting long [274]
sana	m.	offering, gain, acquisition [274]

So, it would be: bala + sana → balsana → Bolsena

Meaning: LONG-LASTING GIFT or LONG LASTING POWER etc. This could be taken in an agricultural, religious and political sense.

So, which translation of Velzna is right?

Is it one of them, several or even all of them?

Or none?

4.2.12 VETLUNA OR VATLUNA

The Etruscan Vetluna was called Vetulonium by Romans. Today, it is a village called Vetulonia.

Pallottino talks about Vetulonia[275] while the Bonfantes also list variants Vetluna and Vatluna[276].

vAtUla	adj.	entirely devoted, bent upon [277]
+		
oNi	m.	protection, shelter

vAtUla + oNi → vatuloni + A → vatulonia

This gives us the translation ENTIRELY DEVOTED TO PROTECTION. There might be other ways.

vATa	m.	enclosure, wall, fence [278]
Ali	adj.	secure, pure, honest [279]
oNi	m.	protection, shelter

vATa + Ali + oNi → vataloni → vataluna → vatluna

The literal meaning is WALL-SECURE-SHELTER and it should be read as SHELER WITH PROTECTIVE WALLS. The second word, 'Ali', has another meaning, too.

AlI   f.   ditch, dike [280]

This would give us a SHELTER FORTIFIED WITH WALL AND DITCH. But there is a cleaner reconstruction.

holati   { hul } verb   cover [281]

vATa + hul + oNi → vathuloni + A (name ending)

After H is dropped and O regularly turned into U, we get VATULUNIA → VATLUNA.

The literal translation is WALL COVERED SHELTER.

4.3 CONCLUSIONS WE CAN DRAW FROM SANSKRIT RECONSTRUCTIONS OF ETRUSCAN CITY NAMES

All names of the Dodecapoli cities are responsive to Sanskrit. It is harder to decide which exact translation we should choose. Sometimes, the situation seems to be clear and it looks obvious that a Sanskrit translation is correct, as it was in the case of Capeva and Nepete.

Two patterns appear to repeat. First, it is a "CAPITAL-pattern", that suggests a regional seat of power. Second, it is a "FORT-pattern".

For us, these are city names. But my idea is that they were just nouns, words invented to describe "the thing". They grew into city-names later.

However, some of those names a reconstructable with Sanskrit in other ways and those reconstructions do not fit the patterns I have shown. That complicates everything.

Why did we stick to patterns? Because we learned on names of Tuscan and Italian rivers that people who named them used clear and straightforward words, describing those rivers in the most basic and precise way. They called things for what they were.

The majority of Etruscan city names are reconstructable with Sanskrit., but this also applies to many other settlements in ancient Italy. There is nothing special, isolated or non-Indo-European in them. They are a part of an Italic, Mediterranean and Euro-Asian context.

The weirdest thing here is that according to the established linguistic story none of this should be possible. Western scholars consider Sanskrit as a contemporary of Greek and Latin. For them, Sanskrit is just another branch of the Indo-European tree. Therefore, Sanskrit should not have any special power when compared with Latin or Greek. According to this belief, it is equal to Greek and

Latin. Therefore, we should not expect Sanskrit to be capable of explaining Latin and Greek terms better than these languages.

I am starting to believe that Sanskrit, if not that tree itself, is closer to the trunk than any other Indo-European language. It could be that Sanskrit is a result of much longer religious and intellectual tradition than we can even assume. Somehow, Sanskrit preserved old linguistic material better than any known ancient European language. If it was not so, we would not be able to translate with Sanskrit Etruscan, Latin, and Greek names which are otherwise not translatable with those languages.

It is not a question if the names of Etruscan cities are Indo-European or not. The question is if these names or words were assigned by Etruscans.

Pliny the Elder wrote that the Etruscans *"vanquished three hundred Umbrian cities"*. [282]

It is believed that many Etruscan cities were previously Pelasgian. Did those Pelasgians, Umbrians, and others become Etruscans? It had to be so. Maybe it was less dramatic than how Etruscans later dissolve into "Romans", but it certainly happened.

So far, it looks to me that Etruscans are generally very similar to other peoples of the Mediterranean. Their material culture certainly confirms that view.

Even though it is frequently challenged in modern times, the opinion that the Etruscan language was "foreign" or non-Indo-European stayed strong and prevailed for over two thousand years.

We can take a few more moments and examine how correct it is.

We must check the vocabulary of the Etruscans.

5 ETRUSCAN VOCABULARY: RECONSTRUCTIONS

This is the main battlefield! A majority of Etruscan words we analyze here is taken from *"The Etruscan language: An Introduction"* by Giuliano and Larissa Bonfante. They list almost 400 Etruscan words, including personal names, words that come out of root-words, names of gods, some cities, etc.

Initially, this chapter was much longer. Just like in the case of names of Tuscan rivers and cities, I often found many ways to reconstruct with Sanskrit a certain word.

First, Sanskrit has so many short words and stems that quite often have many meanings. This itself offers you a huge choice of various "lego-blocks" from which you can make many words. There is a good chance that you trick yourself and start seeing what you want to see. The situation is similar to the one I faced while reconstructing the name of Sava River. You might get many reconstructions that make sense and even find yourself incapable of deciding which exact reconstruction is the right one.

But, with rivers, we had some tools of deduction we

were able to use, we could even identify possible patterns.

You cannot count on that kind of help when you try to analyze Etruscan vocabulary. You can attempt to identify a pattern only if you have available multiple Etruscan words that belong to the same theme. But this happens rarely.

For example, various Etruscan, Greek, and Italic words for pottery and ceramics seem to express the same or similar ideas. Still, that type of help is not generally available.

One characteristic of the Etruscan language further complicates reconstructing attempts.

As it has been constantly repeated, the Etruscan language does not have the sounds B, D, G, and O. They replace them with P, T, K, and U. This means that if you search a hypothetical word PUK (invented for this example), we would have to search PUK, PUG, POG, POK, BUK, BOK, BUG, BOG. Even though it is just a three-letter word it could still be a compound. So, we have to extend the search to PA, PU, PO, PE, PI and then UK, UG, OK, OG, UKA, OGA etc. Our hypothetical word PUK could be a compound formed from BU + KHA, BA + UG, PA + OG, POG + KA, etc, etc.

The problem is that you might find many of these in the form of short words or stems. Some of them will have two or three meanings, some will have five to ten and some might have dozens! This will result in too many possible reconstructions and translations.

So, how do you navigate through this jungle?

I never established a complete set of rules regarding how sound changes happen between Etruscan and Sanskrit, but I was generally guided by the Bonfantes' insights. While doing reconstructions, I also mostly tried to find a confirmation of the meaning of a certain word that is offered by the Bonfantes, only occasionally by somebody else (like Steinbauer for example). I rarely challenge the translations of Giuliano and Larissa Bonfante, I build upon it and I challenge only their general conclusion about the non-Indo-European nature of Etruscan. When I say the Bonfantes, then it also includes numerous other scholars whose work they synthesized into their own.

It is possible that there are some techniques and methods of linguistics not known to me, that I could have used, but didn't. I am an amateur and I never forgot that limitation, one that helped me stay modest.

So, what was my method?

It was mostly based on ordinary logic and so-called common sense. This is something that cannot be recognized as a method, I am fully aware of that. What we call common sense is a collection of thoughts and attitudes of our time that are real in the meaning of reality as something that we partially invented. In short, while we might laugh at the superstitions of the Etruscans or the concept of flat Earth, we also base our picture of reality on many imaginary "facts". If it wasn't so, no progress in science would be possible.

It is not my fault that the cream of professionals somehow missed that the name of Arno River means *river* in Sanskrit or that Nepete or modern Nepi, a city famous for its mineral water, has Sanskrit word for *water* in it.

Hmm!

I already believe that the Etruscan language is Indo-European and tightly related to Sanskrit, but I still need to prove it.

If everything was as easy as Arno, my discussion would be very short. But it wasn't. Etruscan and Sanskrit are different languages and it is not always a simple process in which you just translate a word from one language with a word from another language. It rarely works in that way.

ARYAN ITALY OF THE ETRUSCANS

5.1 TESTING THE WATERS

One of the favourite words of those who claim Indo-European ties is 'mi'. In Etruscan, it means 'I' (like in 'I am'). A perfect place to start!

MI

Giuliano and Larissa Bonfante say that this is an Etruscan pronoun that means *"I"*.[283] Here is a comparison, not with words for "I" in other languages, but with object pronouns that replace "I", like the word *me* does in English.

ETRUSCAN: mi
SERBIAN: mi, me (mean 'to me'; 'me', 'of me', 'upon me', 'from me')
ENGLISH: me

The Bonfantes also mention the following inscription *'mi arathiale zichuche'* (p. 101; this they translate as *"I was written to Arath"* or *"by Arath"*).

In my opinion, they translate it well. But there is a possibility that this means 'me', not 'I'. Their translation would still be correct. They also mention the passive participle form of 'mi'. It is *'mini'*. (*"mini alice velthur"*, p. 101). I see another parallel with Serbian.

Etruscan: mini
Serbian: mene, meni

They don't even have to match in a grammatical sense, they have the same meaning and they sound almost the same. If we follow the Etruscan word order literally, an alternative translation to Serbian would be: 'mene Arath napisa'. In English, it would sound like "ME BY ARATH WAS WRITTEN". It is grammatically correct in Serbian. All the attempts to make a connection of this word with the Indo-European language family were discarded with the argument that similar words with the same meaning exist in many languages. But let's take a look at another word in the inscription *"mi arathiale zichuche"*. This is what the Bonfantes say *zichuche* means.

ZIC, ZICH   *"book, writing, document, inscription"*
(p.220)

The verb in the same sentence is in the form ZICHUCHE (*"mi arathiale zichuche"*). They translate it as *written*.[284] But the Etruscan *zichuche* has a cousin in Sanskrit.

zikhaka   m.   scribe, writer [285]

With this comes a warning! In the Harvard-Kyoto Sanskrit transliteration, Z represents SH (like in English word 'shore'). So, this is pronounced as "shikhaka'. But, the two words are still very similar.

AM- (p.214)

The Bonfantes say that AM means *'to be'* in Etruscan (p. 214).
How AM I supposed to comment on this?

Doesn't AM in English "I am" represent the verb 'to be'? It is so similar.
Could this be accidental?

ARYAN ITALY OF THE ETRUSCANS

AN (ana, ane, anc, ancn, ananc)

According to the Bonfantes, this is the relative pronoun *HE, SHE, THIS, THAT* (p.214).

I see a similarity with the Serbian pronouns ON, ONA, ONO that mean HE, SHE, IT.

ANA (Etruscan)
ONA (Serbian)

Both the Etruscan and Serbian rendition feel like versions of the Sanskrit word for 'he' or 'she' or 'it'. Let's take a look!

ena pronoun   he, she, it, that, this [286]

CEHEN

The Bonfantes translates it as *'this one here'* (p.215). That might be correct. This could be closely related to the Sanskrit word for ka[287], meaning *who, what, which*. In some contexts, the word kaH appears as WHO.

kaH m.   who

For example *Who are you?* you can say in these ways.

bhavAn kaH ?   Who are you?
kaH tvam ?   Who are you?

The second word would be *enA*.

enA ind.   here[288]

kah + enA → kahena → kahen

KAHEN (reconstructed)
CEHEN (Etruscan)

The literal translation is WHO (is) HERE or WHICH-HERE. The Bonfantes said THIS ONE HERE.

One of the Sanskrit forms of the word that means *who* is *ka*. In Serbian, it is *ko!* Spokensanskrit.com says that *ko* means *"but who?"* Now, I understand why Svetislav Bilbija saw in Etruscan an ancient form of Serbian. Ko, who ka...

ETH, ET (*'thus', 'in this way'*, adverb) (p.216)

iti   adverb   thus, in this manner [289]

'Et' and 'iti'?

Almost the same!

ITA

"this" (p.216)

I will propose several similar Sanskrit words to be considered as related. I think they are.

yat	ind.	that [290]
etat	n.	this [291]
idam	n.	this [here]
ataH	indecl.	from this

Also, look at the Latin words for 'this' and 'that'. You can easily check it on Google Translate.
Pronoun: ID (that, this, it).[292]

ARYAN ITALY OF THE ETRUSCANS

You can see the connection between Latin ID and English IT and Etruscan ITA. One thing is certain: the Etruscan ITA belongs to the Indo-European family.

5.2 FAMILY RELATIONS AND SOCIAL TERMINOLOGY

When linguists are looking for the kinship of languages they usually pay attention to words for family members. The common belief is that those words are relatively resistant to change. It will be interesting to see they relate to Indo-European terminology.

ATI, APA, PAPA, CLAN

The most known Sanskrit word for mother is *mAtR⁹*, similar to the English word *mother* or Latin and Serbian *mater*. But there are other Sanskrit words for mother. We use the term "umbilical cord" and we believe that "umbilical" (meaning 'related to navel') comes from the Medieval Latin *umbilic*. Nobody thought of the Sanskrit word that explains everything much deeper.

| ambA | f | mother [294] |
| ambAlikA | f. | mother (vocative case) [295] |

And what now? An umbilical cord is a mother's cord. If our culture could not recognize *ambA* and *ambAlikA* in the umbilical cord, it would not be a surprise if it were incapable of seeing the Indo-European features of the Etruscan language. There are other Sanskrit words for mother: *alla, anas, atta*... Did I just mention *atta*?

attA f.   mother [296]

An Etruscan word for *mother* is ATI. It is 'attA' in Sanskrit! The Etruscan word for *father* is not 'papa', but APA (the Bonfantes. p.214) but the Etruscan word PAPA means *grandfather* (the Bonfantes, p.218). In Etruscan, *son* is CLAN (the Bonfantes, p.215). Why did nobody dare to think that our word 'clan' could mean *sons?*

TETA means *'grandmother'* in Etruscan (the Bonfantes, p.219). In Serbian, *teta* is how you address a woman who is much older than you when you want to speak in a warm and respectful manner. But, in Serbian, your mother's or father's sister is *tetka*. Words do not have to be the same and even when they are, they do not have to mean the same thing, but if those meanings stay in the same constellation it can be proof of kinship between languages. *Stolica* is *chair* in Serbian, it is *capital* in Polish. If you think of a throne, a royal chair, a seat of power, you will understand how the meaning of *stolica* shifted. Teta-tetka, apa-papa, ati-atta – are these minor or crucial differences? They might be big in everyday conversation, but they are minor when you are looking for a kinship of languages.

By the way, *daughter* is SECH or SEC (pronounced as SEK) in Etruscan (the Bonfantes, p.218). In Serbian, sister is "sestra", but a warm word for sister is *seka*.

SECH (pronounced as SEK) and SEKA!? Daughter and sister?

The Etruscan NEFTŚ means 'nephew' and 'grandson'. Its similarity to the English *nephew* was spotted long ago! Are these accidental similarities?

PRUMATHŚ, PRUMTS

The Bonfantes translate this as *"great-grandson"* (p218).

We can see here an "Etruscan corruption" of words at work. PRUMATHŚ becomes PRUMTS. The word is shockingly Indo-European. We just need to put its meaning upside-down and it will show its heritage. I am not even questioning the Bonfantes' translation, so I will translate it as OF GREAT GRANDMOTHER, which might mean great-grandchild.

The MATH part of PRUMATHŚ looks akin to the Latin and Serbian MATER, Slavic MATI, etc. The PRU part is the same word you find in the Serbian 'prababa' (great grandmother) or the English word 'prehistory'.

pra   adverb   before, in front [297]

So, *prababa* is 'before baba' (since 'baba' is grandmother, *prababa* is 'before grandmother') and 'prehistory' is before history. Interestingly, the same word gives birth to our word PRO (like in 'pro-life', 'pro et contra', etc).

pra   adverb   forward [297]
pra   ind.   in nouns of relationship = great- see pra-pitāmaha-, pra-pautra-[297]

MATH in PRUMATHŚ should not be doubted. It is related to a Sanskrit word.

mAtuH   indecl.   of mother [mother's] [298]

So, the formula is very clear now.

pra + mAtuH → pramatuh → Etruscans drop some vowels in ending part of words → pramath

PRAMATH (reconstructed)
PRUMATHŚ (Etruscan)

The sound Ś at the end of PRUMATHŚ might be forming the Etruscan genitive (which is very similar to the way it is expressed in English, this is well explained by the

Bonfantes).

So, my Sanskrit based literal translation is OF PRE-MOTHER, or OF GREAT MOTHER or just GREAT MOTHER'S. The Bonfantes translate it as GREAT GRANDSON. Not the same, but not too different either!

The Indo-European nature of this word is unquestionable even if I or the Bonfantes made some mistakes. This means that the Etruscans had a word for mother that was identical to one of the Sanskrit words for mother; just as the Latins had the Sanskrit word *AMBAlika, mother,* at some earlier, forgotten time.

ATERŚ, ATURS, ATRS, ATRUS

These words, according to the Bonfantes, mean *'descendants', 'ancestor'* (p.214).

They put the word 'ati' in brackets, reminding us that it is an Etruscan word for mother. Regarding ancestors, I find that the word 'attA', that same word I mentioned as a word for 'mother, also has another meaning.

attA f.   elder [299]

Elders, ancestors... The Etruscans pluralize by adding an R at the end of the word. Now, we get ATTAR or ATAR or ATR, which would mean ELDERS. We only need an S now! This would indicate the genitive form. So ATERŚ would mean OF ELDERS or COMING FROM ELDERS or, why not, DESCENDANTS.

CILT

The Bonfantes translate it as *people, nation* (p. 215). The connection I see might not be correct, but it should be considered.

kIlita   adj.   tied [300]

Apply an Etruscan word-ending corruption and you will get 'kilta' or 'kilt' (cilt), which eventually means *a group that is tied or bound*. The idea to explain *cilt* in this way came from my translation of the name of the Alans, who were one of Iranian Aryan peoples.

AlAna   n.   tying, binding [301]

Nobody can guarantee these are valid parallels, but they do look logical.

CLAN, CLENAR (plural) *"Son"* (p.216)

glahate { glah }   verb   receive, take [302]
anas n.   offspring, birth, mother [303]

glah → h is dropped, G always becomes K → kla

kla + anas → klanas → klan ???

According to this reconstruction, this should mean RECEIVED OFFSPRING (?), WHAT MOTHER RECEIVED. We should keep our doubts, but if you look at having children as a gift received from the gods it is not far from the concept of son or daughter.

SNENATH *'maid'*, *'companion'* (p. 219)

I followed here associations from Serbian where the

words 'snaha' and 'snaya' mean 'daughter-in-law' and 'sister-in-law'.

I don't know if these Serbian words are currently identified to be related to Sanskrit, but it wouldn't be a surprise since most Serbian words for family members are similar to those from Vedic Sanskrit.

sneha   m.   friendship with [304]
nAdhate { nAdh }   verb   seeking help [305]

sneha + nAdh → snehnadh → H is dropped, DH becomes TH → snenath

The literal translation would be FRIEND-HELPER. This could fit the idea of a COMPANION or a MAID.

There is another and more complicated Sanskrit explanation of the Serbian word *snaha*, but this is not a place to discuss it.

ATI NACNA *"grandmother"* (p.214)

I am not getting the meaning of grandmother from Sanskrit, but it is not far from it. I have already shown that the Etruscan *ati* (mother) is related to Sanskrit.

attA f.   mother, mother-in-law [306]
+
nahyati { nah }   verb 4   bind, tie [307]
gnA f.   wife, woman [308]

nah + gnA → nahgna → no G in Etruscan, becomes K ; H is dropped → nakna

The literal translation of ATI NACNA should be MOTHER-IN-LOW "WIFE-TIE".

So, it is MOTHER OF A FEMALE SPOUSE or MAN'S MOTHER IN LOW.

Also, instead of *nah* we can use *na* (gift)[309], and then ATI NACNA would mean MOTHER WHO GIFTED (man's) WIFE (less probable).

TUSURTHIR

The Etruscans were family-oriented. The position of women in their society was much better than it was in Greece and Rome. We see it as a real achievement of their civilization but Greeks and Romans saw it as scandalous and immoral. Etruscan art shows married couples in a manner that suggests love, harmony, and equality.

The Bonfantes tell us that TUSURTHIR is a word that means *"married couple"* (p.219).

Tu   m.   love, god of love [310]
 surati { sur }   verb   rule [311]
 tarati { tRR }   verb   live through, carry through, attain an end or aim, attain an end or aim, accomplish, fulfill[312]

Tu + sur + tRR → TUSRTRR

TUSRTRR (reconstructed)
TUSURTHIR (Etruscan)

The literal meaning is LOVE RULE LIVE-THROUGH which we can translate as RULED AS LOVE FOR LIFE. It sounds like the traditional concept of marriage, of wedLOCK. You can also translate it in other meaningful ways, one of them being GOD OF LOVE RULE LIVE THROUGH, etc.

The third word in the compound could easily be 'dhira' (would become 'thir').

dhIra   adj.   steady, constant, strong, firm [313]

This would give the literal translation LOVE RULE CONSTANT.

LAUTAN, LAUTN

While searching for the etymology of LAUTN, which means *'family'* (the Bonfantes, p.217), I found something else, a handy example of how words in European languages took a different direction and why because of the difference in only one sound we don't even recognize them as relatives. Here is that example.

lIDhe { lih } verb   lick [314]

Obviously, the verb is *lIDhe*, but its stem is almost identical to the full English verb that has the same meaning - LICK. Also, it is almost the same in Serbian but the last sound is different. Let's see it!

LIH (Sanskrit stem that means 'to lick')
LIK (spelt as LICK, English verb and noun)
LIZ (Serbian noun, means 'lick', the verb is 'lizati')

Having this in mind, we can reconstruct LAUTN in the following way.

lAva   adj.   gathering, reaping [315]
+
tan   m.   offspring, posterity, propagation, uninterrupted succession, continuation [316]

lAva + tan → lavtan → V changes into W or U → lautan → Etruscans compress word endings because of the strong accent they put at the beginning of words (this is explained well by the Bonfantes) → LAUTN

The literal Sanskrit meaning is "GATHERING-OFFSPRING". Can we see it as an expression of the idea of a family? Is this a good explanation? Maybe. But there could be other Sanskrit words at play here. Remember, D becomes T.

UDha   adj.   married, led home [317]

This Sanskrit D, as you know, becomes T. This could be a simpler path for understanding the second word in the compound.

The literal translations this LAUTA would be "GATHERING-MARRIED" and "HOME - GATHERING", suggesting 'marriage union'.

By the way, the Serbian verb 'udati' means 'to get married' and is applied only when we talk about females.

5.3 SOME RANDOM ETRUSCAN WORDS

CELA *"room, Latin cella'* (p.215)

There is a Sanskrit verb with its stem that looks similar. It has many meanings, but we present the one that could be related to the Etruscan word.

kalayati { kal }   verb   furnish with [318]

Another similar Sanskrit word offers another perspective.

kAla   m.   part, a section [319]

The Sanskrit 'kAla' (meaning 'part') has some logic if you think of a 'room' as a part of the house, a division of the house. Even dictionary.reference.com defines the word 'room' as "a portion of space within a building or other structure". [320]

CEL

The Bonfantes translate this as *'earth'* and they are correct (p.215). But there is an undetected Sanskrit relation.

keli f.   earth [321]

It is very interesting that they also list another related Etruscan word: CELTI (p.215) which they translate as *'on the land'* (makes you think of the Celts?).

It looks obvious that the Sanskrit 'keli' (earth) is tightly related to these Etruscan words.

CAR-, CER *"make, build"* (the Bonfantes, p.215)

Both words have a similarity to some Sanskrit words.

kara	adj.		maker, doer, causer[322]
karoti { kR }		verb 8	to do[323]
kr̩	doing / karaṇa[324]		

This is one handy word to mention.

Etruscan:	car- (or 'kar-')		make, build
Sanskrit:	kara	adj.	maker
Sanskrit:	kara	m.	hand [325]

The word *kAra* could be found in some Sanskrit compound words that are connected building.

gRhakAraka	m.	house-builder [326]
gRhakArin	m.	house-builder [327]

The word 'gRha' means 'house', therefore 'kAraka' and 'kArin' have to stand for 'builder'. Its relation with Etruscan is clear.

CULSCVA *"door', 'gate"* (p.215)

A possible Sanskrit connection is in the stem *kUl*.

kUlati   { kUl } verb   cover, keep off, hide, obstruct [328]

This would go along with the idea of a door as a "cover" to an opening in the wall. We should break it down in this way: CULS + KVA.

ARYAN ITALY OF THE ETRUSCANS

The sound 'S' at the end of the first word should be attributed to Etruscan grammar (if 'cul' is a noun, 'culs' should be its genitive form,). This is already explained well by the Bonfantes. The word 'cva' is similar to Latin 'quo' (meaning 'where') and might have the same meaning. Both Latin and Etruscan words are related to Sanskrit words which are identical to the Etruscan word.

kva ind. where? [329]
kva ind. to whatsoever place, to some place [329]

So, I will translate 'culscva' literally as COVER OF "IN-PLACE" or WHAT COVERS "TO-PLACE", therefore what COVERS THE ENTRANCE, which is a 'door' or 'gate'. There is also another option that looks convincing.

kula n. house, front [330]

kula + S (Etruscan genitive, 'of house') → kuls + kva → kulskva

The literal meaning is "WHERE" OF THE HOUSE or "OF-THE-HOUSE IN", "TO THE HOUSE"; therefore HOUSE ENTRANCE or DOOR or GATE.

While searching this, I accidentally reconstructed the Serbian word *vrata,* which means 'door' (by the way, the English word 'door' is so similar to the Sanskrit *dur*[331] that we can see them as the same word).

Let's take a look at VRATA. We have two approaches here.

vRtti f. occurring or appearing in, rolling [332]

vRtti → vrata ? [331]

By the way, *vRtti* as *rolling* is very close to Serbian verb *vrtiti*, which means *spinning, moving, revolving*. But what if VRATA is a compound? Let's try that path.

vAra { vR } m.   anything which covers or surrounds or restrains, doorway, cover [333]

Now, we can conclude that VRATA is a development that came from stem *vR*. Stems are only used in compound words as a short representation of the full word. Therefore, we need to look for the second element.

AtA m.f.   frame of a door [334]

vR + AtA → vrata

We can see how *vR* as 'cover' could represent a wooden board or moving part of the door while *AtA* is the frame of the door. Together, they make the whole thing, Serbian VRATA (door).

Did I just reconstruct a contemporary Serbian word with Sanskrit? I think I did. The origin of the Serbian word VRATA seems to be explained. But do I know which of two reconstructions is the right one? I don't.

FARTHAN, FARTN

The Bonfantes give the meaning of *'generate'* (p.216)

This word comes from a Sanskrit verb that gives us the stem 'vRt'. In this case, the Etruscan F came from the Sanskrit V, but this change does not happen always. Often, the Etruscan F corresponds to the Sanskrit P.

ARYAN ITALY OF THE ETRUSCANS

vartate { vRt }   verb 1   originate, be, become, act, live, arise from or in [335]

aNu   m.   life, soul [336]

And the meaning is ORIGINATE LIFE!

The stem 'vRt' might explain the Serbian noun 'vrt', meaning 'garden' (think of stem 'vRt' as 'arise from or in'), though it might be connected to the stem 'vRdh' (foster).

There is a simpler and better Sanskrit match for FARTHAN.

vartana   adj.   causing to live or be [337]

Do you think this is close to 'generate'?

MAL-   *"to look, watch, guard, oversee"*   (the Bonfantes, p.217)

As I was searching for a word or stem that would be similar in Sanskrit and would also mean "to look", I found something else. LOOK at this.

lokate { lok }   verb 1   see, perceive [338]

The stem LOK would be pronounced by Etruscans as LUK ('look')! Here, based on another Etruscan word, 'malena', the Bonfantes translate MAL as *to look, to watch*. Let's take a look at *malena* and challenge their explanation.

MALENA, MALANA, MALSTRIA

The Bonfantes say that these three variants mean

"mirror" (p.217).

Around three hundred hand-held Etruscan mirrors are preserved. They all have pictures on their back, showing scenes from mythology, with inscribed texts.

This proved that Etruscan women were literate and Etruscan society was more advanced and humane than Greek or Roman societies of that time.

Here is my first reconstruction of *malena*.

malate { mal }   verb   hold, posses [339]
ena pronoun   she [340]

I know, the literal meaning sounds clumsy! HOLD-SHE! But it makes sense! First, it was a hand-held mirror that was unmistakably made for females, therefore it is something that SHE HOLDS, but it can also be something that was HOLDING HER, since the picture of the lady who owned it was always in there, whenever she looked at it. Am I sure? No, I never was. My job is not to be sure, but to examine. In this case, we got lucky. There are three known forms of this word: MALENA, MALANA, MALSTRIA. "Malena' and 'malana' are essentially the same so we will focus on *malstria*. To me, the STRIA part sounded similar to the Serbian words 'strina' ('aunt', a wife of your father's brother) and 'striye' (spelt as 'strije', skin-stretchmarks that are a result of pregnancy).

strI   adj.   female, lady, woman, wife [341]

mal + strI + A (word-ending) → malstria

The literal meaning is the same as the meaning of 'malena': WOMAN-HOLD (*holds a woman, what a woman holds*).

One thing is positive, the second word in MAL-ENA means SHE, and STRIA in MALSTRIA means WOMAN.

ARYAN ITALY OF THE ETRUSCANS

But the MAL part has a better option.

   mAyate { mA }   verb   display, show, measure [59]

MAL would be a noun or an adjective made from this verb and it would simply mean DISPLAY.

So, MALENA and MALSTRIA are most likely WOMEN'S DISPLAY, a "DISPLAY" FOR FEMALES, or a mirror meant to be used by women. By the way, the Serbian word 'strije' probably has another Sanskrit explanation!

   striyate   { stR } verb pass.   be spread or strewn [343]

AVIL *"year"* (p.214)

   avi m.   sun [344]

Observing the Sun had to be important in forming the concept of a year. This way of thinking, which connects year with one cycle in the movement and "behaviour" of Sun, we can find inside Sanskrit in word *sava*[345]. It means 'sun', but it also means 'year'!

AR-, ER- *"to make, move"* (the Bonfantes, p.214)

   Irte { Ir }   verb 2   move, go [346]

The Sanskrit stem *Ir* means 'move' and is almost identical to the Etruscan ER-, but...

   Arpayati { Ar }   verb caus.   cause to move, cause to partake, settle, annex, inflict, fix [347]

However, SanskritDictionary.com offers one root in the shape of singular accented R.

ṛ   going, moving / gati [438]

The Etruscan verb/stem is identical to the Sanskrit stem! And it matches one of two existing translations!

RESTM, *RASTUM   *"land (cultivated?)"*   (the Bonfantes, p.218)

Here, the Bonfantes rely on an analogy with Rasenna and Rasna, which is how the Etruscans called their land. I will explain these words later and in detail. Since they are names for Etruscan land, there is a strong logic behind the Bonfantes' translation. What is more important is the support that Sanskrit gives to it.

rasA   f.   earth, soil, ground [439]

My explanation of *rastum* goes well up to this point, but we can debate about the second word. There are two options.

dunoti { du }   verb   be burnt [440]

rasa + du → rasdu → D becomes T → rastu (BURNT LAND)

This could be in the context of burning agricultural fields to increase their fertility. Or it is about...

dhUma   m.   wheat [441]

It would give LAND-WHEAT or FIELDS OF

WHEAT. Again, am I sure? Not really. But it is close to the Bonfantes' suspicion that this might mean "cultivated land". Besides, RAS in *rastum* is explained clearly.

TUR- *"to give"* (the Bonfantes, p.219)

There is a Sanskrit noun that is related to the Etruscan 'tur-'.

dura   m.   giver, granter [442]

dura → no D in Etruscan, it becomes T → tura → tur

PENTHUNA, PENTHNA

"cippus, stone?" (the Bonfantes, p.218)

The Bonfantes are not sure. Cippus or stone? The closest Sanskrit reconstruction has no 'stone' in it, though stone makes sense because cippus is a boundary stone, tombstone, etc. It is always there to give a message, to communicate something.

bhaNati { bhaN }   verb 1   speak, call, say to, name, declare [443]
tUNa   m.   bearer [444]

bhaN + tUNa → bhantuna → B always becomes P in Etruscan → panthuna → PENTHUNA

The meaning is WHICH BEARS A DECLARATION and that is the function of any cippus. We can also see at as BEARER OF "SPEACH", therefore BEARER OF TEXT.

This might even explain the very word 'boundary'.

bhaNati { bhaN }   verb 1   declare[443]
dharA   f.   earth, bearer, supporter [445]

This would give BHANDHARA the meaning of "DECLARED" LAND.

Or it might directly express a 'boundary'.

dhAra   m.   edge, boundary [446]

The meaning would be "DECLARED" EDGE, "DECLARED" BORDER, DECLARATION OF A BOUNDARY.

NERI   *"water"*   (the Bonfantes, p.217)

Obviously, this is very similar to the Greek *nero* for water. Both of them are related to Sanskrit.

nAra   m. pl.   water [447]
nIra   n.   water [448]

KANA, KANNA   *"gift"*   (p.216)

There are two ways to view this word through the glasses of Sanskrit.

ka   n.   happiness, joy, pleasure [449]
Na   m.   gift [450]

Meaning: PLEASURE-GIFT, PLEASING GIFT.

But there is a similar reconstruction that also works.

kanati   { kan } verb   be satisfied or pleased, to agree to, accept with satisfaction [451]

kan + na → kanna (PLEASING OR SATISFYING GIFT)

Let me make a little digression. Sanskrit 'Na' means 'gift', but in Serbian "Na!" is a colloquial way to say "Take it! It's yours." This Serbian "Na!" is not explainable by the Serbian language. But it is by Sanskrit!

MELICRATICCE *"honey and wine"* (p.217)

It is easy to recognize honey in the MELI-part of the word, it means 'honey' in Greek. For the CRATICCE-part, the closest in Sanskrit. is

klaitakika   n.   wine, a fermented liquor prepared from the Klitaka root, spirituous liquor [452]

Not very similar? Think of switching between L and R between early Indo-European and Classical Sanskrit. And think of vowel corruption that happens in the Etruscan language and two words will not look that different.

But, for the sake of supporting the claim, I invite you to look at the English word COCKADOODLEDOO, a word for the sound a rooster makes.

Through 'cockadoodledoo' a rooster communicates with hens. A hen is KOKA in Serbian (pronounced the same as COCKA in 'cockadoodledoo'.

Now, the Serbian equivalent of the English COCKADOODLEDOO is KUKURIKU. But 'rooster' in Sanskrit is *kRkavAku* [453]!

KUKURIKU (Serbian)

KRKAVAKU (Sanskrit)

Sometimes, you have to think of words as shape-shifters. Then you might conclude that Sanskrit is a rooster of Indo-European languages. It is interesting that the Serbian words for 'rooster' are PETAO and PEVAC. "pevac" comes from the Serbian verb 'pevati (means 'to sing') while 'petao' cannot be explained by the Serbian language. But it is explainable by Sanskrit! It comes from the Sanskrit verb 'petati'!

peTati   { piT } verb   sound, assemble or heap together [454]

A rooster makes sounds (cockadoodldoo) and makes an assembly of hens!

LAIVE   *"left"*   (p.216)

It is similar to the Serbian 'levo' or 'liyevo' (spelt as 'lijevo'), meaning 'left'.

LAIVE (Etruscan)
LIEVO (Serbian, spelt 'lijevo')
LEVO (main Serbian variant)
LEFT (English)

MATH   *"honey, honeyed wine"*   (p.217)

madhu   n.   honey [455]

Since D becomes T in Etruscan...

madhu→ mathu → math

They are both similar to 'med' (which is 'honey' in several Slavic languages), it is also similar to 'mead'.

TALITHA *"girl"* (the Bonfantes, p.219)

tallI f.   young woman [456]

If TALLI is 'young woman', TALITHA could easily be 'girl'. Besides, *lATa* means 'childish' and these two can give TALLATA or 'young-woman-childish'. Another option might sound vulgar to some because its literal translation is "WOMB-CHILD".

ta   m.   womb, breast [457]
laTati   { laT } verb   be a child or to cry [458]

WOMB-CHILD? I base this approach on another Indo-European parallel. The Serbian word for MAN or MALE is MUŠKARAC. In Sanskrit, *muSkara* means 'having testicles'!

TIUR *"moon"* (the Bonfantes, p.219)

This could be reconstructed in several ways.

dideti { dI } verb 3   shine [459]
uru adj.   large, broad, wide, excellent [460]

dI + uru → diuru → no D in Etruscan, becomes T or TH → tiuru → Tiur (SHINE-BROAD or maybe, interpreted, FULL MOON)

Another option comes with the stem 'vR'.

varate { vR }   verb 5 9   obstruct, cover,

veil, conceal, hide [461]

dI + vR → divr → V is sometimes equal to W or U in Etruscan → diur → D always becomes Tin Etruscan → Tiur

The meaning is SHINE-COVERED, SHINE-OBSTRUCTED.

The Moon is not obstructed or covered for just one day per lunar cycle.

US-, USETI *"scoop, ladle, draw (water)"* (the Bonfantes, p.220)

This looks like a stem followed by its verb (US-, USETI). It is very similar to the Serbian verb UZETI, which means 'to take'.

Do you scoop or draw water or do you take water? It all depends. But in the end, the meanings are not very different. There is a similar Sanskrit verb.

aSati { aS }   verb 1   take or receive[462]

USETI (Etruscan)
UZETI (Serbian)
ASATI (Sanskrit)

Etruscan, Sanskrit and Serbian words look like dialectal versions of each other.

TUPI

"punishment"
(Dieter H. Steinbauer, http://www.etruskisch.de)[463]

If this translation is correct, the Etruscan word developed from the Sanskrit word *tupati*.

tupati { tup }　　　verb 1 6　　　hurt [464]

Punishing? Hurting? Connected?

VERS - *"fire (or ladle?)"*　(the Bonfantes, p.220)

The Bonfantes are not sure if it is 'fire' or a 'ladle'. It might be a ladle.

varSati { vRS }　　　verb　　　pour forth, shower down, rain [465]

Well, the verb is about liquids, but is it close enough? One of the many Sanskrit words for water contains all the consonants in the same order as in VERS.

vRSa　　　m.　　　water [466]

VERS can also simply come from the Sanskrit word *vAr*, which means 'water'. I can also see this word for water as the part of the Serbian word 'varyacha' (varjača), which is a shallow wooden spoon for stirring. We can reconstruct 'varyacha' with Sanskrit.

vArya　　　　　　adj.　　watery [467]
ca　adj.　　　　　moving to and fro [468]

vArya + ca → vAryaca

The character C in 'ca' is pronounced as 'CH'.

But there might be a better reconstruction of 'varyacha'.

Pay attention to Y in this word. It doesn't change much if we replace it with I.

varyacha → variacha

Now, take a look at this.

vArI f.   water [469]
aja m.   mover, driver [470]

vArI + aja → variaja (with J as in word 'jam')

So, a spoon used for stirring called 'varyacha' means WATER-MOVER. One can say that all the sounds are not the same because I got VARIAJA with J, not VARYACHA with CH. OK, that is a legitimate question. But the meaning suggests that the reconstruction is right and makes me think that Sanskrit J sometimes ended up as Serbian CH (Č), not just as ZH (Ž).

Why is this relevant in a book about Etruscan vocabulary? It is because I use the same method on the Etruscan language, trying to figure out linguistic processes by sorting out meanings and patterns, rather than going in the opposite direction.

The Etruscan word 'vers' is clearly Indo-European, related to Sanskrit. At the same time, The Bonfantes' "water or fire" dilemma is also strongly supported by Sanskrit.

vIra   m.   fire, sacred or sacrificial fire [471]

What counts are consonants and they are the same (V and R).

So, my Sanskrit parallels did not bring a complete resolution, but they did show an undeniable Sanskrit affiliation!

SVELERI *"living creature"* (the Bonfantes, p.219)

The closest I found to their proposal is a reconstruction that gave me MEN, PEOPLE, PEOPLE OF THE LAND and maybe even TRIBAL LAND.

sva m.   one's own, man of one's own people or tribe, kinsman, relative [472]
lR m.   earth [473]

sva + lR → svalr → E is inserted 'lR' → svaler → svaleri (possibly plural form of 'svaler')

The Bonfantes propose 'living creature', I got "tribal man of land". Again, I might be wrong. Or perhaps they are? Also, some very different translations are available here.

sva adj.   of self [472]
sva n.   property, wealth, riches [472]

It could be about LAND-PROPERTY or PRIVATE LAND. The Serbian word 'svoyina' ('svojina'), meaning 'property', comes from one of these Sanskrit words.

5.4 RELIGIOUS TERMS

TRUT, TRUTH *"libation, sacred action"* (the Bonfantes, p.219)

It seems that the Bonfantes translated it correctly. Read the words below.

driyate { dR }   verb   honour, respect [474]
+
undate { ud }   verb 6   flow or issue out, wet, bathe [475]
uda n.   water(only at the beginning or end of a compound) [476]

dR + ud (or *uda*) → drud → no D in Etruscan → becomes TRUT or TRUTH

The literal translation is HONOUR-FLOW, RESPECT-FLOW, "HONOUR WETTING". It could also be HONOUR-WATER, RESPECT-WATERING (indicating a libation, pouring a liquid in honour of a god or the dead).

The only surviving Etruscan book, Liber Linteus, contains several words related to TRUT or TRUTH. One of them is **TRUTANAŚA**. At first, it looked so easy to reconstruct it. I was sure that NAŚA stands for the dead, deceased.

nAza   m.   death, desertion, annihilation, disappearance [477]

This *nAza* is pronounced as *nasha*, with SH as in 'shore'. So, TRUTANAŚA must be a LIBATION FOR THE

DEAD. Then I caught myself that I am assuming that the A in TRUT-A was added like some kind of inflection, just like it would be in Serbian. But what if it is about a word?

anAza   adj.   living, not-dead [478]

So, could it be a LIBATION FOR LIVING ONES? Does such a thing exist? Could it be some equivalent of lighting a candle for your dead and a candle for your living ones, just as you do in the church?

Or the word is actually TRUT-TA-NAŚA?

TA f.   earth [479]
dA adj.   giving [480]

LIBATION TO THE EARTH OF THE DEAD, LIBATION-GIVING TO THE DEAD? This sounds good to me, but I will leave it to others to decide what would be the exact translation. I am satisfied if I made you think that the Etruscan TRUTANAŚA is indeed an Indo-European, Sanskrit related word.

CECHA *"ceremony (right, law)"* (the Bonfantes, p.215)

A short word, but it still could be a compound.

kagati { kag }   verb   act, perform [481]
khaga   m.   deity [482]
kha   n.   action, cypher, understanding [483]

khaga + kha → khagka → no G in Etruscan, it becomes K → khakkha → H is droped → kaka

The Etruscan word is CECHA, it should be pronounced

as KEKA. The literal meaning is "DIETY-CYPHER", we can see it as a DIVINE CODE and interpret it as a DIVINE LOW. We can opt to reconstruct the word using the stem KAG (act, perform). In that case, the word means ACTING CODE or some kind of "code" or rule of performance (rite). It can also be "UNDERSTANDING OF PERFORMANCE".

Another way is to use 'kha' twice, as two separate words that form the compound 'CECHA.

kha	n.	action, cypher, understanding [483]
kha	n.	heaven [483]

The literal meanings are ACTION-HEAVEN, CYPHER HEAVEN etc.

The Bonfantes also mention ZILCH CECHANERI. Likely, the NERI-part came from the word for people, mortals.

nR	m.	people [484]
nara	m.	man [485]
nAra	adj.	human, mortal, spiritual [486]

You can choose your translation, but these are "Sanskrit words" found in the Etruscan vocabulary. It is something like DIVINE CYPHER (for) HUMANS. Or the literal translation is "DEITY-PEOPLE" suggesting some kind of religious community, maybe a congregation?

But, looking at 'cechaneri' one already can get other ideas.

ga   adj.   relating to or standing in connection with, reaching to [487]

khaga + ga + nara → kagganara → G changes into K → kakkanara → kekaneri

This would mean DIETY RELATING TO HUMANS. Laws? There are also other options in Sanskrit.

CLEVA (the Bonfantes translate this as *"offering"*, p.215)

The word 'cleva' was identified as Etruscan, but I don't think it was exclusively an Etruscan word, it belongs to a much wider Indo-European heritage.

There are not many words similar to 'cleva' in Sanskrit dictionaries. Without denying the possibility that 'cleva' meant 'offering', I want to propose a little theory.

The first three letters in the word 'cleva' are identical to the first three letters in the Greek word CLEOS. It is known that in classical Greek the sound V did not exist. Sometime after the 12th century BC and the Bronze Age collapse, the Greeks lost their literacy. Also, the sound V, present up to that time, disappeared from the language. I want to show that it is possible to think that those pre-Greek inhabitants of Greece most likely had this word 'cleva' in the same form we find in the Etruscan language. My "formula" is shown below.

CLEVA → Greeks drop or substitute V → CLE(v)A → CLEA

CLEA + OS (common ending of nouns in Greek, also prevalent after Greek Dark Ages) = CLEOS

The result is CLEOS, the Greek word for GLORY, FAME or BEING TALKED ABOUT.

'Cleos' is usually earned in wars and battles...We are playing with the idea that Greek and Etruscan might have some common roots. Considering that Etruscans lacked G and always used K instead of it, we can attempt to find the "original" word and stem!

glevate { glev }   verb   worship, serve [488]

This Sanskrit stem 'GLEV' Etruscans would pronounce as 'KLEV' ('clev' in their spelling).

In a way, it confirms the existing opinion that 'cleva' means offering because 'glevate' can also mean 'serve' and we can see an 'offering' as a 'serving' to a god, or as an expression of worshiping a god. Even the meaning of WORSHIP can work here. How?

Here is one analogy. Every Serbian family has a family saint, which they celebrate through generations. That celebration is much bigger than the celebration of Christmas; family, friends, and neighbours are invited. The noun that marks this celebration is SLAVA, which means FAME or GLORY in all Slavic languages. By the way, the word is very similar to CLEVA, but we will not discuss that here (it is very hard to see how K and S would be switched). The closest English translation of SLAVA as a celebration of a saint is not GLORY, word PRAISING works better. Praising? Worshipping? Offering?

It all could make sense regarding Etruscan CLEVA (offering), but how about Greek CLEOS (fame)? I am not sure Sanskrit GLEV explains CLEOS and I also believe that CLEOS and CLEVA are two versions of the same word. There is another Sanskrit option.

First, you need to remember that the same word that contains L in some Indo-European dialects can have R instead of L in some other dialects. We already used this option while reconstructing the name of Clevsin. Let's do it again!

gRNAti   { gRR }   verb 9   praise, announce, mention with praise [489]

Theoretically, this stem *gRR* could be *gLL* or *gL* in some other dialect.

ARYAN ITALY OF THE ETRUSCANS

This very GL would become KL in Etruscan. We need a second word in this possible compound.

avi   adj.   favourable, kindly disposed [490]

avati { av }   verb 1   favour [ved.] [491]
av   Ved. to promote, favour, (chiefly Vedic or Veda) to satisfy, refresh; to offer (as a hymn to the gods) [491]

That would give something similar to KLEVA or CLEVA.

KL + av → klav

KLAV (reconstructed)
KLEVA (Etruscan, spelt as *cleva*)

The literal translation is MENTION-WITH-PRAISE-FAVOUR(ED)   or   MENTION-WITH-PRAISE-PROMOTE(ED. It feels close to Greek CLEOS, which is translated as FAME or TO BE TALKED ABOUT. We can also read it as "PRAISE-OFFER".

If any of these approaches is correct, the existing understanding of the relation between Etruscan and Greek must be wrong.

'Cleos' could only come to be if the Sanskrit G was rendered by speakers who could not pronounce it and used K instead. I am not talking here about the language of Mycenean Greeks, who had the sound G as well as the sound V. My suspicion stretches back to the mysterious people that inhabited Greece before the Greeks – the Pelasgians. We know that Pelasgians also settled in Italy, but we don't know what happened with them. It is reasonable to suspect that part of the Italian Pelasgians ended up in the Etruscan melting pot. These are ideas, but they needed to be touched.

SAC The Bonfantes translate it as *"carrying out a sacred act"* (p. 218). Sacred, divine, heavenly...

It is hard to ignore the similarity between Etruscan SAC and our words like *sacred, sacralize,* etc.

If we would try to get rid of one half of it, what would we drop and what would we keep to preserve the meaning? What should we erase in *"carrying out sacred act"*? I simplify it to SACRED ACT. Let's see if we can recreate it wits Sanskrit.

Sa   m.   heaven [492]
kha n.   action [493]

Sa + kha → sakha → H is dropped → saka

SAKA (reconstructed)
SAK (Etruscan, spelt as SAC)

The literal meaning is HEAVEN ACTION. We can see it as DIVINE ACTION and, why not, SACRED ACTION. So, we got SACRED ACT from the Bonfantes and HEAVEN ACTION from Sanskrit.

Now, let's take a Sanskrit look at Latin verb *sacro, sacrare*[494] (means *make sacred, consecrate*) and adjective *sacer*[495] (means *sacred, holy*, but also *detestable* and *horrible*).

Sa   m.   heaven [492]
karoti { kR }   verb 8   to do [496]

Sa + kR → sakr → sakra

The literal translation of this SAKRA is HEAVEN-DOING.

It is interesting that if we translate them with Sanskrit, both the Etruscan and the Latin word give the same meaning!

SACNICLERI

The Bonfantes say that the word is in the accusative plural form and that it means *'sanctuary'* (p.218).

It could be. ERI at the end of SACNICLERI indicates the Etruscan plural form and that is just one of several reasons to take the Bonfantes' translation very seriously. But I want to take another path and examine the word in a slightly different manner. Actually, we will examine just half of the word.

On the surface, it looks like SACNICLERI is a two-word compound made of SACNI and CLERI. But each of these words might also be a compound word. The first word, SACNI, has been identified as a word by itself. The Bonfantes list it in the glossary section of their book (p.218) and they translate it as *"holy, consecrated"*.

Let's accept this and focus on CLERI. It is very similar to our words 'clerical' and 'clergy' and that is what interests me. It is my feeling that CLERI simply means PRIEST(S) or PRIESTHOOD or CLERGY or OFFICES OF CLERGY (which would confirm 'sanctuary', the meaning proposed by the Bonfantes).

This Etruscan CLERI should be the very same word that is known to us from Latin. Website Latin-Dictionary.net shows the word in this way:

CLERUS, CLERI (noun; 2nd declension; masculine gender)
Definitions: *clergy, clerical order* [497]

Let's try to reconstruct CLERI! Just like in the case of CLEVA, there are two ways.

We can connect it to verb *glevate* and its stem *glev* (meaning 'to serve', 'to worship'). But what do we do with V in *glev*? How and why would it disappear? We do find particle CLE in Hercle, which is the Etruscan name of Greek Heracles or Roman Hercules. Scholars translated Heracles as Hera's Glory. Again, the meanings of WORSHIP and GLORY are not that much different, we don't have to exclude this option. We can try to treat as equal Sanskrit GLEV and Etruscan CLE, but the disappearance of V stays unexplained. With that in mind, we can try to reconstruct the word.

SACNI + CLE → SACNICLE (this would be "HOLY WORSHIP" or "WORSHIP OF SACRED")

ER, ERI, or RI ending would be explained by Etruscan plural and we would get SACNICLERI.

Another path is also already presented under the discussion of the word CLEVA. It would rely on that old Indo-European L that later became R in Sanskrit.

gRNAti   { gRR }   verb 9   praise, announce, mention with praise [498]

So, this *gRR* would be *gLL* or *gL* but because Etruscans always turn G into K, it would end up as *kL*. We can attempt to identify ERI part of CLERI.

ari   m.   faithful or devoted or pious man [500]

kL + ari → klari

The literal translation would be PRAISING PIOUS MAN, where we need to see PRAISING as actively celebrating gods. We are very close to Latin CLERUS-

CLERI, which means CLERGY! By the way, this might explain the personal female name Clara, the meaning of it would be similar to the meaning of Theophil.

Is it possible that these Sanskrit based reconstructions are wrong? It is. But it is hard to believe that all of them are completely wrong. Etruscan, Latin, Greek and Sanskrit words do look like members of the same family, but it is Sanskrit that repeatedly shows the ability to explain the others.

VACAL, VACIL, VACL *"libation?"* (the Bonfantes, p.220)

A libation is pouring of a drink as an offering to a deity or the dead.

The simplest reconstructions are always the best, but there are several simple options here.

va   m.   water [501]
kAlayati { kal }   verb   throw [502]

va + kal → vakal

This would mean WATER-"THROW". Could it be this was just a word for 'pouring a liquid'?

More likely, it means what it looks like: pouring on the ground.

va   m.   water [501]
khala   m.   earth, soil, ground [503]

va + khala → H is dropped → vakala → vakal (spelt as 'vacal')

The literal translation is WATER-SOIL, which could be read as WATERING THE SOIL. That is what a libation is.

TURA *"incense"* (p.219)

Since 'incense' is a material that is burnt to produce smoke with a scent, it is more likely that it is in connection with

dunoti { du }   verb   be burnt   [by fire, pain, sorrow, etc.], burn, consume with fire [504]

As it was already repeated so many times, the Etruscans did not have a D sound, they used T or TH instead.

du → tu

But there are other approaches, too.

tu   adverb   pray! I beg [505]
ra   m.   heat, fire [506]

tu + ra → tura

This would mean "PRAYING-FIRE". We should not be too confident about this, there is a simpler option.

dhur   f.   spark of fire [507]

dhur → thur → tur → tura

5.5 POLITICAL TERMS

Just like in other societies from the dawn of history or late prehistory, political terminology can also be viewed as religious terminology. Religion and politics were much closer than at later times, they were different faces of the same way of life and view of the world.

LAUCHUME

This word is translated by the Bonfantes as *'king'* (p.217) and *consul* (p.111), which is the title of one of the chief magistrates in the Roman Republic.

Lauchume is believed to be an Etruscan word, while *lucumo* would be its Latin version. The main meaning of it is 'king'.

Livy mentions Lucumo as the name of one of the important figures of early Roman history, the legendary fifth king of Rome Lucius Tarquinius Priscus. He wrote that *"During the reign of Ancus a wealthy and ambitious man named Lucumo removed to Rome, mainly with the hope and desire of winning high distinction, for which no opportunity had existed in Tarquinii, since there also he was an alien. He was the son of Demaratus a Corinthian, who had been driven from home by a revolution, and who happened to settle in Tarquinii."* [507]

There is a widespread belief in modern scholarship that Livy confused Lucumo to be a personal name because it means 'king'. We will touch this later.

LAUCHUME and/or LUCUMO look as compound words. We might divide them in this way:

LAUCH-UME
LUC-UMO

Bear in mind that CH in *lauchume* is just one of the ways

in which Etruscans write letter K. This means that there is only one letter difference between two variants. While the Etruscan version has LAUK (*lauch*), the Roman variant is shorter – LUK (*luc*).

Now, we search Sanskrit for words similar to LAUC and LUC.

laukya   adj.   worldwide, commonplace, global, general, common, belonging to the world [508]

lokya   adj.   worldwide, free space or sphere, everyday, ordinary, granting a free sphere of action, customary, usual [509]

These two words are very similar and their meanings overlap significantly. What could be the second word in the compound?

uma   m.   city, town [510]

Don't forget that those rulers were not kings of countries in our sense of the word, they ruled city-states.

laukya → there is no letter Y in Etruscan → becomes LAUKIA

LAUKIA + uma → laukiuma → Etruscans corrupt ending parts of words → laukuma

LAUKUMA (reconstructed)
LAUKUME (Etruscan, spelt as *lauchume*)

We can reconstruct the Roman variant in the very same manner, the result would be LOKUMA. If this would be correct, the word would have to be borrowed from Etruscan, because Etruscans turn every O into U, thus we end up with LUKUMA.

LUKUMA (reconstructed)
LUKUMO (Latin, spelt as *lucumo*)

Both reconstructions look alright, but the literal translations are "GENERAL-CITY" (for *lauchume)* and FREE-SPHERE-OF-ACTION CITY (for *lucumo*). It is not impossible to eventually see a ruler or king in these translations, but they are quite foggy. They don't fit the general pattern of Etruscan "Sanskrit compounds", where words are simple, direct and meanings are clear.

Maybe another second word would fit better?

Uma   m.   helper, friend, companion [511]

The translation GENERAL HELPER sounds like it rather fits a housemaid, a social worker or even some kind of a communist functionary! But there is another way, not as elegant, but very possible.

loka   m.   people, folk, region, district, province, common space, community, mankind [512]
+
oma   m.   protector [513]

loka + oma → lokoma → Etruscans always turn O into U → lukuma

LUKUMA (reconstructed)
LUCUMO (Etruscan and Latin, spelt as *lucumo* in Latin)

The meaning is PEOPLE'S PROTECTOR, COMMUNITY PROTECTOR, PROTECTOR OF THE REGION.

Could this express an idea of KING? It could, but it

sounds exceptionally soft, quite democratic. It is interesting that, at least in theory, Sanskrit offers the same translation for just slightly different reconstruction that would explain the first sound U in LAUCHUME.

laukika   m.   people, men in general, mankind [514]

oma   m.   protector, friend, helper [513]

laukika + Uma → laukikuma

We got 'laukikume" not 'laukume' (lauchume). How to come to 'laukume'? If we apply a process known in linguistics as haplology then it might become 'laukume'. Haplology is when two identical or similar syllables are placed in the word next to each other, just like in my reconstructed "lau-KI-KU-me", and one of them is dropped, so the remaining syllable represents both of them. This works perfectly here.

lau-KI-KU-me → lauKUme

The meaning is the same – PROTECTOR OF THE PEOPLE.

If this is the real translation of the Etruscan LAUCHUME (translated as KING), then it is very sophisticated. We can argue that political and military elite presented their privileges as public service from the earliest times, or we can speculate that this was an early hint of the emerging republican concept of the society. What we do need is some kind of confirmation of the meaning.

The list of Sanskrit words that mean 'king' is very long but we find something interesting there.

lokanAtha   m.   protector or guardian of the people, lord of worlds, king, sovereign [515]

lokapAla	m.	protector or ruler of the people, king, prince [516]
lokapālaka	m.	king, sovereign, world-protector[517]

This analogy confirms our translation. There are words in Sanskrit that mean both PROTECTOR OF THE PEOPLE and KING. And there is a word with the same meaning in the Etruscan language! All three listed Sanskrit words are compounds. In all three of them, the second word means PROTECTOR!

nAtha	m.	protector, lord [518]
pAla	m.	protector, guard [519]
pAlaka	m.	protector, guardian [520]

In fact, old Livy was probably not mistaken. Lucumo could be a personal name, too. This very translation PROTECTOR OF PEOPLE is the very translation of the name Alexander.

It is considered as non-scientific and dilettante work when you quote Wikipedia, the free encyclopedia, but that is what I am going to do here, supporting (with all its flows included) one of the noblest cultural projects after Library of Alexandria.

"The name Alexander is derived from the Greek "Ἀλέξανδρος" (Aléxandros), meaning "Defender of the people" or "Defending men" and also, "Protector of men", a compound of the verb ἀλέξειν aléxein, "to ward off, to avert, to defend" and the noun ἀνήρ anḗr, "man" (GEN ἀνδρός andrós)." [521]

PURTH *"name of magistrate or magistracy: dictator?"* (the Bonfantes, p.111)

Being responsible, the Bonfantes put a question mark.

We will keep on mind that question mark and examine this word with Sanskrit. Before we start that, we need to see what word DICTATOR meant at the dawn of history.

"Originally an emergency legal appointment in the Roman Republic, the term 'Dictator' did not have the negative meaning it has now. A Dictator was a magistrate given sole power for a limited duration." (Wikipedia) [522]

What are similar Sanskrit words that might make sense in this context?

parthayati { pRth }   verb   extend [523]

We can argue that it could be about EXTENDED POWER, but it doesn't feel like a sufficient explanation.

It could also come from some other words. Read them slowly.

pUrti   f.   reward, satisfaction, granting, completion, ending, coming to an end [524]
tha   m.   protector [525]

pUrti + tha → purttha → purth ?

If a king was "protector of the people", we can speculate that literal translation COMING TO AN END PROTECTOR meant that a person who became *purth* was given a power of a king, but for a limited time.

Or we can use another similar word.

pUrta   n.   granting, rewarding, a reward, merit, a meritorious work [526]
pūrta   n.   keeping, guarding [526]

ARYAN ITALY OF THE ETRUSCANS

Does this mean HONOURARY PROTECTOR? Is it about a political function that was received as an honour, based on past achievements? That is very possible.

Ellen Macnamara wrote that *"(...) an inscription from Vulci tells of a man who had been zilath seven times and purth once and who died at age of seventy two."* [527]

Zilath seven times and purth once! This tells us that both functions were elected. Massimo Pallottino wrote that from the fifth century BC a social change happened in Etruria, leading towards a republican type of organization (Pallotino, The Etruscans, 2nd edition, p.131-133).

'Purth' as a dictator? Maybe, but this type of "dictator" would have to be elected. Sanskrit itself gives different clues.

pur f.   town, stronghold, city, fortress [528]

pur + tha → purtha → purth

Is it some kind of 'mayor' who is still under the king? Is it PROTECTOR OF THE CITY? Or is it PROTECOR or COMMANDER OF THE FORTRESS, which might suggest that he was given the power to rule in a military manner under circumstances of an emergency?

What exactly 'purth' meant is still an open question, but it is a Sanskrit related word.

ZILATH or ZILACH *"praetor, ruler"* (the Bonfantes, p.111)

If the reconstruction of LUCUMO was convincing and the reconstruction of PURTH imposed some challenges, reconstructing ZILATH with Sanskrit turned out to be much more complicated. Approach with caution!

First, there is no sound Z in Sanskrit. That means that we need to go with its closest relative – S.

Second, there is a poor choice of Sanskrit words that start with S and that would make sense in the context.

```
si    f.         service [529]
lAti { lA }      verb    obtain, take, give, receive [530]
tha   m.         protector [525]
```

si + lA + tha→ sialatha → silath

The eventual meaning is SERVICE GIVING PROTECTOR. Since we already established that MEANING of PROTECTOR overlaps with the meaning of KING we can maybe read this as WHO SERVES AS A "KING". It would be somebody who is at the top of political hierarchy, with responsibilities similar to the responsibilities of a king, but who is elected and exercises that function for a limited time.

Generally, there are many similarities between the political systems of our time and Roman political institutions and functions. But the Roman political and legal system was a build-up and continuation of the Etruscan system. Our politicians still SERVE their terms and call what they do "public service". It is interesting that one of the Etruscan kings of Rome, thought to be a descendant of a servant or slave, ruled under the name of Servius Tullius.

So, SERVING PROTECTOR should not be an impossible option, not to mention that a bunch of Sanskrit words mean both *protector and king!*

Etruscans sometimes use ZILATH and sometimes they go with ZILACH. Pay attention to endings of these two: zilaTH, zilaCH

Optionally, ZILATH would come from ZILA + THA

(where *tha* means *protector*), and ZILACH would be the result of ZILA +KA (Etruscans sometimes write K as CH).

ka   m.   king [531]

ZILA + ka → zilaka → zilak (spelt as ZILACH)

Therefore we get "SERVING" (as a) KING.

So, because there is no Z in Sanskrit, we went with S. But some Sanskrit words that start with S appear in a slightly different form, starting with the sound close to SH (as in 'shore'). This sound is presented in IAST with character Ś, while Harvard-Kyoto transliteration uses Z.

You find word *sil* having a version of itself as *śil* (also written as *zil*).

sil   (also written śil-) cl.6 P. śilati-, to glean [532]

It looks like dialectal versions, they start with different sounds but it is still the same word. We are mentioning this as a potential justification for a different reconstruction.

zIla n   practice

This *zIla* does not have its version with S, but I am still mentioning it because I like the meaning. It would give ZILATH and ZILACH meanings of "PRACTICING PROTECTOR" and "PRACTICING KING". Just do not forget that this is all under a big question mark.

CAMTHI *"censor"* (the Bonfantes, p.111)

In the Glossary of *"Etruscan Language: An Introduction"*,

the Bonfantes say that CAMTHI is a *"name of magistracy"* (p.215).

However, on p.111 they translate it as *"censor"*. First, let's do some quick learning.

"The censor was a magistrate in ancient Rome who was responsible for maintaining the census, supervising public morality, and overseeing certain aspects of the government's finances.[1]

The power of the censors was absolute: no magistrate could oppose their decisions, only another censor who succeeded them could cancel it." [534]

Censors had big power, they controlled the behaviour and morals of the population. Sanskrit stem GAM might fit the concept of a censor (every G becomes K in Etruscan). It has many meanings, we list those that fit.

gamati { gam }   verb 1   approach with an accusation, ascribe guilt to a person, observe [538]

CAM in 'camthi' is therefore explained by GAM, while the THI ending could be attributed to *dhI*.

dhI f.   thought, (especially) religious thought, reflection, meditation, devotion, prayer (plural Holy Thoughts personified) [539]

dhI f.   mind, disposition, intention, design (in fine composition or 'at the end of a compound' intent upon)

dhI cl.4 A1. dhIyate-, to contain, hold (Passive voice of 1. dhā-?); to slight, disregard ; to propitiate (?)

gam + dhI → gamdhi → by rule, G turns into K, D becomes T → kamthi

KAMTHI (reconstructed)
CAMTHI (Etruscans, K written as C)

ARYAN ITALY OF THE ETRUSCANS

We can combine the meanings of two words in several ways and get some interesting results.

One is "OBSERVING RELIGIOUS THOUGHT". This "religious thought" we can easily read as *moral conduct that should be in harmony with the religion*. We can see in it OBSERVING (or observer) OF DISREGARD (wrongdoing).

Another option is ASCRIBE GUILT OF DISREGARD or APPROACH WITH AN ACCUSATION OF DISREGARD.

The Etruscan political system feels like some kind of republican theocracy, it is soaked in religious ideas.

METHLUM

Another word that is frequently mentioned is 'methlum'. The Bonfantes think that it means *"district, people, nation, territory"* (p.217).

UM at the end of 'methlum' is something we frequently find as the ending of Latin nouns, but it also might come from 'uma'.

uma m.   city, town [537]

UM ending, somewhat mysterious, is often placed at the end of Roman city names (like Singidunum, Viminacium, Lugdunum, Turicum, Mancunium. etc).

When you look in Sanskrit dictionaries you conclude that it must be marking a city, but the word *um* or *uma* does not exist in Latin dictionaries.

What would be the first word?

maTha   adj.   temple [538]

maTha + AL (genitive ending)

This MATHAL becomes MATHL after it went to through a typical Etruscan shortening of words.

MATHL + uma → mathluma → mathlum

MATHLUM (reconstructed)
METHLUM (Etruscan)

This suggests a temple's territorial unit. In Etruscan society, it would be the same as the territory of a city, so it could be read as TEMPLE'S CITY or, if we interpret it, as WHAT IS CITY'S AND TEMPLE'S TERRITORY.

We have to admit: this translation is very confusing.

The Bonfantes claimed that 'methlum' is a 'district'. My result combined with their translation gave me another idea.

What if *methlum* was POMERIUM?

Here is what *pomerium* means.

"The pomerium or pomoerium was a religious boundary around the city of Rome and cities controlled by Rome. In legal terms, Rome existed only within its pomerium; everything beyond it was simply territory (ager) belonging to Rome." [539]

The Romans probably adopted the concept of pomerium from the Etruscans. A pomerium was a religious shield that protected the city and its people from evil forces outside of it.

Cities were planned to be a materialization of faith and to provide protection of gods. When you lived in such a city you lived in the middle of the Etruscan or Roman religious narrative. A pomerium was precisely defined and that is how, if needed, city walls were erected. So, even city walls

ARYAN ITALY OF THE ETRUSCANS

had a religious meaning attached to them. There was an exact procedure that defined city lay-out. This is how H.H. Scullard wrote about it, paraphrasing Livy.

"Lacking much direct Etruscan evidence, we must see what the Romans thought about the Etruscan procedure. This was a matter which greatly interested them, since they believed that they themselves had inherited this Etruscan Ritus in the founding of their own cities: thus even early Rome itself, the urbs quadrata on the Palatine (see p. 246), was reputed to have been laid out on these lines. According to Plutarch the method which Romulus, advised by Etruscans, followed was this: first a centre was chosen, where a pit (mundus) was dug, into which first fruits were thrown." [540]

Let's stop here! This chosen centre that Scullard mentions will be in the middle of the main intersection of the future city. This reminds of an Indian custom mentioned by Nanditha Krishna in "The book of Demons : including a dictionary of Demons in Sanskrit literature". She wrote that *"Bhutas are found at crossroads and on the boundaries of villages. It is customary, all over India, to plant an iron stake at crossroad and bury grains beneath it for crows to eat. An image of Ganesha may also be installed as a detterent to spirits who would otherwise haunt the place."* [541]

H.H. Scullard continues *"From this centre a circle was marked around it. The founder, having fitted a bronze share to a plough and having yoked to it a bull and a cow, cut a deep furrow round the boundary lines, while those behind turned the clods inwards towards the city and allowed none to lie turned outwards. With this line they marked out the course of the wall; it was called pomerium.*
[...]
The Romans, however, believed that their earliest settlement, Roma Quadrata, had been laid out in the same way as their later colonies and camps by a process which went back to Etruscan augural methods. The augur after taking the auspices orientated the site by use of a surveying instrument, the groma (...)

[...]
Placed at the centre, the mundus, the groma provided the cardinal points; from it two main exes were marked out, the cardo running from north to south and the decumanus from east to west. These two lines intersecting at right-angles, formed a frame on which a regular grid-system of lesser streets could be constructed." [540]

The more I look at my reconstruction of 'methlum' that gave the literal meaning TEMPLE'S-CITY, the less I believe in it. Let's forget the UM-ending and reconstruct METHL again.

mADate	{ mAD }	verb	measure[542]
Alī	f.		line, row, ditch, range [543]

mAD + Ali → madal(i)

This would be changed because the Etruscans always turn D into TH or T. We get MATHALI. And, since Etruscans corrupt word endings by dropping vowels, we end with MATHL.

Remember, a *pomerium* was defined by a line that was established by augurs using geometry (even the word 'geometry' suggests measuring of land).

Along that line they ploughed, making a furrow (ditch?). We can translate this 'MATHALI' as MEASURED LINE OR DITCH or MEASURED BY A DITCH. This is simple and descriptive.

MATHALI + uma (meaning 'city') → mathaluma → MATHLUM

This is how the comparison looks.

MATHLUM (reconstructed)
METHLUM (Etruscan)

ARYAN ITALY OF THE ETRUSCANS

The literal translation is MEASURE-LINE-CITY or MEASURE-RANGE-CITY, but it could be read as DEFINED BORDER OF THE CITY.

The word DITCH relates to FURROW, but we can use another Sanskrit word here.

hali m.   furrow [544]

So it goes in this way.

mAD → mat

mat + hali → mathali → mathal → mathl

mathl + uma → mathlum

We can translate it as FURROW MEASURE OF THE CITY or FURROW(ed) BORDER OF THE CITY.

Both METHLUM and POMERIUM end with UM. This means that we should question the current etymology of 'pomerium'.
Here it is.

"The term is a classical contraction of the Latin phrase post moerium, literally "beyond the wall". The Roman historian Livy writes in his Ab Urbe Condita that, although the etymology implies a meaning referring to a single side of the wall, the pomerium was originally an area of ground on both sides of city walls. He states that it was an Etruscan tradition to consecrate this area by augury (...)" [539]

So, Livy shows that *post moerium* is not describing a pomerium accurately. Also, there are some other questions we must ask. If Rome was founded by an Etruscan procedure, then the word for that procedure could be

Etruscan. Or it could come from a forgotten layer of Latin? What if we try to reconstruct POMERIUM as if it was a Sanskritic word?

bhUmi	f.	earth, land [545]
arya	adj.	devoted, true, attached to [546]
uma	m.	city [537]

bhUmi + arya + uma → bhumaryum

As always, B becomes P, Y becomes I (as in 'tin'), H is dropped. The result is PUMARIUM.

PUMARIUM (reconstructed, hypothetically Etruscan)
POMERIUM (Latin)

This would mean LAND DEVOTED TO CITY, TRUE CITY LAND, etc.

But, again, there is a better Sanskrit option!

bhU	f.	earth, land, ground, soil [547]
maryA	f.	mark, limit, boundary [548]
uma	m.	city, sky [537]

bhU + maryA + uma → B becomes P, Y becomes I → pumarium

PUMARIUM (reconstructed, hypothetical, Etruscan)
POMERIUM (Latin)

The literal translation is simple and precise: LAND MARK CITY (or MARKED LAND OF THE CITY). We can also translate it as BOUNDARY OF CITY LAND or even better LAND BOUNDARY OF THE CITY.

Technically speaking, we can reconstruct METHLUM

with a similar meaning in mind.

mADate   { mAD } verb   measure [542]
+
halA   f.   earth [549]

mAD + halA → madhala

Since Etruscans turn D into T or TH we get MATHALA. Then, because Etruscans corrupt word endings by dropping vowels, this *mathala* would become MATHL.

mathl + uma → mathluma → mathlum

The literal translation is MEASURE LAND CITY.

But the story of Roman Pomerium became more complicated as the city expanded and Pomerium ended up defining just a special district of Rome.

Hilary Becker wrote, *"A different picture is presented by a boundary marker installation at Bolsena (Volsinii Novi) that was found before one of the main entrances into the city. The inscription reads THVAL METHLUM, and while the meaning of the first word remains unknown, the second word METHLUM describes the URBS. Thus this stone marked the entrance to the 'pomerium' of Bolsena, the boundary inside which an augur could take his readings (see Chapter 26)."* [550]

Regarding THVAL METHLUM the solution could be very simple.
Why THVAL looks so mysterious?
It is because scholars divorced Etruscan from Indo-European languages. This was based on observation of certain Etruscan words, especially words for numbers,

which don't even remotely resemble their Indo-European "counterparts".

My inspiration came from the Serbian and generally Slavic word for number two. It is DVA. In Sanskrit, two is *dvi* [551] (*dva* in compounds).

How would Etruscans pronounce 'dva'?

It would be THVA or TVA. Treat V in this 'thva' as close to W and you will come to English TWO. 'Two' is 'duo' in Latin. It appears that, because it ends with L, THVAL is made from DVA (two) + L (being either genitive or an adjective ending).

Simply, THVAL seems to mean DUAL.

If we accept that METHLUM meant *pomerium,* THVAL METHLUM would be DUAL POMERIUM, or maybe 'double pomerium'.

Why? We can only guess. Sometimes, when discussing 'pomerium', authors wrote about both sides of the wall that are considered sacred but there could be another parallel

If you picture the Etruscan city-planning procedure that Scullard described, you will remember that they would determine a central point and, referencing to it, draw a circle. Through that central point, one line would go in North-South and another in an East-West direction. This symbol, which we can describe as a circled "plus sign", appears throughout Etruria. Often, this circled cross is encompassed by two concentric circles. An example of this you can see on an Etruscan vase shown in a news item about an exhibition of Etruscan artifacts.

(Check it on YouTube at *abnewsTV* Channel, clip: https://youtu.be/CpFRDWTV6U0, at 1:31)

Variations of it you can see even on Etruscan jewelry, though instead of a cross there would often be a flower shape in the middle that actually might suggest the Sun and an idea of cosmic order, of the divine... My impression is that the Etruscan obsession with concentric circles has a meaning that comes from their religious system. But this symbol is not only Etruscan and you can find it elsewhere (think of Celtic cross). Or, take a look at this example of Daunian pottery (550-440 BC) exhibited in the museum in Düsseldorf. You will see the same "Etruscan symbol"!

LINK:
https://en.wikipedia.org/wiki/Daunians#/media/File:Daunisch-subgeometrischer_Kyathos_3,_Hetjens-Museum_Düsseldorf_(DerHexer).JPG

Well, again and again, maybe my translations of 'thval' and 'methlum' are not correct, but the very fact that I constantly offer Sanskrit interpretations of Etruscan terminology should be taken seriously.

MACSTREV or MAKSTREV

The Bonfantes translate it as *"name of magistracy"* (p.217), but we can speculate that it could mean *magistrate*.

If we break the word in two, MAKS and TREV, we might get something.

magha   m.   power [552]

Since Etruscans do not have 'G', their rendering of the word would be 'makha'. 'Maks' is likely a genitive form (the Etruscan genitive is often identical to the Saxon genitive in English; i.e. Peter's). The second part is TREV.

trA   m.   protector, defender [553]

maks + trA → makstra → K spelt as C → macstra

In this case, MACSTRA becomes PROTECTOR OF

POWER (of political order), maybe POWERFUL PROTECTOR. But we do miss EV at the end of the word. Let's try to explain that!

  avati { av }   verb 1   govern [said of kings or princes][554]
  avati { av }   verb 1   promote [ved.] [554]

The formula is changed.

maks + trA + av → MAKSTRAV

The literal translation is POWER PROTECTOR GOVERN. It might be too general. We can read it in a couple of ways: RULING PROTECTOR OF POWER (order) or POWERFUL PROTECTOR OF GOVERNMENT (order).

This is not the end of our trouble with multiple options. We can use stem tRR which has numerous meanings but some of them might apply here.

  tarati { tRR } verb   perform, accomplish, fulfill[555]

tRR + av → trav (literally PERFORM-GOVERN)

magha → maka → mak → maks (genitive form)

maks + tRR + av → makstrav

The literal layout is OF-POWER PERFORM GOVERN.

Also, as the Etruscan word for people was MECH (or MEKH) it could be PROTECTOR OF PEOPLE (but one vowel is different). Yes, we are translating one language with another, so imprecision is to be expected. Etruscan vocabulary seems to be related to Sanskrit, but the Etruscan language is not equal to Sanskrit, though it likely descends from the same language base as Sanskrit. But, what is shocking is how strong this relationship is. Just think of this: while we didn't have any etymology of 'macstrev', we now have too many.

We should probably discard the option with MECH (people) and go with MAGHA (power) simply because related Latin words like *magisterium* contain G. Romans lived with Etruscans and in the beginnings of Rome they were often schooled in the Etruscan language. It is reasonable to assume that Romans knew when an Etruscan K (C) was coming or not coming from G.

MECH

"people, league, district" (the Bonfantes, p.217)

There is no similar Sanskrit word or possible compound that would give us these meanings directly, but there are words that are not that far from 'mech' in how they sound, and we can maybe associate their meanings with 'people'.

mAkha   n.   any relationship based upon an oblation offered in common[556]

Looking from this angle, MECH would be about the common way of worshipping gods so it might mean *congregation* or mark members of the religious *community* (which in Etruscan society would be everybody, therefore it would apply to people).

Regarding sounds, much closer is another word.

megha   m.   mass, multitude [557]

This would become MEKHA and then MEK(h) (spelt as MECH in Etruscan).

Mass? Multitude? Masses? People?

PARNICH

"magistracy or priesthood" (the Bonfantes, p. 218)

This title is mentioned in an Etruscan text and it looks like it has Sanskrit references. Sanskrit does offer a possible insight.

parNa   m.(pl.)   of people [558]

Could this be an explanation of *parnich*?

Early Romans were very similar to Etruscans in their way of life, religion, culture, social organization. Let's try it in this way: we will assume that Sanskrit *parNa* is the right etymology and then try to fit its meaning in some known political function of Rome. Which one would it be?

It would have to be TRIBUNE.

Wikipedia says that *"Tribune (Latin: Tribunus) was the title of various elected officials in ancient Rome. The two most important were the tribunes of the plebs and the military tribunes."* [559]

Latin *tribunus* comes from *tribus*, meaning 'tribe'. *Tribal* and *of people*? These meanings are the same.
Website dictionary.com defines a tribune as *"a person who upholds or defends the rights of the people"*.[560] The main idea behind the function of a tribune was defending of interests of common folks (plebs) from the aristocracy (patricians).

ARYAN ITALY OF THE ETRUSCANS

ATHUMI *"nobility"* (the Bonfantes, p.214)

attA   f.   elder[561]
oma m.   protector[562]

attt + oma → attoma → double T becomes single T → atoma

Etruscans turn every O into U → ATUMA

ATUMA (reconstructed)
ATUMI (Etruscan)

The literal meaning is ELDER-PROTECTOR(s).

However, if UMI in ATHUMI comes from *uma* in the meaning of *city*, we get CITY ELDER(s).

RATUM, RATM

The Bonfantes translate it as *"according to law, ritual (rite?)"* (p.218).

The Etruscan RATUM is already quite similar to Latin 'ritus' (rite, ceremony).

raThati { raTh }   verb   speak[563]
Uma   m.   sky, heaven[564]

raTh + Uma → rathuma → ratum

We get 'SPEAK-HEAVEN'. This can be read TALKING OF HEAVEN. It clearly might mean WORD OF HEAVEN, 'word of god', law.

We can also find support in Sanskrit for the eventual meaning of 'ritual' or 'rite.'

rAdhyati   { rAdh }   verb caus.
    perform, accomplish, carry out [565]
+
Umam.   sky, heaven

rAdh + Uma → radhuma → radhum

There is no D in Etruscan, it becomes RATHUM or RATUM. The literal translation is PERFORM-HEAVEN, therefore it really can be PERFORMANCE (FOR or ACCORDING to) HEAVEN or a RITUAL. The same might apply to a 'performer' for HEAVEN, a priest.

But let's not rush in making conclusions! There is a third way. Both the Etruscan word RATUM and the Latin word RITUS might have a parent or an uncle in this Sanskrit word.

Rta   n.   sacred or pious action or custom [566]

This word also has numerous additional meanings and most of them match the meaning of 'ratum' that The Bonfantes offered: LAW, RITUAL, RITE.

Rta   n.   divine law, divine truth, truth personified sacrifice, law, faith, fixed or settled order, oath, sun [566]
Rta   n.   (Rtam- i-, to go the right way, be pious or virtuous)[566]

We should not doubt that Sanskrit *Rta* is either a parent of Etruscan *ratum* and Latin *ritus* or that all of them together are linguistic triplets.

5.6 CULTURE AND ENTERTAINMENT

ISTER *"actor"* (gloss: Latin 'histrio') (p.216)

More often than not, the Etruscans drop H.

hasitR   adj.   one who laughs, a laugher, smiler[567]

All the consonants are in the exact order as they are in Latin and Etruscan words. The meaning is not too bad - 'laugher'. The first actors were simply entertainers, clowns, jokers. But a 'laugher' could be somebody who is in the audience, watching a comedy. Let's try something else.

hasati { has }   verb   laugh, ridicule, mock [568]
tarati { tRR }   verb   perform, carry through, accomplish [569]

has + tRR → hastrr → Double R becomes single R → hastr + IO (word ending in infinitive) → hastrio

HASTRIO (reconstructed)
HISTRIO (Latin word)

This means RIDICULE PERFORMER or, if you want, COMEDY PERFORMER.

The Etruscan word ISTER went through a similar process, but the H was dropped and one of the accented double Rs was replaced by a vowel.

PHERSU

"mask, masked person, actor", Latin 'persona' (The Bonfantes, p.218)

There is a Sanskrit noun that is similar to the Latin 'persona'.

puruSa   m.   person, man, personal and animating principle in men and other beings, soul, spirit [570]

After we drop H from the Etruscan word, all three consonants are in exact order: P-R-S. Let's try it on the Latin word and provide the consonant N.

puruSa	m.	person [570]
Ana	m.	face [571]

puruSa + Ana → purusana

PURUSANA (reconstructed)
PERSONA (Latin)

This would mean "PERSON'S-FACE", maybe suggesting a mask that actors of the era used (also translatable as "face of the soul").
Is there more?

puras	indecl.	in front [572]
puras	adverb	before [572]
Ana	m.	face [571]

puras + Ana → purasana → pursana

PURASANA
PERSONA

The meaning we get is IN FRONT OF FACE, suggesting a MASK. Latin *persona* means *character* and *mask*.

Along with the idea of a mask is another reconstruction.

puruSa	m.	person [570]
oNi	m.	protection [573]

puruSa + oNi → purusoni → pursoni

PURSONI (reconstructed)
PERSONA (Latin)

The meaning is PERSON-PROTECTION. Are we stretching it too much if we interpret it as MASKED PERSON?

There are so many Sanskrit words you can play with!

para	adj.	other, another, strange [574]
pAra	m.	particular personification [575]
sU	adj.	bringing forth [576]
Ana	m.	face [571]

para + sU + Ana → parsu + ana → parsana

PARSUANA
PERSONA

Literal meaning: ANOTHER BROUGHT FORTH FACE could be seen as MASKED PERSON.

Well, most of these reconstructions must be wrong, maybe all of them are, but this demonstrates how possible it is to reconstruct these words with Sanskrit.

Look at this one!

bhAratI   f.   Sanskrit speech of an actor, literary composition, speech [577]

There is no stem offered here that we can use in compounds, but if we would like to enforce one it would have to be BHAR. As you know, Etruscans don't have B, this would be PHAR for them. Add the word *sU* to it.

sU   adj.   bringing forth [576]

PHAR + Su → pharsu → phersu

Literal meanings would be "BRINGING FORT" OF SANSKRIT SPEECH BY AN ACTOR and DELIVERY (vivifying) OF A LITERARY COMPOSITION. What do you think? Does it make sense? It does, but the reconstruction was doctored by using a hypothetical stem.

We should try again. Maybe this word is relevant.

bhara   m.   raising the voice, shout or song of praise [578]

For the end, let's just notice that one of the Sanskrit words for an actor is partly similar to PHERSU.

bharata   m.   actor, dancer, tumbler [579]

The Etruscans would pronounce this as PHARATA.

Even if we cannot or should not decide which etymology is correct or most relevant, there is enough evidence that confirms the Sanskrit affiliation of Etruscan PHERSU and Latin PERSONA.

Also, we encountered two words for an actor:

ARYAN ITALY OF THE ETRUSCANS

HISTRIO-ISTER and PHERSU-PERSONA. We can speculate that they were about two kinds of acting. In Latin, HISTRIO also marks an actor that performs pantomime and it might generally be applied to performers of comedy and physical humour. PHERSU should probably be about acting in dramas.

*SUPLU *"flutist (Latin 'subulo')"* (The Bonfantes, p.219)

The Bonfantes do put an asterisk in front of 'suplu' because nobody was sure if the word was of Latin origin. It seemed to be Etruscan.

sunoti { su } verb 5 press out [580]
savati { su }   verb 1   urge, impel, incite [581]
+
plavate { plu }   verb   blow (as the wind) [582]

su + plu → suplu "(PRESS OUT BLOW" or PRESS OUT WITH BLOW)

A flute is a wind instrument, it makes sounds because a player is blowing into the instrument. SUPLU, reconstructed in this way, could mark any wind instrument, including bagpipes. The same stem PLU must be the root of the English word 'flute'. We can see how the Sanskrit P becomes the English F, and F is the sound that came to Italic languages from the Etruscans!

SLICA- ? Regarding its meaning, The Bonfantes just put a question mark (p.218)

This time, there is no English word to compare with, but Serbian. In Serbian, the word 'slika' (pronounced the same as the Etruscan 'slica') means 'image', 'picture'. Why am I mentioning English or Serbian words? English and Serbian are Indo-European languages, they are relatives of Sanskrit. If Etruscan is an Indo-European language, they are also relatives of Etruscan.

The word below must be a root of the Serbian words 'slika' (image) and 'slikati' (verb, 'to paint an image').

likhati { likh }   verb 6   draw a line, scrape, paint, scratch, engrave, sketch, write [583]

The comparison looks like this:

LIKHATI (Sanskrit)
SLIKATI (Serbian)

The oldest layers of the meaning of 'likh' must be 'draw a line' and even more likely 'scratch'. Then, through the first pictorial writing, it came to mean 'to write'.

In Serbian, the sound S which is added at the beginning would indicate doing WITH or BY something. One of the Sanskrit words for WITH is

saha indecl.   together with [584]

It looks like the Serbian *sa* and its short form *s*, meaning WITH, are also identical in meaning with the Sanskrit *sa*, which also means 'with' and is actually the same word. The website *sanskritdictionary.com* says that *sa* is in connection to *saha-*, *sam-* and *sama-* and that it can be translated as 'with', but also expresses a conjunction, 'sameness'.[585] Take a look at this Sanskrit word and its English translation.

sama   adj.   same, equal [586]

These parallels are grounded. Now, I understand the

Serbian 'slika'. It is when you draw and the result looks like something real, it is a depiction of it. For example, you can draw abstract geometrical patterns all over the wall and it will not be 'slika'. If I have to go over two thousand years back to understand the formation of Serbian or English words, I think my Sanskrit chances with Etruscan are great. Take a look at these words from Sanskrit, English, and Serbian.

SANSKRIT: grAbha   m.   what is seized, grasp

ENGLISH: *to grab*

SERBIAN: *grabiti* (means 'to grab'; but it is interesting that there is no similar verb in Sanskrit while the Serbian verb, like all Serbian verbs, looks like a Sanskrit verb!)

These do not prove that the Etruscan 'slica' really means 'drawing' or 'painting', but there is a reasonable doubt based on other parallels and direct ties between Sanskrit and Etruscan and even quite often Serbian or English and Etruscan, and Sanskrit. The Serbian word is related to the Sanskrit *likh*, but we cannot be sure about the Etruscan word *slica*.

5.7 FUNERARY CUSTOMS

THAURE, THAURA – *"tomb"* (The Bonfantes, p.220)

This is a short word, but it could be a compound.

TA f.   earth [589]
uru n.   room, space [590]

TA + uru → tauru

This means EARTH-ROOM, UNDERGROUND ROOM. It is a tomb. But reconstructed TAURU is missing that H which is present in the Etruscan word! TH at the beginning of THAURE might substitute an earlier D.

dA f.   (de-), protection, defence [591]

This would make THAURE a PROTECTION ROOM (or SPACE). It is an open question if this is an acceptable explanation. Maybe we should try another second word. Sanskrit stem *vR* might fit. It is written in IAST as

vṛ

and in Harvard-Kyoto as

vR   covering [592]

dA + vR → D becomes TH, V turns into W or U → THAUR

THAUR (reconstructed)
THAURE (Etruscan)

The literal translation is PROTECTION COVERING. Could this be a grave, a grave chamber or a tomb? It could. But the meaning is not direct so we cannot be completely confident about it.

HINTH, HINTHI, HINTHIS

"below" (The Bonfantes, p.216)

According to The Bonfantes, the adjective is HINTHIU and means *'underground'*, *'infernal'*. Let's take a look at similar Sanskrit words. You should read them slowly.

hIna   adj.   low, lower, brought low, devoid, deprived of [593]
+
dha adj.   placing, putting, holding [594]
dha mf(ā-)n. (1. dhā-; see 2. dhā-) (in fine compositi or 'at the end of a compound) placing, putting [595]

Here is one reconstruction.

hIna + dha → hindha (Etruscans do not have D, it becomes T or TH) → hintha → PUT LOW, PLACED LOW, HELD (BE)LOW, etc.

LUP-, LUPU

"to die" (The Bonfantes, p.217)

Massimo Palottino also mentioned 'LUPU' and 'LUPUCE' as words that meant *'to die'*. [596]
Just read this string of Sanskrit words and stems and see if you find a kinship.

lupta   adj.   annihilated [597]
luptatA   f.   non-existence, disappearance [598]
lumpate { lup }   verb 6   cause to disappear, hurt, take away, deprive of, be destroyed [599]

The stem is LUP. The explanation is not needed.

ZIVA

The Bonfantes translate it as *"the dead, deceased"* (p. 220).
Sanskrit does not have an identical word, but it has a very similar word.

zava n. m.   dead body, corpse [600]
zavas   n.   dead body [601]

These words are pronounced as 'shava' and 'shavas'. I already raised a question if what is pronounced as SH in Sanskrit can be an Etruscan Z, TS, or S.

There might not be any connection, but the Etruscan word 'ziva' is almost identical to the Serbian *živa*. This 'Z' with the hook is like 'G' in the French name Gerard or Givenchy. I am toying here with the idea that the Etruscan 'ziva' actually means 'living', like in Serbian *život*=life, *živeti*=to live, *živ*=alive, *živa*=alive).

If this was a mistake, it would be an easy one to make, since the word is taken from tombstones. For example, what if the text translated as "died at 36" was actually saying "lived 36"?

There is no doubt that Serbian words are connected to Sanskrit. In Harvard-Kyoto Sanskrit 'J' is pronounced as J in the English word 'jar' or the name John. But in Serbian, this "Sanskrit J" became Ž, pronounced as G in Givenchy.

JIvA   f.   life [602]

ARYAN ITALY OF THE ETRUSCANS

jIva	adj.	living, alive[603]
jIvat	adj.	living[604]

JIVAT (*living*, Sanskrit)
ŽIVOT (*life*, Serbian)

Does the Etruscan *ziva* mean 'dead' or 'living'? We don't know, but it easily could be related to Sanskrit. It is not a long way from SH to S, and it is even shorter way from S to Z. But the truth is that we need much more insight to determine if this parallel is serious. We can speculate because sound changes between languages are present in our time, too. I talked with a recent immigrant from Greece whose English was fairly decent, but he still could not say correctly Chester Avenue, he said it as "Tzester" Avenue.

The Bonfantes wrote, *"The letter Z in Etruscan always had a voiceless sound, as TS in English GETS, CATS (not as in ZEAL."* [605]

A related word also appears in the famous Lemnos inscription in the form of *'shivai'*. Based on this inscription scholars identified Lemnian as a language akin to Etruscan (Lemnos is an island far from Italy, between Greece and Turkey). Scholars did fail to connect it to Sanskrit and Indo-European languages, they rather put it in the separate group of Tyrrhenian (also called Tyrsenian) languages that are thought to be non-Indo-European.

By the way, it is known that Lemnos was populated by Pelasgians. The amount of Sanskrit evidence in the text on Lemnos Stellae is shocking. This is a funerary inscription and words for death are present in it. Line 2 of Lemnos Stellae says:

"maraš:mav".

It is natural to suspect that *maraš* is related to the Sanskrit word for 'death'.

mara   m.   death [606]

Line 4 says: *"evisθu:šerunaiθ"*. For 'evisθu' I find Sanskrit 'avisthu", which means 'priest'. These are just some words you can actually find in a dictionary, without taking them apart. Scholars did notice that some Lemnian words clearly relate to the Etruscan vocabulary, like *'aviš'* (the Etruscan *'avis'*, meaning 'year'; note that Etruscan uses S where Lemnian uses an SH variant).

But such a word can also be *'murinail'*. It must be related to the Etruscan word we will discuss next. As you can guess, it is connected to Sanskrit. This would mean that if the Lemnos Stele was Pelasgian, and chances are that it was, then Pelasgian was actually an Indo-European language.

It could also mean that the Pelasgians were one of the important ingredients in formation of the Etruscan identity. That would explain the unbelievable fondness that Etruscans had for "Greek" vases and motifs from "Greek" mythology. The number of Greek vases that were found in Tuscany is bigger than the number of Greek vases found in Greece itself!

MURS

Word MURS The Bonfantes identify as a word for *"urn"*, *"sarcophagus"* (p.217).

What they don't see, or say, is that the stem 'mR' is an Indo-Aryan stem that is present in words related to death. We find it in the Latin *'mortem'* (death), Serbian words like *'mreti'* = to be dieing , *'smrt'* = death, *'mrtvac'* = dead man etc. Coming through Latin or not (because it might be directly connected to whatever language or language family Sanskrit and Prakrit descend from) it is present in the English words *'mortal'*, *'morgue'* etc. The stem 'mR' clearly comes from the following verbs.

mrayati { mR }	verb		die [607]
mriyate { mR }	verb		die [608]
mAryate { mR }	verb pass.	kill [609]	
mArayati { mR }	verb caus.	kill [610]	

It is present in many other words, too.

marta m. mortal, man [611]
mRta ppp. dead (compare with Serbian adjective 'mrtav', meaning 'dead') [612]
mRti f. death [613]

Therefore, the Etruscan word 'murs' which scholars take as a word for 'urn' and 'sarcophagus' can easily be related to various Sanskrit words associated with death.

FAVI

The Bonfantes also mention the word FAVI which, according to them, means *"grave, temple vault"* (p.216).

All these meanings are derived from the context of inscriptions, using the internal method.

I will treat the Etruscan word FAVI as a compound, assuming that the Sanskrit P or PH will become an F in Etruscan.

But, please, do not forget that however probable the change of P to F can be, it still needs much more verification. In favour of this sound change are some well-known examples, one of them being the name of the city Pupluna or Fufluna

pAti { pA } verb keep, preserve, protect [614]

vyeti { vI }   verb   perish, disappear [615]

pA + vI → pavi → P becomes F → FAVI

The literal meanings are KEEP-DISAPPEAR(ED) ONE, PRESERVE-PERISH(ED) ONE. We can agree that this can express the concept of a grave.

APER

The Bonfantes translate it as *"funerary sacrifice? (Latin parentare)"* (p.214), but they put a question mark.

The Sanskrit stem 'ape' can be easily put in connection with the death and is the real root of this word.

apaiti { ape }   verb   to go away, retire, vanish, disappear [616]

If this was about 'dying', then we would have to notice the use of gentle words when talking about the loss of loved ones. We do the same in our time. When somebody dies we say that he or she 'passed away' (stem *ape as go away*), for the one who is buried we say 'resting' (stem *ape as retire*).

CAPRA

We will include here a noun that maybe should not be in this section, but is a part of another word that relates to a vocabulary for funerary customs.

The Bonfantes write: (p.113): *"The word capra, 'urn', was perhaps derived from Greek kamptra, 'box'."* On page 215, they translate 'capra' as *"urn, container"*. They do not wonder what happened with M and T contained in the Greek *'kamptra'*.

A much cleaner etymology is offered by Sanskrit.

khapura   n.   water-jar [617]

khapura → attested feature of Etruscan to drop vowels in the ending part of the word → khapra → kapra (spelt as 'capra')

Generally, we can see an urn as a 'jar'. There is a possibility here.

SATH-, ŚAT- *"put, establish, be put?"*, p.218

This word is similar to the English verb SET, "to set" something. The meanings that The Bonfantes offer are similar to the English 'set'. Let's play with these words for a moment. When you SET something you 'establish' it, you make it "sit" at the place. Look at this Sanskrit word and its stem!

sIdati   { sad } verb   sit [618]

sad → Etruscans always use T or TH instead of D → sath

Sanskrit *sIdati* is pretty much the same as Serbian *sedeti* (meaning *to sit*). There is no doubt the English *sit* and Serbian *sedeti* are cognates.
Generally, SET seems to be a decent explanation of SATH or ŚAT.
Merriam-Webster Dictionary says that the main meaning of the verb TO SET is
'to cause to sit: place in or on a seat'. [619]
We have to think of meanings that slightly shift inside and between words and translations offered by the

Bonfantes become quite realistic. SIT, SET, SATH!

ŚUTH-, SUT- *"to stay, place?"* (the Bonfantes, p.219).

The closest Sanskrit word is

sUti   f.   lying in [620]

This 'sUti' might explain everything, especially when we read how The Bonfantes translate other Etruscan words related to it. Here is how exactly they present them on p.219.

ŚUTHI - *"seat, tomb"*
ŚUTHINA - *"having to do with a grave, sepulchral gift"*
SUTHIU - *"is placed"*

The Sanskrit *sUti*, meaning 'lying in', can accommodate all of these translations. But there is a big problem here. The main set of meanings of the word *sUti* is related to *giving birth* and *offspring*. It is important to keep this discussion open and avoid making final conclusions, but Sanskrit parallels do exist. For example, The Bonfantes say that ŚUTHINA means s*epulchral gift*. I don't know if this is the right translation, but I am sure that ŚUTHINA might contain one of Sanskrit words for *gift*.

na   m.   gift [621]

Or, take a look at Dieter H. Steinbauer's translation of ŚUTHI (he wrote it as *shuti*): *"vault, grave (building)"*.[242] It is the same as the one offered by The Bonfantes, but also adds the meaning of *building*. [622]

Again, there is a Sanskrit word that might support his

ARYAN ITALY OF THE ETRUSCANS

view, but indirectly.

    sudhA   f.   earth, plaster, brick [623]

But there is a word that actually means *building*.

    saudha   n.   any fine house, palace [624]

OK, you can say that SAUDHA is not the same as SUTHI. We already know that Etruscans replace the sound D with T or TH. So, SAUDHA becomes SAUTHA. But they also had a habit to merge vowels that were placed next to each other. The Bonfantes wrote about the trend in the Etruscan language *"toward the simplification of two different vowels forming a diphthong into a single vowel" (p.80)*. And that is how SAUTHA (previously *saudha*) can become SUTHA.

Generally speaking, The Bonfantes might be right or almost right. Looking from the Sanskrit point of view ŚUTHI might be about something else.

    sudhI   adj.   religious, pious [625]

As for the word SUTHIU, a possible reconstruction could be made by using the word 'yu'.

    yauti { yu }   verb   honour, worship [626]

sudhI + yu → sudhiyu → suthiu

The translation of 'suthiu' could be RELIGIOUS WORSHIP. Do not forget, these are possibilities, not answers.

Let us take a look at SUTHIUSVE. On page 219, The Bonfantes ask if this might mean PROPERTY. Look at this

Sanskrit word!

sva　　n.　　　property, wealth, riches [627]

If Giuliano and Larissa Bonfante and many other scholars didn't deny the Indo-European nature of Etruscan language, you would think that they sometimes used Sanskrit dictionaries! But 'property' is just one of many Sanskrit meanings of *sva* (the base meaning is 'of self'). By the way, one of the Serbian words for 'property' is 'svojina'.

Finally, they also list the word SUTHIVENAS and put a question mark next to it. This is reconstructable in a couple of ways, but one option looks very clean.

sUti　　　f.　　　lying in [620]
vana　　　n.　　　abode [628]

So, this might be an ABODE IN WHICH SOMEBODY IS LAID. It could easily be an underground chamber-tomb. But if we use Sanskrit word *sudhi*, then it becomes RELIGIOUS ABODE or TEMPLE. But, again, like in so many other cases, we cannot always just translate an Etruscan word with Sanskrit. For example, the word *vana* has ten to fifteen other meanings. Still, the option we show does exist.

So, even if we avoid deciding what translation is right (if any), we cannot deny that Sanskrit continues to offer meaningful translations.

MUTANA, MUTNA *"sarcophagus"* (p. 217)

The Second variant, 'mutna', is the result of a known Etruscan shortening of word-endings by dropping vowels. The accent in Etruscan seems to always be on the first syllable. There are several options here.

| mUta | adj. | bound [629] |
| anna | n. | earth [630] |

mUta + anna → mutana (EARTH-BOUND, EARTH-BINDING)

Or, take a look at this.

mU	adj.	binding [631]
mu	m.	funeral pile or pyre, final emancipation [632]
tha	n.	preservation [633]
Na	m.	gift, ornament [634]

mU + tha + na → muthana → mutana

The meanings differ, but if we allow a looser approach it can be "BINDING-PRESERVATION-ORNAMENT" (or ORNAMENTED PRESERVATION CONTAINER, thus 'sarcophagus'), or ORNAMENTED FUNERAL PRESERVATION). There are other ways, too.

| dhAna | adj. | holding, containing [635] |
| dhAna | n. | the site of habitation |

mU + dhAna → mudhana → muthana → mutana

Literally, it is FUNERAL (pile) CONTAINING, or a FUNERAL "CONTAINER" (or a 'sarcophagus' or a 'coffin').

Another option is FUNERAL (pile) HABITAT.

TAMERA

Another confusing word! Here are two views regarding the meaning of TAMERA.

"name of magistracy" (The Bonfantes, p.219)

"grave chamber" (Steinbauer) [636]

Let us try to justify The Bonfantes' guess. This the closest to 'magistracy' we could find (D would become T).

DAmara   m.   lord [637]

But Sanskrit can also accommodate a very different translation proposed by Steinbauer.

TA	f.	earth [638]
tha	n.	preservations [639]
mara	m.	death [640]

Is it TA + mara or tha + mara?

Is it 'EARTH-DEATH' (interpreted as 'burial ground') or is it 'PRESERVATION OF THE DEAD'?

It also could come from

dama	m. n.	home, house [641]
mara	m.	death [640]

dama + mara → dammara → damara → no D, becomes T → tamara

DEATH-HOME is the literal translation. GRAVE CHAMBER is Steinbauer's.

However, this same Sanskrit reconstruction can give another meaning because *dama* can also mean 'punishment'. So, damara-tamara might be 'death punishment'. If the Sanskrit approach is relevant, then the meaning of this Etruscan word can be determined only by examining the

ARYAN ITALY OF THE ETRUSCANS

context in which it appears.

MAN, MANI

Not every Etruscan word has a confusing Sanskrit translation. Sometimes, everything is simple.

The Bonfantes said that MAN, MANI means *"the dead"* and they connect it to the Latin word 'Manes' (p.217).

Online Latin Dictionary gives this meaning for *manes* [642]:

1 spirits of the dead
2 lower world
3 mortal remains

Sanskrit has similar words with many meanings, but some directly correspond to Latin words

manas   n.   the spirit or spiritual principle, the breath or living soul which escapes from the body at death [643]

manyu   m.   spirit, grief, sorrow [644]

There is a parallel between Sanskrit, Latin, and Etruscan words. It's a family!

LEIN-

On page 216, The Bonfantes wonder if this means *"to die"*. The Sanskrit word *laya* has so many meanings but these are relevant here.

laya   m.   death, extinction, destruction [645]

5.8. WORDS FOR ANIMALS

ARAC *"falcon"* (The Bonfantes, p.214)

ara	adj.	swift, speedy [646]

+

AjigAti { AgA }	verb	come towards or into, overcome [647]

ara + Aga → araga → G becomes K → araka → arak

This would make 'arac' "SWIFT COMING TOWARDS" or WHICH OVERCOMES SWIFTLY. The word is based on an observation of a falcon's attack.

Another option, where an H would be dropped, also matches a falcon's hunting style.

haraka	m.	seizer, taker [648]
hAraka	n.	robber, thief [649]

CAPU

The Bonfantes translate it as *"falcon (Greek 'capys')"* (p.215).

This would be the second word for a 'falcon' so one can wonder if one of them might be a word for an 'eagle'.
There are many ways to reconstruct CAPU as a two-word compound and to translate it.

kha	n.	sky, heaven [650]
ka	m.	air [651]

pAti { pA }   verb   govern, rule [652]

kha + pA → kahpa → H is dropped → kapa + U (word-ending) → kapu

The meaning is RULER OF THE SKY. If we exchange 'kha' for 'ka' we get WHO RULES IN THE AIR. If this reconstruction is right, the CAPU would probably be an eagle. Etruscans would never call a falcon RULER OF THE SKY. That title had to be reserved for the bird that is one of the main symbols of this god who rules the sky, which is Tin or Tinia, the Etruscan Zeus.

But the word 'kha' (sky) also means 'action'. And there is another option for PA which brings back the possibility of 'falcon'.

pAti { pA }   verb   watch, observe [652]

It can now mean SKY-WATCHER, or WHICH OBSERVES FOR AN ACTION or maybe OBSERVER FROM THE AIR.

KRANKRU

On his website, Dieter H. Steinbauer asks if 'krankru' is a 'CAT' or a 'PANTHER'. Steinbauer wrote a book about the Etruscan language, *Neues Handbuch des Etruskischen* (1999), which is in German. Not knowing German, I could not read it, but I consulted his English website. [653]

The word *krankru* is first mentioned by George Dennis as being inscribed below the picture of the cat that tears off its prey. [654]

There are many Sanskrit options here, but we will focus on one parallel. One of the Sanskrit words for 'cat' is very similar.

krandana   m.   cat, crier [655]

KRANKRU (Etruscan)
KRANDANA (Sanskrit)

This already shows the Indo-European nature of the word. Let's take a look at the Sanskrit 'krandana'.

krandati { krand }   verb   cry piteously, call out piteously to anyone, weep, roar [656]

aNati { an } verb   sound [657]

krand + an → krandan + A (as word ending)→ krandana

We can translate this as CRYING SOUND, maybe ROARING SOUND. So, this is about a cat's 'MEOW' or 'MIAOW', maybe about the roaring of a panther.

Often, nouns from different languages that mark the same thing are based on the same perception of those "things". So, let us examine if KRANKRU means something that carries the same idea.

    krandanaM karoti   { kR }   verb   cry [658]
    aNati { aN }   verb   sound [659]
    aṇ   sounding / śabda [659]
    kAru   m.f.   maker [660]

kR + an + kAru → krankaru → Etruscans drop vowels in the ending part of words → krankru

This would mean "CRY-SOUND MAKER" or

MAKER OF CRYING SOUNDS. It appears that the words are slightly different, but the logic behind them seems to be the same.

Even though the reconstruction of KRANKRU could be partially wrong or not completely correct, it is clear that KRANKRU is a Sanskrit related compound.

Here is another reconstruction of KRANKRU. The Sanskrit verb *karoti* means 'to do', 'to make'.

karoti   { kR }   verb 8   do [661]
+
Anaka   energetic [662]
+
ru   crying, howling, sounding in general / śabda [663]

kR + Anaka + ru → kranakru → krankru

The literal translation is MAKER OF ENERGETIC CRIES (this would suggest a bigger and more dangerous feline which roars).

TUSNA   "*swan*" (Steinbauer)

The Sanskrit stem 'tus' carries meanings that describe the human perception of a swan, his elegance.

tuSyati { tuS }   verb 4   appease, become calm, gratify, please, be satisfied or pleased with anyone or anything [664]

This looks correct.

5.9 VESSELS, CERAMICS

ACIL   The Bonfantes: *"work, thing made"* (p.214)

While The Bonfantes translate it as "work, thing made", Steinbauer proposes this translation.

acil(u)   *"producer, potter"* [665]

If you consult Sanskrit, it is Steinbauer who might be right.

aga   m.   water-jar [666]

There is no G in Etruscan, it always becomes K...but...

PATNA

"name of vase, Greek 'patane', Latin 'patina'?" (the Bonfantes, p.218)

pAtha	n.	water [667]
pAtha	m.	fire, sun [667]
anna	n.	earth, water [668]

patha + anna → pathana → patana → patna

This can simply mean pottery, the literal meaning would be EARTH-WATER, therefore likely to be CLAY because clay is "earth and water" or a kind of watery earth. But the same "formula" gives us FIRED-EARTH or BAKED "EARTH".

It can also be "WATER-SERVING" or SERVING

ARYAN ITALY OF THE ETRUSCANS

FOR WATER or "FOR SERVING WATER" based on

    patyate { pat }   verb   be fit, serve for [669]

If you add 'anna', which means 'water', you get 'patanna'. It is not a problem here to re-assemble the word with Sanskrit, but how to translate it. There is no proof that this was a Greek and not an Etruscan word. Here is another side-result, a possible explanation of the Serbian word for 'pottery', which is 'grnčarija'. It is impossible to pronounce for English speakers because of four consonants in a row (Č is the same as CH in 'church').

    ghRNi   m.   water, flame [670]
    caru   m.   a kind of vessel (in which a particular oblation is prepared), saucepan, pot [671]

Harvard-Kyoto 'C' is pronounced as 'CH' in 'church'.

ghRNi + caru → H is dropped → grncaru (WATER-POT) → grncaria or grncharia is plural form

CUPE *"cup (Greek 'kupe'?; Latin 'cupa')"* (the Bonfantes, p.215)

The English word 'cup' did not have to come from Latin, it might be of an independent, native origin. The same applies to the Etruscan 'cupe'.

    kUpa   m.   well, cavity, hole [672]

Think about 'well', which is a cavity or a hole filled with water. Is it possible to fit a 'cup' into the same general concept? If this is too much of a stretch, there is another Sanskrit path to take.

| ku | f. | earth [673] |
| pa | m.f. | act of drinking [674] |

It appears 'kupa' could be "DRINKING (from) EARTH" and this explains the Sanskrit 'well'. It can also explain the Etruscan 'cup', but we need to think of patterns that appear in various words. Essentially, pottery was made of baked earth (or clay) and my argument here is that the word 'earth' in the compound stands for 'ceramics'. Along this idea comes another word for 'vase'.

MATA *"vases"* (the Bonfantes, p.217)

| ma | n. | water [675] |
| TA | f. | earth [676] |

ma + ta → mata

The literal meaning is WATER-EARTH which, as previously shown, we can interpret as "CERAMIC THAT HOLDS WATER" or simply as CLAY (for example, English speakers call a vessel for drinking a 'glass').

Just like in the case of the word 'patna', that also means 'vase', we can see it as

| ma | n. | water [675] |
| tha | n. | preservation [677] |

It gives us WATER-PRESERVATION. We can also use an adjective.

| Atta | adj. | seized, taken, obtained, grasped [678] |

This would mean WATER "SEIZED".

PRUCH, PRUCHUM

The Bonfantes, *"jug (Greek 'prochous')"* (p.218)

pArayati   { pRR } verb caus   fill up [679]
+
ukha   m.   vessel, caldron, any saucepan or pot or vessel which can be put on the fire [680]

pR + ukha → prukha → prukh → pruch

It looks like "FILL-UP" VESSEL.

SPAN-, SPANTHI

The Bonfantes, *"dish; plain, fields"* (p. 219)

Dish? It is very similar to the English word 'pan'. Other meanings they offer ('plain' and 'fields') fit into the geometrical and visual idea of 'pan'.

Do Etruscans add 'S' or does Sanskrit removes it? The analogy I will repeat might be shallow, but I know that the Etruscan word for city is SPUR. How about Sanskrit?

pur   f.   city, wall, town, stronghold, fortress [681]

Then, there is another Sanskrit word.

pAna   n.   cup, drinking-vessel [682]

OK, 'pAna' is a 'cup, not exactly a 'pan', but are they that different as, for example, 'rock' and 'butterfly' are? Did Etruscan for some reason add S in front of a word like they might have done with 'slica' and 'spur'?

LARNAS

"vase" (the Bonfantes, p.216) They noticed a similarity with the Greek 'larnax'. But let's first reconstruct 'larnas'.

lAti { lA }   verb 2 Par   take, receive, obtain [683]
arNas   n.   water, river, stream, flood [684]

lA + arNas → larnas

This Sanskrit reconstruction of an Etruscan word is spotless. The literal meaning is RECEIVE-WATER. How about the Greek word? Why is that X-ending different?

It could be the remnant of the whole word.

kSA f.   earth [685]

larnas + kSa → larnaks (larnax)

But what if this 'arnaks' in the Greek word stands for the idea of ceramics? Water-earth, clay?

Let's examine the very word CERAMIC. This is the current explanation of it.

"The word "ceramic" comes from the Greek word κεραμικός (keramikos), "of pottery" or "for pottery",[4] from κέραμος (keramos), "potter's clay, tile, pottery".[5] The earliest known mention of the root "ceram-" is the Mycenaean Greek ke-ra-me-we, "workers of ceramics", written in Linear B syllabic script."
Wikipedia [686]

We are told that 'ceramic' comes from the Greek 'keramikos' and 'keramos', but the Greek words were not explained, we have no clue how they came to be. The Sanskrit dictionary knows how. It is quite easy to see two words in 'keramos' (which means 'potter's clay' in Greek). Those words are 'ka' and 'rAma'.

| ka | n. | water [307] |
| rAmA | f. | red earth [308] |

ka + rAmA → karama → kerama + OS (Greek ending of words) → keramos

The literal meaning is WATER-RED-EARTH or simply just WATER-EARTH, clearly indicating a mixture of the two, which is CLAY. When we mix water and red earth we get REDDISH MUD or CLAY which is a material needed to make terracotta objects. Terracotta itself is of a brownish, pale yellow or reddish colour. *Terracotta* means 'baked earth' in Italian. Isn't it simple?

According to sanskritdictionary.com word *ka* can also mean 'sun' and 'fire'. Then ka + rAmA gives us FIRED (or BAKED) RED EARTH, therefore BAKED EARTH.

Now, let's take a look at one well known Italian type of ceramics the Etruscans were known for.

BUCCHERO

"Bucchero (Italian pronunciation: ['bukkero]) is a class of ceramics produced in central Italy by the region's pre-Roman Etruscan population. This Italian word is derived from the Latin poculum, a drinking-vessel, perhaps through the Spanish búcaro, or the Portuguese púcaro.[1]" [689]

As you can guess, we look for a deeper and different explanation. Is the same pattern we find in other words related to pottery present here? If so, it should be simple and descriptive.

bhU	f.	earth [690]
ka	n.	water [687]
ra	m.	fire [691]

EARTH + WATER => CLAY (bhuka)

CLAY (bhuka) + FIRE (ra) => BAKED CLAY or BUKARA

Well, that is one theory! The word BUCCHERO could not be an Etruscan word in this exact shape because Etruscans did not have sound B. It would have to be PUCCHERO or PUCHARA. That brings it close to Portuguese *púcaro*.

PUT-, PUTH-

The Bonfantes, *"vase, pot, vessel, well?"* (p.218)

They list 'pot' as one of the possible meanings of PUT-. If the Etruscans would write the English word POT, they would turn it into PUT (no O in Etruscan).

Another meaning that the Bonfantes offer is VESSEL.

pota	m.n.	vessel, ship, boat [692]

The Sanskrit 'pota' must be about ships and not about drinking vessels or kitchen, but there is a significant similarity here. For the Etruscans, it would be PUTA.

Then, there is another option that involves two sound changes, both of them well known and attested.

bhU	f.	earth [690]
+		
uda	n.	water [693]

bhU + uda → bhuda → H is dropped → buda

Etruscans always turn B into P and D into T or TH.

buda → puta → put

The resulting word is PUTA or PUT. Its meaning seems to repeat the pattern, it is EARTH-WATER, which we interpret as CLAY and CLAY can simply be a word for CERAMICS.

VERTUN

The Bonfantes, *"vase"* (p.220)

The Sanskrit word 'vAr, water, is recognizable in *VERtun*.

This means that a Sanskrit A often becomes an Etruscan or Italic E or even I. Therefore, the Italian river Verdura could have the same name as the Macedonian Vardar River.

vAr n. water [694]
tUNayate { tUN } verb 10 fill [695]

vAr + tUN → vartun → vertun

The literal meaning is WATER-FILL.

ZAVENA

The Bonfantes, *"vase"* (p.220)

sA f. giving, granting [696]
vana n. water [697]

SA + vana → savana

SAVANA (reconstructed)
ZAVENA (Etruscan)

Literal meanings: GIVING WATER, GRANTING WATER.
But, it is tricky again. Another reconstruction fits the pattern.

zava n.   water [698]
anna   n.   earth [699]

zava + anna → Z stands for SH → shavana (WATER-EARTH, CLAY?)

Again, is the Sanskrit sound SH an equivalent to the Etruscan Z? Maybe not. But could the name of the River Sava come from the Sanskrit *zava* (shava)? Why not?

Now, let's reconstruct the Serbian word 'vaza' (means 'vase') that appears in the same or similar shape in many Indo-European languages. Here are two options!

va   m.   water [700]
+
sa   adv. possession [701]
Asa   m.   seat [702]

va + sa → vasa → vaza ('vase' in Serbian)

SUNTHERUZA

The word SUNTHERUZA was found on a small round container (8 cm high). The text on it says MI

SUNTHERUZA SPURIAS MLAKAS. The Bonfantes translate it as I (AM) THE LITTLE CONTAINER OF SPURIA THE BEAUTIFUL (p. 137). The name Spuria could belong to the LIGHT-pattern of Indo-Aryan names (like Slavic name Svetlana which is based on word *svetlo*, meaning 'light').

sphurati   { sphur }   verb   shine, glitter, be brilliant or distinguished [703]

They translate *suntheruza* as *"little container"* (p.219), where -UZA is a diminutive-making ending. How about SUNTHER- ?

sUnA   a woven wicker-work basket or vessel of any kind [704]
dhAra   containing, holding, preserving [705]

Every D becomes T or TH in Etruscan. This gives us SUNTHARUZA.

It means "CONTAINING" VESSEL, "HOLDING VESSEL" or VESSEL THAT CONTAINS or simply as the Bonfantes translate it – a CONTAINER.

5.10 NAMES OF MONTHS

The list of Etruscan months is taken from the Bonfantes' book (p.224).

They note that some months are not identified. The names of months that we know came from glosses. Therefore, "US" at the end of some words for months came from Latin.

January, February, July, November, and December are not identified. The names of two months are known but have not been assigned completely. They think that Masan or Masn could be December. Another unassigned month is Thucte.

VELCITANUS (*VELCITNA)

The Bonfantes, *"March"* (p.220)

Here is a funny translation and the best explanation of the name of March.

valgita   n.   spring, leaping for joy, leap [706]

Well, Spring is 'spring' in English. It starts in March.

valgita → No G in Etruscan, it becomes K → valkita

We are still missing the second word.

aNu   m.   life, soul [708]

valkita + aNu → valkitanu + US (as Latin word ending) → Valkitanus

ARYAN ITALY OF THE ETRUSCANS

We got VALKITANUS, Etruscan is VELCITANUS!
The literal meaning would be SPRINGING OF LIFE, LIFE SPRINGING.

We can also use a word for 'earth'.

anna   n.   earth, food [709]

Then it would be EARTH-SPRINGING.

You are also tempted to imagine "dancing Etruscans" celebrating an awakening of nature at this time of the year.

velA   f.   season, time [710]
gIta n.   song, singing [711]

velA + gIta → velgita → velkita

You get SINGING SEASON.

And this is the problem with Sanskrit and Etruscan! Often, too many options make sense. Like this one:

valgati { valg }   verb   spring, leap, dance, eat [712]
idAni   n.   a measure of time (the fifteenth part of an etarhi-) [713]

valg + idAni → valgidani → valkitani + US → valkitanus

VALKITANUS (reconstructed)
VELCITANUS

The meaning would be SPRING "MEASURE OF TIME", SPRING TIME or THE SEASON OF SPRINGING. By the way, it is hard not to notice a possible connection between the Sanskrit 'idAni ' and the Latin 'idus' (like in 'Ides of March').

CAPRE *"April"* (the Bonfantes, p.215)

ka m.   sun, joy, time, happiness, pleasure [714]
khA adj. khā mfn. digging (in fine compositi or 'at the end of a compound' exempli gratia, 'for example' kūpa--; bisa-kh/ā-[715]
piparti { pR }   verb   advance, promote, bring out[716]

ka (or 'kha') + pr → kapr → kapre → capre

Is it PROMOTED DIGGING (agricultural spring works) or ADVANCING SUN or ADVANCING PLEASURE, PROMOTING SUNSHINE?

How was the weather in Tuscany in April two thousand years ago?
I assumed that it was generally similar and checked the website At Home In Tuscany (athomeintuscany.org) for contemporary weather information.

"April is the first really spring-like month, with warm temperatures, long days and bright colors in the countryside." [717]

AMPILES *"May"* (the Bonfantes, p.214).

Ampa   m.   sunshine [718]
+
ilati { il } verb come, send, cast [719]

Ampa + il → ampil → ampiles

We can translate it as COMING OF SUNSHINE.

This is what the website Unseen Tuscany says:

"May is one of the best months to visit Tuscany. Weather in Tuscany is good, with most sunny days and only few rainy days as well." [720]

ACLUS (ACALE)

"June" (the Bonfantes, p.224)

Again, a word for Sun is a candidate.

aga   m.   sun [721]

It looks like we should either follow weather characteristics or the time-line of agricultural works. Some other Sanskrit words that could easily be ancestral to Acale or Aclus.

AkAla   m.   at right time, just at the time of [722]

It could mean RIGHT TIME. This should be understood in relation to fruits or even harvest!
But you can reach a similar idea with other words.

AjigAti { AgA }   verb   approach, come towards or into [723]
lunAti { lU }   verb   reap [724]

AgA + lU => agalu → akalu → aklu + US

The literal meaning is "COMING TOWARDS REAP" which could be read as APPROACHING HARVEST.

The harvest of different crops comes at different months, but some of it does happen during July.

TRANEUS *"month, July"* (p.219)

In the glossary, the Bonfantes translate Traneus as July, but on page 224 they say that the Etruscan name of July has not been assigned.

These are the best options available in Sanskrit for Traneus.

dhArayati { dhR }   verb 10 Pa   employ, practice, undergo [725]
anna   n.   earth, food, cereals [726]

dhR + anna + US → dhrannaus → H is dropped, D becomes T → trannaus → tranaus

The literal meaning would be "EMPLOY-EARTH" and PRACTICE-EART. It could be read as FIELD WORKS or maybe WORK RELATED TO FOOD. We can also employ some other stems.

tarati { tRR } verb   gain, perform, accomplish, acquire, fulfill [727]
or
drAhate   { drAh }   verb   deposit [728]

They would give *t*RR + *anna* → *trranna* → *trana* (ACQUIRE FOOD)
and
dr*Ah* + *anna* → *H is dropped, D becomes T* → *tranna* (DEPOSIT FOOD)

If any of these is correct, then this would have to be

about WHEAT HARVEST.

The inspiration for this approach came from Slavic names of months that contain a reference to harvest, like Old Serbian name of July – *Žetvar* (means Harvest-month) or Croatian *Srpanj* (based on word *srp*, meaning 'sickle', pointing at harvest). Some other Slavic nations name August in this very manner because they have slightly different climate and the different time of wheat harvest. So, we find Belorusian *Žnivień,* Sorbian *žnjenc*, Ukrainian *Serpeń*, *Žitar* (month of wheat), etc.

We can also combine stem *drAh* with the noun *nava* [729] (one of its meanings is 'new grain'). This would end up as TRANAVUS or TRANAUS (DEPOSIT NEW GRAIN).

THUCTE

The Bonfantes, *"name of month (August?)* (p.220)

This month is not identified, but the Bonfantes raise a question if it could be August. On the list of months, they say that August was called Ermius, so Thucte would be another name of August. Sanskrit gives some options.

dUyate { dU }	verb 4 afflict [730]
gadayati { gad }	verb 10 thunder [731]

du + gad → dugad → D always becomes T or TH, and G becomes K → thukat + E (word-ending) → thukate → Etruscans corrupt the ending parts of words by dropping vowels → thukte

This means AFFLICTING THUNDERS, which is common in August at this latitude. The website At Home in Tuscany describes the weather in August,
"(...) typically, some summer storms are to be expected during the

second half of the month. By the end of the month, you are likely to get some cooler days, when the weather starts to change." [732]

Another eventual reconstruction is

duh	adj.	granting [733]
dogdhi{ duh }	verb	squeeze out, milk, extract [734]
gAtu	m.	welfare, progress, increase [735]

duh + gAtu → G becomes k, D turns into T or TH → thukatu → thuktu

This means GRANTING WELFARE. Even though all the sound changes and dropping of vowels are in harmony with known features of the Etruscan language, we must doubt these reconstructions. Let's not forget that there is no agreement regarding which month Thucte marks.

What if THUCTE was November? You can ask why not January or February because the names of these two months are unknown. The early Roman calendar was probably mirroring the Etruscan calendar and Romans did not use any names for January and February. They were two nameless months and that period was simply called Winter. The reasons for this probably comes from the religious narrative of the Etruscans. On December solstice, Sun "dies". It is the shortest day of a year in the northern hemisphere. The goddess of love descends to the underworld to try to save her lover and the world is rendered barren until she completes her mission. So, the simple logic suggests that if Thucte is not August, then it must be November.

Now, all reconstructions presented here are inspired by assumed analogy with names of Slavic months, where November and December are frequently called The Cold Month and The Month of Begging (or poverty). This is a possibility because certain ideas and themes constantly repeat through various Indo-European cultures

dugdha	adj.	sucked out, impoverished [736]
duHkha	n.	misery, sorrow, suffering [737]
duHkhatA	f.	discomfort, uneasiness, pain [738]

If rendered by the Etruscan speech, all of these words could end as Thucte.

ERMIUS

The Bonfantes, *"August"* (p.224)

Again, we focus on agriculture, but the options are too many.

Irayati { er } verb caus.   procure, obtain [739]
ma   n.   welfare, time [740]

er + ma → erma → ermius

The literal meaning is PROCURE-TIME, PROCURE-WELFARE. However, the Ermius could easily come from words that at first don't look that promising.

Aharati { A- hR }   verb 1   pick up, deliver, bring, fetch, appropriate [741]
harati { hR }   verb   fetch, sever [742]
+
ma   m.   time, welfare [740]

A-hR (or 'hR') + ma → H is dropped or in a case of 'hR' replaced by a vowel → ARMA or ERMA

This would mean PICKING TIME, DELIVERY OF WELFARE, FETCHING TIME, "SEVERING" or REAPING TIME... Again, this might be about HARVEST.

The third option would require an interpretation.

Irma   m.   arm [743]   [ZM: note the similarity with the English word 'arm']
+
yauti { yu }   verb 2   unite   [744]
yAvayati { yu }   verb caus.   join[745]

Irma + yu → irmyu → irmiu + S → irmius

This would mean UNITED (or "JOINED") ARMS or, interpreted, COLLECTIVE WORK, indirectly referring to 'harvest'.

Determining which option is right, if any, will depend on further linguistic expertise and a deeper understanding of the Etruscan agricultural timeline.

CELI (Caelius or Celius)

"September" (the Bonfantes, p.224)

They say it is September, but in the glossary, they translate correctly the word CEL as 'earth'. Sanskrit agrees. 'Cel' means 'earth'. This is a straightforward explanation of the name of Etruscan Earth-goddess Cel Atti (Mother Earth).
But we can only guess if it is in any connection to the name of an Etruscan month.

keli   f.   earth [746]

CHOSFER

kAla   m.   meal-time [747]

"October" (the Bonfantes, p.224)

They listed Chosfer, but they warned us that it came from glosses. This had to be pronounced CHUSFER (KUSFER) since the Etruscans did not have the vowel O. Now, the sound F would have to be related to P or PH in Sanskrit, eventually to V.

ku   f.   earth[748]
sphAra   n.   abundance[749]

ku + sphAra → kusphara → kusfara → kusfar (EARTH ABUNDANCE)

KUSFAR (reconstructed)
KUSFER (spelled in a gloss as Chosfer)

There is another way.

kuSNAti { kuS }   verb   extract[750]
peru   adj.   drinking[751]

kuS + peru → kusperu → kusferu → kusfer

Now, it means TIME OF "EXTRACTING" DRINKS.

The Etruscans were wine-makers and there is evidence of their wine export to Gaul in the seventh century BC. Wine in Tuscany is made in September and October so this explanation might apply. It is also phonetically "clean".

NOVEMBER – The Etruscan name of this month is not determined.

MASAN , MASN

"name of month: December" (the Bonfantes, p.217)

Finally, one easy month! Even though they don't put 'masan' on the list of Etruscan months (p.224), Giuliano and Larissa Bonfante claim on page 217 that it is December. Here is one interesting Sanskrit word.

mAsa   m.   moon, month [751]

The explanation is that in the northern hemisphere, the shortest day of the year or winter solstice falls in December when the Sun is the "weakest" and the night is the longest. It looks like the Moon rules the sky, while the Sun must be seriously sick or even dead. After the winter solstice, the Sun is reborn and that itself is an event of great importance in any sky-religion.

The word 'masan' is documented in the Etruscan Pyrgi Tablets (around 550 BC) which refers to a prayer or a rite that the ruler Thefarie Velianas conducts at the temple. There is the Punic-Phoenician version of the text and it is translated. It mentions "Sun-sacrifice", making it likely that event at the temple is connected to the winter solstice. The word from Pyrgi Tablet 1 that might mean Sun-sacrifice is VATIECHE (vatieke). I could be wrong, be careful because it could also mean 'temple', but here is a possible reconstruction of it.

vadhyA   f.   killing, murder [752]
aga   m.   Sun [753]

vadhyA + aga → no D and G in Etruscan, they become T and K , while Y (like in 'yolk' becomes I like in 'tin') → vatiaka (MURDER OF THE SUN, KILLING OF THE

SUN, DEATH OF THE SUN)

This would connect to "SUN-SACRIFICE", but there is another possible "death-of-the-sun" word in Pyrgi Tablets. When it comes to the name of the month, Masan, there is additional Sanskrit support.

mAsa   m.   a symbolical name for the number twelve, month or the 12th part of the Hindu year [751]

Any month is certainly a twelfth part of the year, but it could be that Etruscans did not have twelve, but rather just ten months in their calendar. We can speculate about this based on what we know about Latin words for months. The name of December comes from Latin decem, meaning 'ten' because December was the tenth and last month in the early Roman calendar. The time of our January and February was not counted by Romans as months, that came later. Each year started in March, with "springing of life", birth. Or it was rather a rebirth of the Sun, which would die in December, at the time when our winter starts. This nameless and monthless period of Winter is the time of Death. The calendar had a religious narrative that was tied to the journey of the Sun, the most important source of light we ever knew. The Sun is divine and the Etruscan religion was a sky-religion, revolving around the concept of Light (just like Roman, Greek, Illyrian, Celtic, Thracian, Hindu and more or less all religions of Indo-European and Semitic world).

So, when the Bonfantes said that Etruscan names of January, February, and November were not identified, it could be that we are missing only the name of November. Likely, the names of January and February did not exist. And that is not the end of our Masan story! This word could be about HURTING and that 'hurting' might not be just about hurting of the Sun, but conditions of Winter, the lack of resources.

| maSati | { maS } verb | hurt [754] |
| masana | n. | hurting [755] |

We can make a parallel with some Slavic names of December: Bulgarian and Czech *prosinec* and Croatian *prosinac* They come from the verb 'prositi', meaning 'to beg', suggesting beggars and poverty. The same idea is in Masan: the Sun is hurting, humanity is hurting. It is also about the Moon and its rule during hurting time.

| mAsa | m. | moon, month [754] |

But there is a connection between the Moon and hurting. Moon is complete only one day per lunar month, when it is Full Moon, at all other times it is clipped, parts of it are cut off, it is hurting. Let's repeat those words.

| maSati | { maS } verb | hurt [754] |
| masana | n. | hurting [755] |

This is not an accidental similarity. It is a story. Think of Latin word LUNA, which means MOON, and look at these Sanskrit words that explain this Latin word!

| lUna | n. | clipping, cutting [756] |

lUna   adj.   severed, wounded, pierced, clipped, cut, annihilated, destroyed [756]

Now, we know how Latin LUNA came to be, but also Portuguese *mes* and Serbian *mesec* (moon, month)

Researching this, I just found out the background story of *srp*, the Serbian word for 'sickle'.

ARYAN ITALY OF THE ETRUSCANS

sRpa   m.   moon[757]

The explanation is simple: a sickle looks like a crescent moon.

Again, which of my reconstructions of Etruscan names of months are correct? Some were confusing, some looked pretty good (Velcitanus, Masan), some meanings that we got repeated too much (harvest) and some of the offered reconstructions are not that convincing (Thucte?). However, the overall feeling was that Sanskrit had something to say.

We like to think that the general foundation of our calendar was Roman, but the Romans kept building on the base of what was either the Etruscan calendar or a calendar that was a result of a broader Italic and even Indo-European tradition. We owe to the Etruscans so many things we attribute to the Romans.

If it is interesting to you, I can tell you what kind of grudge I keep against the Romans who did many great things, i.e. provided free water for every citizen, which is a human right we don't enjoy even today.

It is not the Romans that bother me, but rather the presence of some of their ways in our time. When I say that, I think of their open preference to live without working, to profit by conquest and by exploiting other social classes and peoples, and their willingness to commit genocide to achieve these goals. And what about slavery? Alright, to be a slave in ancient times was often much better than to be a black American slave or even an industrial worker, but it doesn't mean the whole concept was not inhumane.

The idea that Rome is one of the main foundations of our civilization is truthful... and troubling!

5.11 WORDS BELIEVED TO BE IMPORTED TO ETRUSCAN FROM OTHER LANGUAGES

Giuliano and Larissa Bonfante list some words that the Etruscans took from other languages, mostly from Greek. Every language borrows words and Etruscan should not be an exception. But if we examine the Bonfantes' list with Sanskrit we can see that some claims from their chapter "Foreign Words in Etruscan" (p. 112-113) can be questioned.

QUTUN or QUTUM

On page 112, the Bonfantes say that the Etruscan word for a *hand-held jug* was *qutun,* coming from the Greek *kothon* (letter Q in this Etruscan word is equivalent to K). On page 218 they also list *qutum* as a variant of this word. The question is: What if the Etruscan 'qutun' and Greek 'kothon' came from the Sanskrit 'kUTa'?

kUTa   m.n.   water-jar [758]

The Bonfantes translate it as *hand-held jug*. Sanskrit translates it as *water-jar*. Now, the Etruscan word is closer to Sanskrit than to the Greek word.

CULICHNA or CULICNA

The Bonfantes claim that the Etruscan word for *'cup'*, CULICHNA, comes from the Greek word *kylix* (p.113).
We should not doubt that at some point Greek words entered Italy but I would think that if Etruscans took this

word from Greeks they would render it as CULICS or CULCSA, maybe CULCS.

There are Sanskrit words that show kinship with Etruscan CULICHNA and Greek KYLIX, suggesting that it might as well be about a wider Indo-European context.

Here are some examples.

kullnasa   n.   water [759]

kulija   n.   particular vessel [760]

At least, KULI-part is the same. But that is not all.

golaka   m.   globular water-jar [761]

This GOLAKA would be pronounced as KULAKA (CULACA) by Etruscans. Culaca, culicna? This could be it!
But, technically, there is another option!

gu   n.   water [762]
lagna   adj.   sticking or remaining in [763]

This gives GULAGNA, which would be pronounced as KULAKNA (spelt in an Etruscan way as CULACNA or CULACHNA).

It would mean WATER REMAINING IN, therefore it is WHAT HOLDS A WATER.

ASKA

"(...) from Greek ASKOS, 'leather bag', 'wineskin' comes ASKA, a flask for oil, wine or other liquids (...)"
(the Bonfantes, p.112)

Asyate { As }   verb   pour in[764]
go   m.f.   leather [765]

As + go → asgo

As we know, the Etruscans do not have G, they use K.

Asgo → asko → aska

The literal translation is POUR-IN LEATHER, or a LEATHER IN WHICH YOU POUR LIQUID, a leather flask. And it could also be based on...

ka   n.   water[766]

As + ka → aska (Meaning: POUR-IN-WATER)

ULPAIA

"vase for wine, Greek 'olpe' " (the Bonfantes, p.220)

valate { val }   verb   cover or enclose or to be covered [767]
peya   n.   drink [768]
pAyya   n.   drinking, water [769]

val + peya → valpeya → V becomes U or W → Y becomes I → ualpeia → ulpeia

This process is not completely impossible in Etruscan, because the Etruscan V is close to W and W is close to U. It became UALPEIA → ULPEIA or ULPAIA

Certainly, it is easier if we look at the Etruscan 'ulpaia' as a rendition of the Greek 'olpa'. That would explain U at the beginning of 'ulpaia'.

The Greek word itself could have a partially different reconstruction.

pA   adj.   drinking [770]

val + pa → valpa (the literal meaning is "ENCLOSED DRINKING", we can see it as a "DRINKING CONTAINER")

But the Greeks sometimes substitute V with a vowel. It could be that they turned VA into UA and the merger of U and A gave O. Both the Greek and the Etruscan words are compounds and the second word in both of them is a Sanskrit word that has the same meaning (drink or drinking), but they are still different Sanskrit words.

ETERA

On p. 113 the Bonfantes give us the word 'etera', which means *"client"* or *"stranger"*. They think it might be borrowed from Umbrian. Why not?

Maybe Sanskrit can offer something.

dharA   f.   earth [771]

dharA → no D in Etruscan, it becomes TH; H is dropped → tara

Since the Etruscans always make T out of D, this would be 'thara' or 'tara'. In Sanskrit, by adding an A at the beginning of word we form a word of opposite meaning, just like in English (example: septic & aseptic).

A + THARA = NOT-EARTH, NOT-LAND

Words for earth, land, and country are synonyms on many languages (overlapped meanings are present in English, too). Therefore ADHARA or A-TARA might mean NOT FROM THIS LAND, NOT-"LANDER", NOT-COUNTRYMAN, "outlander", FOREIGNER, outsider, stranger.

Again, no D in Etruscan.

adhara → atara → etera

However, there are other ways in which 'etera' might be related to Sanskrit. This one might relate to a person who comes from another side of one of the boundary rivers.

Atara   m.   crossing over a river [772]

Another word could apply to a CLIENT or a customer who is always welcome.

Adara   m.   regard, respect, honour, love, fondness[773]

FANU

The Bonfantes say that the Etruscan 'fanu', *"sacred place, sanctuary"*, comes from the Latin 'fanum' (p.113).
What if they come from a third, common source?

panU	f.	admiration [774]
pANa	m.	praise [775]
pAna	n.	protection [776]
paNa	m.	house [777]
+		
Uma	m.	sky, heaven [778]
umA	f.	light, reputation, fame [779]

paNa + Uma → panuma → panum → fanum

These would be some literal translations: PRAISE LIGHT, PRAISE HEAVEN, PROTECTION HEAVEN, HOUSE LIGHT, HOUSE (of) HEAVEN, etc.

HOUSE OF HEAVEN or HEAVENLY HOUSE as well as "PROTECTION (of) HEAVEN" come close to an idea of a sanctuary. Certainly, UM at the end of Latin FANUM could be just a noun ending.

5.12 WORDS IN OTHER LANGUAGES THAT MIGHT BE OF ETRUSCAN ORIGIN

Here, we focus on words in other languages considered to be of Etruscan origin. Some are already presented, like PHERSU or HISTRIO.

We must be very suspicious here because everything examined so far points to common roots of Etruscan, Latin and Greek words. Those roots seem to be preserved in Sanskrit.

ARENA

Website dictionary.com says that ARENA comes *"from Latin harena 'place of combat', originally 'sand, sandy place,' perhaps from Etruscan. The central stages of Roman amphitheaters were strewn with sand to soak up the blood."* [780]

Wikipedia says more or less the same,
"from arēna "arena"<harēna, "arena, sand"<archaic hasēna<Sabine fasēna, unknown Etruscan word as the basis for fas- with Etruscan ending -ēna." [781]

There could be a good hint in the word: "harēna, arena". Sanskrit 'hAra' means 'war' and 'battle'.

| hAra | m. | | battle, war [782] |
| anna | n. | earth [783] | |

hAra + anna → haranna → H is dropped → arana

ARANA (reconstructed)
ARENA (Latin)
HARENA

ARYAN ITALY OF THE ETRUSCANS

The meaning is BATTLE-GROUND or FIGHTING GROUND or BATTLEFIELD.

Now, let's take a look at Sabine *fasēna*. ARENA does not come from FASENA, but its Sanskrit reconstruction is similar. Be reminded that the sound F mostly comes from a previous P.

pauSa		n.	fight, combat [784]
anna	n.	earth [783]	

pauSa + anna → pausanna → pausana

P becomes F. Two vowels, A-U, merge into a single vowel (this process is frequent in Etruscan and many other languages). The result is FASANA.

FASANA (reconstructed)
FASENA (Sabine)

The literal meaning is FIGHT GROUND.

It is interesting that *arena* also means 'sand' in Latin. One of many Sanskrit words for 'sand' is very similar.

reNu   m.   sand [786]

In fact, we can get a word close to *arena* by employing Sanskrit *ha*.

ha   m.   war, battle, dying, blood [786]

ha + reNu → harenu → H is dropped → arenu

The meanings are "BATTLE-SAND" and BLOOD(y) SEND, which would justify the existing etymology!

It could be argued which reconstruction of *arena* is right (I prefer *battleground*), but that is not our concern. The important thing is that *arena,* being either an Etruscan or Latin word, is reconstructable by Sanskrit.

CURIAE

Here is a Latin word that could be partially explained by Latin. Let's consult Wikipedia.

"The word curia is thought to derive from Old Latin coviria, meaning "a gathering of men" (co-, "together" =vir, "man").[3] In this sense, any assembly, public or private, could be called a curia." [787]

In early Latin, V was pronounced as W, so somehow this CO-WIRIA became CURIA. If this hypothesis is correct, half of the word is still related to Sanskrit. Latin *vir,* *"man"* has its Sanskrit twin.

vIra m.   man [788]

So, at least half of CO-VIRIA is Sanskrit related. The front part of proposed CO-VIRIA could have come from Sanskrit *go* [789] (pronounced as *ku* in Etruscan), which means 'voice', 'speech', 'mother'. It may suggest *a place where men discuss things.*

However, if this word came from the Etruscans, it would be hard to discard another option, not less convincing in a phonetic sense.

gRhya   adj.   belonging to a house [789]
gṛhya   m. pl.   inmates of a house, domestics [790]
gṛhya   n.   a domestic rule or affair [790]

This 'gRhya' would always be 'krhia' or 'k-Ria' in an Etruscan pronunciation. Let's compare them!

KhRIA (reconstructed)
CURIA (Latin)

The translation is HOUSE., a GROUP BELONGING TO A HOUSE, even a DOMESTIC RULE. Most of the meanings of word CURIA support this etymology. Curia marks a political group (tribal, in early times), but also a house in which they meet. Curia is the word used for the house of the Senate in ancient Rome and curia is also the papal court.

FASCES

"Fasces (English: /ˈfæsiːz/, Latin: [ˈfa.skeːs]; a plurale tantum, from the Latin word fascis, meaning "bundle";[1] Italian: fascio littorio) is a bound bundle of wooden rods, sometimes including an axe with its blade emerging." [791]

This symbol of power came to Rome from the Etruscans. The word fascism is based on *fasces*.

Fasces is a bundle of rods with an axe placed in its middle. It symbolizes political unity and strength. The existing Latin etymology is even more convincing if we back it with Sanskrit.

pasati { pas }   verb 10   bind [792]
coSkUyate { sku } verb int.collect, gather up [793]
pas + sku → pasku

The Bonfantes say that the consonant F first appears in Italy in the Etruscan language (p.78-79). So, PASCU becomes FASCU. The literal meaning is BIND-COLLECT and it does express an idea of 'bundle'.

But we can also use a different second word.
ku   f.   the number "one"

Now, this PASKU-FASCU means "BOUND IN ONE" or maybe BOUND BY ONE.

MILITARY

"The first recorded use of the word military in English, spelled militarie, was in 1582.[3] It comes from the Latin militaris (from Latin miles, meaning "soldier") through French, but is of uncertain etymology, one suggestion being derived from *mil-it- – going in a body or mass." Wikipedia [795]

It says that **mil-it* means *'going in a body or mass'*. It is the same in Sanskrit.

mIlati { mIl }   verb   assemble, be collected [796]
+
iT cl.1 P.   eṭati-, eṭitum-   () , to go ; to go to or towards [797]

The literal translation of this Sanskrit MIL-IT is "ASSEMBLE-GO" or "BE-COLLECTED-GO".

The whole Latin word is MILITARIS. If we take into account that S or IS is just a common ending of Latin words, it means that we need to look for AR-part. It could easily come from Sanskrit *hAra*.

hAra   n.   battle, war [798]

So, the entire "formula" looks like this

mIl + iT + hAra → milthara → H is dropped → militara
militara + IS (Latin word ending) → militaris

The literal translation is BE-COLLECTED GO WAR or ASSEMBLE GO BATTLE.

This looks very good and there is no need for an alternative reconstruction but we will present one simply because it looks possible.

A soldier is a warrior that is part of a bigger squad. A soldier is trained to fight in co-ordination with his mates. But let's not forget that vowels are fluid, prone to change. Here is one of several possible reconstructions.

mela   m.   company [799]
ta   m.   warrior [800]
arha adj. costing, obliged [801]

mela + ta + arha → melatarha → H is dropped → MELATARA

If we add to this IS, a frequent Latin ending of nouns, we get MELATARIS. It means: COMPANY WARRIOR(s) OBLIGED (or 'costing', paid).

MELATARA (reconstructed)
MILITARIS (Latin, of possible Etruscan origin)

Again, Sanskrit can explain Latin words, but the ability of Latin to explain Sanskrit terminology is much weaker.

COLUMNA (column)

It really doesn't matter if this is an Etruscan word as some suspect. It does sound Etruscan with its UMNA-ending.

The website dictionary.com defines COLUMN as *"an*

upright post or pillar usually having a cylindrical shaft, a base, and a capital" [802]

gola	adj.	cylindrical [Bot.] [803]
gola	n.f.	circle [803]

There are no Gs and Os in Etruscan, so 'gola' becomes KULA. Also, early Latin often uses either G or K in the same word (i.e. Gaius or Caius). Eventually, this KULA or KOLA means CYLINDER. We have to reconstruct the rest of the word.

Uma   m.   sky [804]

KULA + Uma → kuluma

This now means "CYLINDER-SKY" or maybe "TALL CYLINDER(s)".

UM (or even UMN) in COLUMNA might be a noun-ending (as in words *qutum* and *pruchum*), or Etruscan *vinum*, meaning 'wine'). If that was the case, we need to treat this word as a compound made of COLUM + NA. Here is one way to do it.

Na m.   ornament [805]

COLUM + Na → columna

It would mean ORNAMENTED CYLINDERS. Temple columns were indeed ornamented, but the translation doesn't give us a precise idea of a column or pillar. There is another NA-word that can be useful.

nahyate { nah }   verb pass.   to get fastened together [806]

nahyati { nah }   verb   bind on or round or

together, arm oneself, tie [807]

COLUM + nah → columnah → H is dropped → columna

The literal translation is CYLINDER(s) FASTENED TOGETHER. Those ancient pillars were very rarely made from a single piece of stone, they rather included elements or cylinders that were bound together to form a pillar.

PALACE

Look at this explanation of the word *'palace'*!

"From Middle English paleys, borrowed from Old French palais, which comes from Latin palātium, from Palātium, in reference to the Palatine Hill, one of the seven hills of Rome, where the aristocracy of the Roman Republic—and later, Roman emperors—built large, splendid residences. The name is ultimately either from Etruscan, the same source as Pales ("Pales, the Italic goddess of shepherds, flocks and livestock"), or Latin palus ("stake; enclosure")." [808]

In Europe, we love to attribute everything to the Greeks and Romans. This habit is so strong that we don't even search for other options. Sanskrit can explain the name of the shepherd-goddess Pales.

pAla   m.   herdsman, guard, protector [809]

The Sanskrit origin of the name of a Roman hill and an Etruscan shepherd-goddess is direct, no explanation is needed. This applies to 'palus' (shepherd's stick), to the aforementioned Roman hill; also to Pallas Athena (but in the meaning of Guardian Athena, Protector Athena), to the city of Pale (herdsman) in Serbian Republic, maybe to the Serbian word 'palanka' (town), and eventually even to the

Greek word 'polis' (city) and Macedonian capital Pela, to last name Pallottino etc.

The Sanskrit noun 'pAla' that so nicely explains these words from various European languages comes out of a verb.

pAlayati { pAl } verb denom. protect, guard, observe, govern, rule, support [810]

How about the name of the Mayan city *Palenque* (almost the same thing as 'palanka')? OK, 'palenque' is actually a Spanish toponym.

"From Spanish Palenque, the name of a maroon settlement in Colombia, from palenque ('palisade')." [811]

What is 'palisade'?

Dictionary.com says that it is *"a fence of wooden stakes or iron railings fixed in the ground, forming an enclosure or defence"* [812]

Palenque could be about sticks, but the idea of protection also repeats! And, yes, 'pAla' might even explain 'palace' or the last name, Pallottino. But, in cases of 'palace' and Pallottino there is a competing etymology.

pAli m. ruler [813]

English PALACE is pronounced as PALAS. Let's look for AS-ending!

asti { as } verb 2 dwell, abide [814]

pAli + as → palas
This would mean RULER'S DWELLING.

Powerful people live in palaces, but the origin of the word can be more modest.

palli   f.   house, hut [815]

Wherever you dig, you find Sanskrit, the language of Mahabharata.

VERNACULAR

Wikipedia puts this word on the List of English Words of Etruscan Origin. It is done in this manner:

*"vernacular
 from vernaculus, 'domestic', from verna, 'a native slave'"* [816]

Today, we use the word vernacular to mark the native speech of some region or country and also when we refer to a domestic, informal or everyday speech.

Let's give Sanskrit a chance to sort this out!

| varNa | m. | word, letter, syllable, vowel [817] |
| kula | n. | house, tribe, family [818] |

varna + kula → varnakula + R → varnakular

VARNAKULAr (reconstructed)
VERNACULAR (English)

The literal meaning is DOMESTIC WORD, but it means DOMESTIC SPEECH, TRIBAL SPEECH, FAMILIAR SPEECH. It is EVERYDAY STREET LANGUAGE.

ELEMENT(UM)

Here is another word from the same Wikipedia list of "Etruscan words" in English. It is presented in the following way.

"element
　from elementum, 'letter'" [819]

This is a simple and self-explainable compound.

alam	ind.	equal to, adequate [820]
+		
antu	m.	characteristic [821]
anta	m. n.	end [822]
anta	m.	inside [822]

So, it is:

ALAM-ANTU (OF EQUAL CHARACTERISTICS)
or
ALAM-ANTA (EQUAL to the END or EQUAL INSIDE).

It is something that throughout itself has the same properties and it does not consist of other things. There are many Latin and some Etruscan words that end with UM. In this case, it might not just be a noun-ending, but a word.

um	ind.	interrogation [824]

Therefore, when you interrogate it, you come to an end, you cannot divide it further, it is all the same, it is an ELEMENTUM, an element.

When applied to a language, it is a single sound (a

consonant or a vowel). When applied to an alphabet, it is a letter.

5.13 NAMES OF FAMOUS PERSONS

HANIPALUSCLE

The Bonfantes write *"for (or against?) Hannibal"* (p.216).

This must mean FOR. The name expresses Etruscan support for Carthaginian Hannibal in his march against Rome. They admired him!

An explanation of Hanipaluscle is simple. Hannibal became Hanipal because the Etruscans always use P instead of B. The US-part is just a name ending coming from Latin. To this, Etruscans attach CLE in the same manner they did it in the name of Hercle, the Etruscan name for Heracles or Hercules. The CLE-ending, coming from CLEVA (fame, glory), has been already explained

By adding CLE they indicated that they saw a hero in him. The name expresses Etruscan support for Hannibal in his march against Rome. They admired and loved Hannibal. He brought them some hope.

LARS PORSENA AND HIS SON ARUNS

Lars Porsena (Pursenas in Etruscan[824]), the king of Clevsin, besieged Rome and forced it to a peace treaty. Accounts differ, but Porsena was a powerful figure.

"(...) Roman sources often place the war at around 508 BC." [824]

The name of Porsena's son Aruns has a clear Sanskrit etymology.

aruNa m. dawn (personified as the

ARYAN ITALY OF THE ETRUSCANS

charioteer of the sun), the sun [825]

So, the meaning of Aruns could be the same as the meaning of my own name – Zoran, meaning 'dawn'! How about the name of Arun's father Lars Porsena? Let's start with Lars. What if it came from the root 'lR'?

IR   m.   earth, mother of the gods [826]

This forces us to digress for a moment. It is a seductive idea that Lars means the same as the Roman name Gaius, which can be associated with the goddess Gaia, mother-earth? Take another look at the meaning of 'lR'.

IR   m.   earth, mother of the gods [826]

Gaia is the mother of all life and the ancestor of all gods. Gaia is 'lR'.
What if the root 'lR' had additional meanings like the word 'gaya' did?

gaya m.   wealth, offspring, family, house [827]

I dedicate this article to my dear late uncle Gajo Tabakovic (English spelling would be Gayo).

While we are at it, let's offer the reconstruction of the name of Gaya.

gu   f.   earth [828]
go   f.   earth [829]
+
ya   m.   fame [830]

go + ya → goya

GOYA (reconstructed)
GAYA (name of the goddess)

Gaya means EARTH-FAME or GLORIOUS EARTH.

Now, let's take a look at the Porsena-part of Lars Porsena.

para   adj.   supreme, chief [831]
sana adj.   old, lasting long [832]

para + sana (or 'sanA') → parsana → Porsena

It turns out that that translation of the name Lars Porsenna is: "LAND'S LASTING CHIEF. or maybe SUPREME OLD, SUPREME ELDER? This is a possibility.

Clearly, he could not be Porsena because Etruscans had no vowel O. It was probably Pursena or Pursana or, as it is believed, Pursenas.

pur f.   city, town, wall, fortress [833]

He could be CITY'S ELDER. However, Sanskrit will also give another attractive option.

purati   { pur } verb   precede, go before, lead
senA   f.   army

pur + sena → PURSENA

This means LEADER OF THE ARMY. It is not easy to decide which optional translation is right, but his "name" is entirely explainable with Sanskrit, probably being a title.

Since we mentioned the Sanskrit word PUR (city), let's discuss a very similar Etruscan word with the same meaning, SPUR-.

Scholars agree about its meaning: *"city"* (the Bonfantes, p.219).

We have two Sanskrit approaches here. First, it is very similar to Sanskrit *pur* , meaning 'city'. The problem here is that we are not sure how to explain starting S.

Another approach is phonetically cleaner.

sphura   m.   = (and varia lectio for) sphara-, a shield[836]

So, Sanskrit *sphura* is more or less identical to SPUR, but it means 'shield'. If we stick to the thesis that first city names were not names but rather nouns created to describe the function of the city (and the main concept of a city was PROTECTION), then Sanskrit *sphura* becomes a serious proposal (*spR* [837] means protecting).

This reminds of the existing etymology of Parma, which is 'shield'. Also, because *sphura* is the identified variation of sphara, this might explain the name of Sparta in Greece (the whole country of the Spartans was called Lacedaemon, while Sparta was the name of the main settlement or city).

THEFARIE VELIANAS (ruler of Caere)

This name was inscribed on golden foils unearthed at the site of the ruins of an Etruscan temple at Pyrgi. Two foils were inscribed in Etruscan, but the third was written in Punic-Phoenician. It read "King Thefarie Velianas".

Experts think that the Etruscan name Thevarie is a version of the Roman name Tiberius. The analogy they establish is offered by the river that flows through Rome - Tiber. The popular name of the Tiber is Tevere which places it closer to the name of the king. Let's take a look at Thefarie. The Etruscan language had no 'D', which is always turned into TH or T.

deva	m.	god [838]
deva	adj.	divine, heavenly [838]
deva	m.	king, prince [838]

The second part of the name comes from the verb 'Aryanti'.

Aryanti { Ar }   verb 4   praise [839]

deva + Ar → devar + IE (name ending)

D becomes T in Etruscan → TEVARIE (or Thefarie)

Or the second word might be *Arya*.

Arya   adj.   noble, respectable, Aryan, worthy, polite, honorable [840]

It really could mean PRAISED KING, HONOURABLE KING (or maybe "HONORARY" KING, elected king) or even NOBLE KING.

But, if this was a name, which is more likely, it can be translated, too. There are several options. One of them is GOD-PRAISING (similar to Theophil or Slavic name Bogoslav). Or it might be WORTHY OF GOD.

devArha   adj.   worthy of the gods, divine [841]

What appears to be the last name, Velianas, is also translatable. Here is one simple version.

| velA | f. | shore, sea-shore [842] |
| anna | n. | water, earth [843] |

velA + anna → velaana → veliana → veliana

We can translate it as "OF MARITIMES or "of seashore", which can be a part of the title or the last name. There is another way to get the same.

valI   f.   wave   [ZM: the same as contemporary Serbian word val, meaning 'wave'] [844]

valI + anna → valiana (literal translation: WAVE-LAND, interpreted as MARITIMES or COASTAL LAND)

What appears to be the last name can also be a part of his title.

vAlayati { val }   verb caus.   cherish [845]
yAna   adj.   leading [846]

vAl + yAna → valyana → Y is always I in Etruscan → valiana

This 'VALIANA' could be CHERISHED LEADER. Again, it is hard to decide if this is a title or a name, not to mention that the first and last names of aristocrats frequently expressed their "social role" of ruling and being privileged., therefore sounding as some kind of titles. The most famous example of such a name is Alexander, *"protector of people"*.

SERVIUS TULLIUS

This is probably the most important name we touch in this section. Before he became the second Etruscan king of Rome, he was known as MASTARNA.

"Servius Tullius was the legendary sixth king of Rome, and the second of its Etruscan dynasty. He reigned 575–535 BC.[1] Roman and Greek sources describe his servile origins and later marriage to a daughter of Lucius Tarquinius Priscus, Rome's first Etruscan king, who was assassinated in 579 BC. Servius is said to have been the first Roman king to accede without election by the Senate, having gained the throne by popular support; and the first to be elected by the Senate alone, without reference to the people." Wikipedia [847]

Roman sources have to be taken with caution, they were written afterward and were politically biased. But they also contain lots of useful information. The Romans did what everybody does, they "fixed" the history to adjust it to their political needs. It could be that Romans of later times were quite upset with Servius Tullius being an Etruscan and having a name that would mean 'a servant' in Latin. An Etruscan 'servant' was a king of Rome!?

Historian Titus Livius Patavinus, called Livy in English, wrote that Servius was a son of a noble Latin woman whose husband was a leader of Corniculum and was killed defending his town from Romans. Even though she was formally enslaved, she was not treated like a slave because of her noble origin and was accepted into the royal household of Lucius Tarquinius Priscus, an Etruscan and the fifth king of Rome. Roman narratives are on the border of legend, but some of it is likely true. What is clear is that Servius Tullius became king in a non-standard way and that the story about him contains layers of ancient propaganda, parts of it could be generated by Servius himself (there are several references in the narrative that he was either chosen by gods or of divine origin). All the versions of his birth look as an attempt to explain his roots as Latin.

Emperor Claudius, who was an intellectual, flatly rejected Livy's storyline.

Based on the Etruscan tradition, he wrote that Servius Tullius was an Etruscan mercenary. According to Claudius, his name was Mastarna and he fought on behalf of the Etruscan noble Caelius Vibenna (this is the Latinized version, the original was Vipina).

It seems that the Romans of Livy's time already could not understand the name Servius. They did connect it to the idea of being a servant. However, in the centuries that follow they will keep using Servius as a noble name, which shows that it did not have any negative connotations.

The list of achievements of Servius Tullius is long. He erected the Servian Wall, giving Rome its first serious fortification, He made important reforms regarding land ownership, instituted census, weakened the role of the aristocracy and extended voting rights to ordinary citizens. To make a long story short, his Servian Reforms gave more political power to common people.

It would be interesting to see what do we get if we translate his name with Sanskrit.

sarva   adj.   everyone, of all sorts [848]

sArva   adj.   fit or good for all, relating to all, universal, general [849]

sarva → Servius

It looks to me that some of his political ideas were compressed in his new name. If this has any ground, it would mean that he was suggesting he would be there for everyone or rule in the name of everyone. He would be universal.

How about his "last name" Tullius?

tulA f.   equality, balance, equal measure, equilibrium [850]

yauti { yu }   verb 2   unite, bind, honour, push on towards [851] tulA + yu → tulyu → Y (like in 'yolk' becomes I like in 'tin') → tuliu + US (Latin name -ending) → tulius

Now, he seems to communicate that he will unite people through a measured, balanced rule which will be equal for everyone. Wow! What a sophisticated political marketing! It sounds very good but we need to stop here. The offered meaning of Servius is still a hypothesis, speculation. Let's go back to the word SERVE as we know it today. Does it mark somebody of lower social status? One can conclude that it does (servant). At the same time, the answer is a big NO. Our politicians serve their terms, soldiers do service for their countries, and we go to churches to worship, to attend service.

So, SERVIUS might have the same meaning we already offered as an optional translation of THEVARIE – GOD PRAISING, WORSHIPING. In a political sense, it suggests SERVING ONE'S COMMUNITY.

This parallel between religious worship and serving is as present today as it was present in the time when Sanskrit was a living language. Here are some examples that show several words that mean 'to worship' and 'to serve' at the same time.

```
glevate        { glev } verb     worship, serve [852]
sevate         { sev }  verb 1   worship, serve [853]
zIlati{ zIl }  verb              worship, serve [854]
niSevate { niSev }      verb     worship, serve [855]
pratibhUSati { pratibhUS }       verb    worship, serve [856]
```

Since Livy already could not understand the name of Servius Tullius, we have to suspect that the Latin of his era was losing comprehension of its "Aryan" roots at an accelerated speed.

Let's examine his previous "name", thought to be

Mastarna or Macstarna (Macstrna). This second variant, Macstarna, is based on scholar's contemplation that a person shown on wall paintings at François Tomb in Vulci was indeed Servius Tullius. That Macstarna was some important warrior and an ally of Vipina brothers.

It might be wrong, but something is interesting regarding the word MACSTARNA. A parallel with the Latin word MILITARY appears. We reconstructed MILITARY as a three-word compound. The first word was either 'mIl' or 'mela', the rest can be done differently.

mIlati { mIl } verb   assemble, be collected [857]
melA   m.   company, association, assembly [858]

The second and third word could be *ta* and *arha*.

ta   m.   warrior [859]
arha adj.   costing, obliged, proper, fit [860]

mela + ta + arha → malatarha → H is dropped → MELATARA

The translation of MACSTARNA might be the same!

makSati   { makS }   verb   collect [861]
ta   m.   warrior [859]
RNa   n.   duty, obligation, debt, money owed [862]

makS + ta + Rna → makstarna

The literal translation of 'macstarna' is COLLECT-WARRIOR-OBLIGATION (or MONEY OWED).

The literal translation of 'military' is COLLECTED (or 'company') WARRIOR OBLIGED (or COSTING).

However, there are other possible reconstructions or

readings of Macstarna. If we use a different meaning of the last word we get something else.

RNa   n.   debt of money [862]

Now, it is COLLECT WARRIOR DEBT OF MONEY, maybe suggesting a paid freelance soldier, a mercenary.

It is also speculated that MACSTARNA is an Etruscan word that is known as MAGISTER in the Roman version. This is possible, too.

However, while some scholars talk about MACSTARNA, Claudius mentioned MASTARNA and Pallottino himself uses this variant[863]. Here is the problem, Mastarna also has a Sanskrit translation, but a different one!

masta   n.   head [964]
RNa   n.   fort, stronghold [862]

This means HEAD OF THE FORT!

Or we can use

masta   n.   head [864]
+
tAra   adj.   protector [865]

and we get MASTARA - *a* HEAD OR A LEADER THAT PROTECTS. It is reasonable to ask if this means MASTER? Ass to it short Sanskrit word na, which means WAR, and you get MASTER of WAR,

There is no doubt we can be tricked by Sanskrit easily, but we can also say that Sanskrit talks to us through Etruscan, Latin and Greek words and names.

Sanskrit talks, but our ears are trained not to hear it.

5.14 THE NAME OF THE ETRUSCANS

The Etruscans called themselves Rasenna, which was later shortened to Rasna or Raśna.

The Sanskrit word *rasa* has many meanings and quite a few of them make sense in this context.

rasati { ras } verb   praise [867]
+
anna   n.   earth, water [868]

ras + anna → rasanna (PRAISED LAND)

RASANNA (reconstructed)
RASENNA (Etruscan)

Some words are not exactly a phonetic match, but they intrigue with their meanings.

rASTra   n.   people, nation [869]
rAzi   m.   group, multitude, mass [870]
rasya   n.   blood [871]

Here is another interesting option.

rasA   f.   earth, ground [872]
+
anas n.   mother [873]

If we add the word 'anas' to EARTH, we get MOTHER-EARTH.

rasA + anas → RASANAS

RASANAS (reconstructed)
RASENNA (ancient name)

The meaning MOTHER-EARTH should be seen as MOTHERLAND.

It was the Serbian scholar Radivoje Pešić who thought that we should check Sanskrit regarding the name RASENNA.
This is what he wrote.
"In Sanskrit, the word *ras* means *to sing*, *rasa* means *juice, water, essence, taste, religious feeling*; *rasana* is *scream, sound*, while *rasa* literally means *earth, state*." [874]

Somehow, this connection of the name of the Etruscans with Sanskrit, which professor Pešić established, was not examined further.
So far, MOTHERLAND is the translation I like the most. The only thing that could be better in gluing together collective identity is a language. Professor Pešić missed the meaning of 'tongue' because most Sanskrit dictionaries show this

rasA	f.	tongue [872]
rasana	n.	tongue [as organ of taste] [875]
rasnA	f.	tongue [876]

This 'organ of taste' makes us forget that the same thing is a speaking tool.
It works in the same way as in English or Serbian where we use word *tongue* or *jezik* as synonyms for *language*.

rasA + anna → rasanna

RASANNA (reconstructed)
RASENNA (Etruscan)

It means TONGUE-EARTH, therefore it is LAND OF SPEECH, LAND IN WHICH PEOPLE SPEAK THE SAME LANGUAGE. This is also a serious proposal for the etymology of the name of Russia (Rasia), the name of Russia should be connected to either 'language' or 'land', maybe even to both.

And, again, you can use 'anas', the Sanskrit word for 'mother', and you will get MOTHER'S TONGUE or MATERNAL LANGUAGE.

Could it be that the idea of territory covered with the same language is the same as the idea of someone's land? The lesson is profound. Does your language define "your land"? Maybe this concept echoes in the English word 'land'.

laNDayati   { laND }   verb   speak [877]

OK, this could be an accident. But are there any parallels in other ancient Italian ethnonyms?

RHAETI OR RHETI

The Rhaeti were people who lived on the Italian side of the Alps. Their language is considered to be close to Etruscan. Where did the ethnonym Rhaeti come from?

raThati { raTh }   verb   speak [878]
reTati { reT }   verb   speak [879]

The Rhaeti were SPEAKERS.
They are not the only ones who are wrongfully classified as Non-Indo-European. Ancient Sardinians were also thought to be non-Indo-European. We should not be sure

about that.

SARDINIANS AND BALARES

sara	adj.		fluid [880]
datte { dA }	verb 3	speak [881]	
anna	n.		earth [868]

sara + dA + anna → sardana

There are other reconstructions of Sardinia (one possible meaning is ISLAND), but this one suggests LAND OF "FLUID" SPEECH or, maybe, LAND OF FLUENT SPEAKERS.

(Side-note: Egyptian records mention Sherden as a group that was part of Sea Peoples who invaded them. The word *zardha*, pronounced as 'shardha', means 'troop' in Sanskrit, while 'na' is 'war'. The literal translation of this Sherden or Shardana is 'war troops'. It might be too early to announce a victory, but Sharden is reconstructable).

Now, we need to check BALARES, people who lived in the northern part of Sardinia.

valhate { balh }		verb	speak [882]
AriNanti { ArI }	verb	pour, flow over [883]	

'Balari' seems to mean FLUENT SPEECH (or FLUENT SPEAKERS)

This is intriguing. Is it possible that so many peoples based their ethnonyms on shared language or dialect? Is there any identity marker that is better than language?

UMBRI

om ind. verily, truly, a word of solemn affirmation and respectful assent [884]

ARYAN ITALY OF THE ETRUSCANS

bravIti { brU }   verb   speak [885]

But the Umbri themselves did not have the sound O. Just like the Etruscans, they always made a U out of it (om + bru → ombru → umbru). The meaning is TRUE SPEECH, CORRECT SPEECH.

Another option would include 'Uma' and would mean "COMPANION-SPEECH".

Uma   m.   companion [886]

BRUTTI

brUte { brU }   verb   speak [887]

This Verb is certainly the root of the ethnonym Brutti. We can only speculate if this double T means that Brutti is a compound word. It could be, the adjective *utta* means 'wet' in Sanskrit. "Wet" Speach, "FLOWING SPEECH", FLUENT SPEECH?

VENETI

vANi   f.   speech, praise [888]

The rest of the word is up for a discussion. But we can make a completely different Sanskrit reconstruction of Veneti.

veNI   f.   current, stream [889]
datte { dA }   verb 3   speak [881]

The resulting VENIDA → VENITA ("stream speech") can be seen as FLUENT SPEECH.

LEPONTII

The most obvious reconstructions are:

lap speaking [890]
anta adj. agreeable, near [891]

lap + anta → lapanta → Lepontii (SPEAKING "AGREEABLE")

But, eventually, there is another option.

lapana n. speaking, talking [892]
TA f. earth [893]

lapana + TA → lapanta → Lepontii

Does this mean "TALKING LAND", LAND OF SPEECH?

LATINI

lATI f. particular style of speech [894]
ina adj. glorious [895]

It gives GLORIUS SPEECH.

Here, we find what I conditionally call the Slavic Sub-pattern (where ideas of glory and speech are present in an ethnonym).

But there is one little flow to this reconstruction. The noun *lATI* means *'particular style of speech'*, so it is not speaking in general. Is this imperfection crucial? That is a tricky question.

We already quoted Michael Coulson who said that classical Sanskrit preserves *"an original Indo-European L, where the Rgvedic dialect (in common with Iranian) changes this sound to R".* Now, we can speculate that the root of the name of Rhaeti and the name of Latins could be the same.

raThati { raTh }   verb   speak [878]

raTh → laTh → H is dropped → LAT

LAT + ina → LATINA

CATARI

kathayati   { kath } verb 10   tell, verbalize [896]
AriNanti   { ArI } verb   pour [883]

kath + ArI → kathari → H is dropped → katar or katari

This "TELL-POUR" I read as FLUENT SPEAKERS.

The Catari were a tribe that was part of the Veneti and the Veneti themselves are sometimes thought to be related to Illyrians. Many historians and linguists reject this view claiming that the language of Veneti is clearly Italic and has no associations with Balkans. But everything looks different once you start looking at things from the Sanskrit point of view. So, let's move to the Eastern side of the Adriatic Sea.

ILLYRIANS

Various Illyrian peoples roughly covered the same territory as the former Yugoslavia.

ilA	f.	flow [897]
irA	f.	speech [898]

ilA + irA → ILIRA

The literal translation is FLOW SPEECH, therefore it is FLUENT SPEECH.

It looks like we are facing a pattern here. Ultimately, the name RASENNA could be a part of this same pattern. Here is how.

rasA	f.	tongue [872]
anna	n.	earth, water [868]

rasA + anna → rasanna

An optional literal translation is TONGUE-WATER. Could this mean "FLOWING" SPEECH or FLUENT SPEECH?

Sanskrit might be "too elastic", but it does give us the same translation for Illyrians. Because *ilA* also means 'speech'.

ilA	f.	speech [897]

Let's look for some other meaning of 'irA'.

irA	f.	water, earth [898]

Now, ILIRA is SPEECH-WATER which eventually means FLUENT SPEECH, the same as that optional translation of RASENNA. And another optional translation, "LAND OF SPEECH", is also the same.

Is this correct? One day we will know the answer because this is just a beginning. It is hard to deny that thanks to Sanskrit we can see meanings raising from the mist of ancient languages.

At the end of this section, let's try to translate two other names of the Etruscans that come to us from Greek sources.

TYRRHENIANS AND TYRSENIANS

Etruscans were famous seafarers known in early history for their thalassocracy or rule at the sea. They were traders, but also pirates.

Tyrrhenians? The question is if they were named after the sea or if the sea was named after them. At this point, we are examining this as an umbrella name for the Etruscans.

dhIra		m.	sea [899]
raNa	n.		war, battle, fight [900]
yAna		n.	ship [901]

dhIra + raNa + yAna → dhirranyana

H is dropped, Y becomes I. We get DIRRANIANA → DIRRANIAN → D becomes T → TIRRANIAN

TIRRANIAN (reconstructed)
TYRRHENIAN

Interestingly, if we would apply the Etrusco-Pelasgian transformation of D into T, we get TIRRANIAN.

Its literal translation is SEA FIGHTING SHIP(S) or SEA WARSHIPS. However, IAN at the end is rather a modern addition, so THYRRENIANS should be translated as SEA-WARRIORS, SEA-FIGHTERS. There is another Sanskrit word that gives the same meaning to the compound, but the whole reconstruction is cleaner.

| raNya | n. | war, battle [902] |
| raNya | adj. | warlike, fit for fighting [902] |

dhIra + raNya → dhirranya → tirrania

The meaning is the same: SEA WARRIORS, SEA FIGHTERS.

Let's take a look at TYRSENIANS. Hesiod called them Tyrsenoi. TYR comes from 'dhIra'. Add to it

senA   f.   army, any drilled troop or band or body of men, armed force [903]

and you will get TIRSENA or SEA-ARMY.

The translation is more or less the same as the translation of Tyrrhenians. These words are synonyms. Early in their history, just like the Greeks, the Etruscans were notorious for their piracy. Maybe Tyrsenians and Tyrrhenians meant PIRATES, maybe it was even about the mysterious SEA PEOPLE, a confederation that raised havoc in the Mediterranean during the Bronze Age collapse. Or is it about their *thalassocracy*, their rule at seas?

But let's try to explain the name of the Tyrrhenian Sea as if it was not named after the Etruscans. What if it is some kind of generic word for a sea, similar to numerous translations of river-names that mean 'water' or 'river'.

dhIra	m.	sea [899]
+		
raNya	n.	joy, pleasure, delight [902]

dhIra + raNya → dhirranya → TIRRANIA

ARYAN ITALY OF THE ETRUSCANS

We can see this as DELIGHTING SEA.

Were TYRRHENIANS called after the sea, or the sea got its name after them?

Again, I want you to read my reconstructions as questions. There is so much that still needs to be sorted out even though some things look obvious.

Whatever the answers turn out to be, they can never be reached if you ignore Sanskrit.

6 THE CONCLUSION

You had to notice my frequent lack of willingness to make a final decision about the exact translations of Etruscan terms, toponyms, and words. Sanskrit has so many short words and stems that you start thinking that it might be possible to reconstruct almost anything with it. There is some ground for this suspicion, but if these are linguistic accidents then they appear quite regularly!

Did it work in this book? I thought it did, but there were problems with multiple reconstructions and many translations.

My impression was that some reconstructions offered here were spectacularly clear, some were puzzling and some of them could be problematic. It would be realistic to expect that some of them are later proved to be ridiculous. God knows what I didn't see or understand. Future researchers will judge it.

But, when it comes to the question of whether the Etruscan language is an Indo-European language or not, which was my main interest, the answer is clear: Etruscan is one of the oldest Indo-European languages that are known to us. The majority of Etruscan words are responsive to

Sanskrit and it would be hard to claim that any language we know is more Indo-European than Etruscan.

The real question is why this connection was not seen before. Why did the myth of the "foreign nature" of the Etruscan language last for two thousand years?

The main reason was set by the Romans. It was in their political interest to erase Etruscans and their role in the development of civilization in Italy. The Roman robbery took the "noble" disguise of freeing the peninsula from the rule of the descendants of those that did not belong to Italy.

The second wave of erasure came from Christianity. It had no interest in preserving "pagan" cultural models, but it needed Roman imperial ideas and its military iron as a protection and a tool of expansion. The Etruscans were positioned to be a perfect victim. Again. The same destiny was later applied to other cultures like Illyrians, Thracians, Celts, Maya, Inca, not to mention Africa, etc. It is needless to say that the Etruscans, like others, did not deserve it.

We owe so much to the Etruscans, to these builders of bridges and cities, these law-makers who put boundaries on human greed, these inventors of the dental bridge which Europe would discover two thousand years later, these regulators of rivers and lovers of life.

All the great achievements of Rome, except their disgusting imperial thinking but possibly even that, had started in Etruria. And that includes the idea of the republic. For the last two hundred years, interest in the Etruscans has been growing at an accelerated speed and the world is recognizing their role.

Why did linguists fail to see that Etruscans were so similar to everybody around them?

The reasons for this are cultural, political and linguistic. We think of history and languages from national perspectives, our point of view is almost always political.

Nations usually want to differentiate themselves from their immediate neighbours. It is not a popular idea that the two nations could be just brands of each other. They would rather pay to research them as separate entities and they only sometimes insist on common roots (if they see a material gain from it). I was interested in what would be the same.

This two thousand years old misunderstanding of Etruscans is a result of the enforcement of imaginary borders between Romans and Etruscans, Etruscans and Greeks and Phoenicians-Carthaginians, and ultimately between Europe and Asia. It has been said many times that Greece and Rome are the foundation of Western civilization. If you read such a statement and you were born in former Yugoslavia, you get the impression that both Greece and Rome have nothing to do with you even though so many Roman emperors were from Illyria.

On the linguistic side of things, words were "re-invented", often wrongly, while they could be found in a Sanskrit dictionary. You probably remember our shocking discovery of the true etymology of the river Arno. Here are some examples of that approach that routinely ignored the Indo-part of Indo-European heritage. This one is about the name of the Drava River.

The Drava starts in Italy as La Drava, flows through Austria where it is called Drau, then it goes through Slovenia, where it is the Drava again and is later shared by Croatia (Drava) and Hungary (Dráva).

Now, let's take a look at the "Western explanation" of this name.

"Drave: in Latin "Dravus", of Thracian or Illyrian origin, probably from PIE *dhreu = 'to flow, to fall'." (Wikipedia) [904]

What does this mean? First thing first: we need to clarify that what is called Proto-Indo-European **dhreu* (supposedly meaning 'to flow') is a re-imagined word, not an attested word, a word thought to be possible.

The second thing to notice is that this imagined PIE *dhreu is practically the same as the German name of Drava, which is Drau.

Third, the name is credited to people that lived in that general area, Illyrians and Thracians.

Fourth, it seems that Illyrians and Thracians used a language that was very close to Proto-Indo-European and judging by the German name Drau that language heritage is best preserved in Germanic and western languages.

There is only one problem here: Sanskrit offers a better explanation. It was Slovenian linguist Marko Snoj who pointed at Sanskrit roots of Drava's name. Snoj proposes Sanskrit verb *dravati*. [905]

dravati   { dru }   verb   to flow

Numerous Sanskrit words support his claim.

drava   adj.   fowing, dripping, running, wet[906]
drava   m.   liquid, liquefaction, fusing[906]
drava   m.   stream, liquid[906]
dravantI   f.   river[907]
dravayate { dravaya }   verb   flow[908]

Now, DRAU appears as a variation, rendering or pronunciation of Sanskrit *drava*.

What more do we need to prove the Sanskrit etymology of Drava?

In fact, there is more.

drAti { drA }   verb   run, verb make haste [909]
va   m.   water [910]

drA + va → Drava

Drava means RUNNING WATER or RIVER.

Now, you can see how linguists chose a "Western" explanation, not having any need to check Sanskrit nor any other "Eastern language". They opt for a German-sounding PIE *dhreu = "to flow", which you cannot find in any dictionary (even if it existed, we have no way of being sure about it).

A very similar case is with the explanation of the name of the River Siret.

"Siret: ancient Thracian "Seretos", probably from PIE *sreu = 'to flow'" (Wikipedia) [911]

The real etymology of Siret is easy.

sirA   f.   water, stream, artery, vein-like channel or narrow stream of river water [912]

O, boy!!!! You would think that the Illyrians, the Thracians, the Dacians or the Etruscans have no connection to Sanskrit. The Etruscans were doomed to receive this treatment, while Illyrians and Thracians, who left no written sources, were simply erased.

In history, the explanations will depend on your point of view and the iron that can protect it.

To see linguistic differences and similarities, you have to compare words from different languages with words from Etruscan. That means that you have to use a comparative etymological method. But that very method has been rejected and ridiculed for over a century!

So, how do you know?

It is not my intention to blame Giuliano and Larissa Bonfante, whose book was my main source of information about the Etruscan tongue, nor I want to accuse Massimo Pallottino. One has to admit that when you look at the Etruscan vocabulary it is not easy to see connections. That is because words were composed of stems and short words, so the resulting combinations looked like something that was on its own, something that doesn't have similarities with known languages.

Besides, why would Sanskrit, which is on the very edge of the vast territory covered by Indo-European languages, be so tightly related to the biggest language of Italy before the rise of Rome?

Seemingly, it doesn't make any sense. That explains how Massimo Pallottino, an excellent scholar, often called the father of Etruscology, could mistakenly spread this approach. Read carefully!

"But the insufficiency of the method of etymological comparisons with other languages only became generally established after the publication of a work by the famous latinist Corssen "Uber die Sprache der Etrusker" (1874), stating that Etruscan belonged to the Indo-European family of languages and, in particular, to its Italic branch, and following this premise (with apparent methodological rigour) with a general attempt towards a morphological analysis and an interpretation of the texts. The thirty nine pages of Deecke's "Corssen und die Sprache der Etrusker.Eine Kritik" (1875) were sufficient to bring down, like a house of cards, the imposing construction erected by Corssen."[913]

The imposing construction erected by Corsen!

Hmm! Poor Wilhelm Paul Corssen (1820-1875) was completely right! Needless to say that Corssen's 1874 theory was rejected hastily. Why the rush? Corssen was a great linguist and we can only guess in which way he would reply to Decke if he didn't die that very same year when his "house of cards" was brought down.

On the surface, Etruscan might not look similar to other languages of ancient Italy, but if you shake the vocabulary of those with Sanskrit you will see that they are related. And they are related not only to each other but to the language of Mahabharata!

The great Bulgarian linguist Vladimir Georgiev (1908–1986) claimed that there was a connection between Etruscan and Hittite. He was ignored. There sure was, they were both very old Indo-European languages. It sometimes looks like ancient languages of the Mediterranean were related to Sanskrit so much that you are tempted to think of them as of dialects that just started their separation.

The Serbian scholar Milan Budimir (1891-1975) recognized connections between Etruscan and Slavic languages. That connection was real. Like many other achievements of Eastern European linguists, it was ignored, too.

So, if Pallottino rejected the thesis about the Indo-European nature of Etruscan, what could you expect from other top etruscologists who continued on his path?

The Bonfantes identified some features of Etruscan as comparable to features of Greek and Latin, but they could not see its general Indo-European essence. At the same time, let me say what should be obvious: without their *"The Etruscan Language: An Introduction"* this book would not be possible.

For the last two millennia, European history has been interpreted from a Greco-Roman point of view. It has served European imperial concepts. Anything that could show Europe as "Asiatic" or even Eastern was coldly ignored. But the time when such huge entities (like Celts, Slavs, Germans, Scandinavians, and others) were swiped under the carpet has passed long ago.

The Bonfantes concluded that *"Etruscan influence on Rome was important, though it never touched the base of the Latin language or the conservative Roman religion"* (p.114).

Regarding religion, the Bonfantes were completely wrong, even from the perspective of current knowledge. Many gods venerated in Rome were the same as Etruscan gods and some of them are thought to be passed to Romans by the Etruscans.

On the other hand, over a hundred years ago, the scholar George Hempl attempted to warn of the similarities between Etruscan and Latin. Maybe his formulation lacked proof, but he was right regarding their kinship.

"The development of the language, from the early stage when it was almost identical with Latin, down to the time when it was so different that the Romans regarded it as a totally alien tongue, can be traced step by step on the chiseled monuments that stand in our museums. In attempting to read Etruscan, scholars have, however, largely confined themselves to a study of late inscriptions, and have permitted the relatively modern forms that they there found to blind them to the original character of the language — much as Old-English scholars once did with West Saxon. The situation in which the philological world at present finds itself with reference to Etruscan is as regrettable as it is extraordinary. The kinship of Etruscan and Latin lies open for all men to observe, and yet this fact is denied by practically all Indo-European philologists." [914]

This was written in 1911! Hempl's claim was never seriously considered nor honoured. Sadly, it had no impact whatsoever.

The Serbian scholar Radivoje Pešić thought that expelling the Etruscans from the Indo-European family had far-reaching political effects, changed our understanding of the historical and linguistic timeline and tragically prevented many ideas of kinship. Contemplating history and languages from national, even religious, and most often imperialistic perspectives, made horrible damages to our understanding of ourselves. It seems that the art of history is mostly a continuation of politics by other means.

But there is one section of the Etruscan language that still looks very non-Indo-European. The Etruscan words for numbers seem as they have nothing in common with Indo-European numbers. That is probably the second main reason why scholars were fooled. Just look at them!

1 - θu
5 - maχ
10 – śar [915]

Why is it that the words for numbers are "non-Indo-European" when everything else is "Indo-European"? The fact that we cannot explain this suggests that something must be wrong with the contemporary understanding of language families.

Yes, it is highly unusual that Etruscan numbers have no similarity to Indo-European. And that's about it! Generally, we can say that Etruscan vocabulary displays Indo-European heritage, but there could be a "non-Indo-European" part of it. We can say that about other Indo-European languages, too.

The question is still shocking: why didn't we see this tsunami of Etruscan, Latin, Greek and Sanskrit ties?

The answer is painful: because the Etruscans got the same treatment as other "pagan cultures" - erasure. That is why we didn't see it. We were raised to forget the past for the sake of future opportunities that smiled at us with their golden teeth of ideology, religion, and profit.

We were raised to erase.

7 NON-SCIENTIFIC CONCLUSION: IT ALL ENDS WITH PROSCIUTTO

There are times when we enter some realms with one goal and finish with another. Initially, I just wanted to prove that people from the former Yugoslavia can also claim prosciutto as a part of their heritage. But the Etruscans took me over and I forgot about that. Let me quote again what Wikipedia said about the etymology of prosciutto.

"The word prosciutto is derived from Latin pro (before) + exsuctus (past participle of exsugere "to suck out [the moisture]"); the Portuguese presunto has the same etymology. It is similar to the modern Italian verb prosciugare "to dry thoroughly" (from Latin pro + exsucare "to extract the juices from")." Wikipedia [916]

Well, I was experienced in eating 'prosciutto' and never saw the process of making it. So I always searched words that are in connection to drying by air flow, but when I carefully read how prosciutto is made I realized there were other paths to search.

This is what an Italian butcher said, *"Today, the ham is first cleaned, salted, and left for about two months. During this time, the ham is pressed, gradually and carefully so as to avoid breaking the bone, to drain all blood left in the meat."* [916]

So, the ham must be pressed! I never thought of that! I decided to give it one more try to find that "common ancestral word" from which Italian 'prosciutto' (pronounced as 'prshuto') and 'prshut' of Balkans (spelled as 'pršut') descended. Sure, I checked Sanskrit.

| prasut | f. | pressing [917] |
| preS | f. | pressing, pressure [918] |

Press! It looks like a pig's leg and our media might have more in common than it was thought.

But let's not celebrate. There is more!

| preS | f. | pressing [918] |
| sut | adj. | extracting juice [919] |

preS + sut → presut (EXTRACTING JUICES BY PRESSING)

And there is even a better and cleaner etymology!

| pArayati { pR } | verb caus. | preserve[920] |
| sut | adj. | extracting juice [919] |

pR + sut → prsut

This one is very similar to both the "South Slavic" and the "Italian" word. It would mean PRESERVED BY EXTRACTING JUICES.

Pršut... my grandfather Risto... my motherland, language, heritage...

ARYAN ITALY OF THE ETRUSCANS

I was always aware that my tears for Etruria were about the country of my birth. Now, it is just another name gone with the wind of history.

I stand before the photograph of my grandfather Risto Tabaković. It was taken in 1916, in Bisbee, Arizona. In that picture, he is around twenty, but he is still older than me. I look at his photo with the deepest love, wishing that he and my grandmother Ana are now proud of me, as well as my paternal grandparents Djoko and Stana Maslić, who I never met and who did not survive World War II.

I hope they are pleased because they know that I know that one simple thing:

SONS ARE NOT OLDER THAN FATHERS.

It feels like my Etruscans are here. They are dancing in the sunshine.

ZORAN MASLIĆ

NOTES

ARYAN ITALY OF THE ETRUSCANS

1. IT ALL STARTED WITH PROSCIUTTO (p.1-9)

1. Wikipedia contributors. "Prosciutto." Wikipedia, The Free Encyclopedia. Wikipedia, The Free Encyclopedia, 27 Feb. 2019. Web. 1 Mar. 2019.

2. The article was about the book "The Old European Language and the Etruscan Alphabet" by Svetislav S. Bilbija

Bilbija, Svetislav S. - "Stari Evropski jezik i pismo Etruraca", published by "Miroslav", Belgrade, 2000.

3. Herodotus - "The Histories", translated by Tom Holland, introduction and notes by Paul Cartledge, Book I, p.48-49, columns 93-94, Viking Penguin, New York, 2014.

4. Pallottino, Massimo - "The Etruscans", p.82-90, the revised and enlarged hardcover edition based on the sixth Italian edition, Edited by David Ridgway, Indiana University Press, Bloomington & London, 1975.

5. Bonfante, Giuliano/Bonfante, Larissa - "The Etruscan Language: An Introduction", p. 50, Manchester University Press and Room 400, Second Edition, Manchester and New York, 2002.

6. Macnamara, Ellen - "Everyday Life of the Etruscans",p.181, Dorset Press, New York, 1987.

7. Barker, Graeme/ Rasmussen, Tom - "The Etruscans", Blackwell Publishing, Malden, MA, 2000.

8. Lawrence, D.H. - "Mornings in Mexico and Etruscan Places", Etruscan Places, p. 9, William Heinemann Ltd., reprinted in Great Britain by Redwood Press Limited, London, 1970.

9. Bonfante, Giuliano/Bonfante, Larissa - "The Etruscan Language: An Introduction", p.73, Manchester University Press, Manchester and New York, 2002.

2. IN THE WATERS OF SANSKRIT (p.10-14)

10. Dictionary.com contributors. Dictionary.com. "6 German Words So Good English Just Had to Borrow Them",

https://www.dictionary.com/e/s/german-compounds/#german, 2019, Web. 13 Mar. 2019.

11. Šašel Kos, Marjeta - "Reka kot božanstvo – Sava v antiki" [River as a Deity – The Sava in Antiquity], p. 46, (PDF). In Peternel, Jožef. "Ukročena lepotica: Sava in njene zgodbe" [The Tamed Beauty: The Sava and Its Stories] (PDF) (in Slovenian). Sevnica, Slovenia: Javni zavod za kulturo, šport, turizem in mladinske dejavnosti. 2009. ISBN 978-961-92735-0-0.

12. "sava." SanskritDictionary.com. Sanskrit Dictionary, 2019. Web. 13 March 2019.

13. "ṣa." SanskritDictionary.com. Sanskrit Dictionary, 2019. Web. 13 March 2019.
(Note that in the body of this book we usedHarvard-Kyoto transliteration where an accented S is written as capital S. The same sound is presented in IAST as ṣ)

14. "va." SanskritDictionary.com. Sanskrit Dictionary, 2019. Web. 13 March 2019.

15. "sā." SanskritDictionary.com. Sanskrit Dictionary, 2019. Web. 13 March 2019.
(Again, accented A is presented in the body of the book in Harvard-Kyoto transliteration standard as capital A, not as IAST standard ā)

16. "śava." SanskritDictionary.com. Sanskrit Dictionary, 2019. Web. 14 March 2019.
(Again, in the body of the book and the word is presented as 'zava' in Harvard-Kyoto transliteration)

3. RIVERS OF TUSCANY

3.1 FIRST ATTEMPTS: BURE, CHIANA, IDICE, LIMENTRA, MAGRA, MARECCHIA, METAURO, SAVENA, SIEVE, TORA (p.16-33)

3.1.1 BURE (p.16-18)

17. Snoj, Marko - "Slovenski etimološki slovar" , p. 66, Second Edition,. Modrijan, Ljubljana, 2003.

18. "bhurati." SpokenSanskrit.com, Spoken Sanskrit, 2019, Web. 14 March 2019.
"bhur." SanskritDictionary.com, Sanskrit Dictionary, 2019. Web. 14 March 2019.

19. "ya." SanskritDictionary.com, Sanskrit Dictionary, 2019. Web. 14 March 2019.

20. "vātṛ." SanskritDictionary.com, Sanskrit Dictionary, 2019. Web. 15 March 2019.
"vAtr." SpokenSanskrit.com, Spoken Sanskrit, 2019, Web. 15 March 2019.

21. Mallory, J.P. / Adams, D.Q. - "The Oxford Introduction to Proto-Indo-European and the Proto-Indo-European World", p.121, Oxford University Press, Oxford, 2006.

3.1.2 CHIANA (p.18-19)

22. Encyclopedia Britannica contributors, revised and updated by Melissa Albert. "Chiana River." Britannica, . https://www.britannica.com/place/Chiana-River, 2019. Web. 17 Mar. 2019.

23. "glāna." SanskritDictionary.com, Sanskrit Dictionary, 2019. Web. 17 March 2019.
"glAna." SpokenSanskrit.com, Spoken Sanskrit, 2019, Web. 17 March 2019.

24. "khyā." SanskritDictionary.com, Sanskrit Dictionary, 2019. Web. 17 March 2019.
"khyA." SpokenSanskrit.com, Spoken Sanskrit, 2019, Web. 17 March 2019.

25. "anna." SanskritDictionary.com, Sanskrit Dictionary, 2019. Web. 17 March 2019.

26. "kheya." SanskritDictionary.com. Sanskrit Dictionary, 2019. Web. 17 March 2019.

3.1.3 ERA (p.20)

27. "irā." SanskritDictionary.com. Sanskrit Dictionary, 2019. Web. 17 March 2019.

"irA." SpokenSanskrit.com, Spoken Sanskrit, 2019, Web. 17 March 2019.

3.1.4 IDICE (p.20-21)

28. "iḍā." SpokenSanskrit.com, Spoken Sanskrit, 2019, Web. 17 March 2019.
"iDA." SanskritDictionary.com, Sanskrit Dictionary, 2019. Web. 17 March 2019.

29. "cah." SpokenSanskrit.com, Spoken Sanskrit, 2019, Web. 17 March 2019.
"cahati." SanskritDictionary.com, Sanskrit Dictionary, 2019. Web. 17 March 2019.

30. "icchā." SpokenSanskrit.com, Spoken Sanskrit, 2019, Web. 17 March 2019.

3.1.5 LIMENTRA (p.21-22)

31. Wikipedia contributors. "Limentra." Wikipedia, The Free Encyclopedia. Wikipedia, The Free Encyclopedia, 4 Sep. 2014. Web. 18 Mar. 2019.

32. "lī." SanskritDictionary.com, Sanskrit Dictionary, 2019. Web. 17 March 2019.

33. "ma." SanskritDictionary.com, Sanskrit Dictionary, 2019. Web. 17 March 2019.

34. "netra." SanskritDictionary.com, Sanskrit Dictionary, 2019. Web. 17 March 2019.

35. "manā." SanskritDictionary.com, Sanskrit Dictionary, 2019. Web. 17 March 2019.
"manA." SpokenSanskrit.com, Spoken Sanskrit, 2019, Web. 17 March 2019.

3.1.6 MAGRA (p.22-23)

36. "ma." SpokenSanskrit.com, Spoken Sanskrit, 2019, Web. 17 March 2019.

37. "gRh." SpokenSanskrit.com, Spoken Sanskrit, 2019, Web. 17 March 2019.
"gr̥h." SanskritDictionary.com, Sanskrit Dictionary, 2019. Web. 17 March 2019.

38. "vārī." SanskritDictionary.com, Sanskrit Dictionary, 2019. Web. 17 March 2019.
"vArI.", SpokenSanskrit.com, Spoken Sanskrit, 2019, Web. 17 March 2019.

3.1.7 MARECCHIA (p.23-25)

39. Digital Atlas of the Roman Empire Contributors, "Marecchia." Digital Atlas of the Roman Empire. http://dare.ht.lu.se/places/44093.html, © 2015 Johan Åhlfeldt, Department of Archaeology and Ancient History, Lund University, Sweden, 2019, Web. 18 Mar. 2019.

40. "Marecchia." Wikipedia, L'enciclopedia libera. 24 ott 2018, 12:29 UTC. 18 mar 2019, 05:57 <//it.wikipedia.org/w/index.php?title=Marecchia&oldid=100535541>.

41. "rā." SanskritDictionary.com, Sanskrit Dictionary, 2019. Web. 17 March 2019.
"rAti." SpokenSanskrit.com, Spoken Sanskrit, 2019, Web. 17 March 2019.

42. "khyā." SanskritDictionary.com, Sanskrit Dictionary, 2019. Web. 18 March 2019.
"khyA." SpokenSanskrit.com, Spoken Sanskrit, 2019, Web. 18 March 2019.

43. "maraka." SanskritDictionary.com, Sanskrit Dictionary, 2019. Web. 18 March 2019.
"maraka." SpokenSanskrit.com, Spoken Sanskrit, 2019, Web. 18 March 2019.

44. "yā." SanskritDictionary.com, Sanskrit Dictionary, 2019. Web. 18 March 2019.

45. "Aramati." SpokenSanskrit.com, Spoken Sanskrit, 2019, Web. 18 March 2019.

46. "āram." SanskritDictionary.com, Sanskrit Dictionary, 2019. Web. 18 March 2019.

47. "ina." SanskritDictionary.com, Sanskrit Dictionary, 2019. Web. 18 March 2019.

48. "vārī." SanskritDictionary.com, Sanskrit Dictionary, 2019. Web. 18 March 2019.
"vArI." SpokenSanskrit.com, Spoken Sanskrit, 2019, Web. 18 March 2019.

49. "mī." SanskritDictionary.com, Sanskrit Dictionary, 2019. Web. 18 March 2019.
"mInAti." SpokenSanskrit.com, Spoken Sanskrit, 2019, Web. 18 March 2019.

3.1.8 METAURO (p.25-26)

50. Wikipedia contributors. "Metauro." Wikipedia, The Free Encyclopedia. Wikipedia, The Free Encyclopedia, 2 Mar. 2018. Web. 18 Mar. 2019.

51. "madā." SanskritDictionary.com, Sanskrit Dictionary, 2019. Web. 18 March 2019.
"madA." SpokenSanskrit.com, Spoken Sanskrit, 2019, Web. 18 March 2019.

52. "ha." SanskritDictionary.com, Sanskrit Dictionary, 2019. Web. 18 March 2019.

53. "uru." SanskritDictionary.com, Sanskrit Dictionary, 2019. Web. 18 March 2019.
"uru." SpokenSanskrit.com, Spoken Sanskrit, 2019, Web. 18 March 2019.

54. "āvṛh." SanskritDictionary.com, Sanskrit Dictionary, 2019. Web. 18 March 2019.
"AvRh." SpokenSanskrit.com, Spoken Sanskrit, 2019, Web. 18 March 2019.

3.1.9 SAVENA (p.26-27)

55. "Savena." Wikipedia, L'enciclopedia libera. 30 nov 2018, 21:12 UTC.

19 mar 2019, 00:04 <//it.wikipedia.org/w/index.php?title=Savena&oldid=101302040>.

56. "savana." SanskritDictionary.com, Sanskrit Dictionary, 2019. Web. 18 March 2019.

57. "sā." SanskritDictionary.com. Sanskrit Dictionary, 2019. Web. 13 March 2019.

58. "vana." SanskritDictionary.com, Sanskrit Dictionary, 2019. Web. 18 March 2019.
"vana." SpokenSanskrit.com, Spoken Sanskrit, 2019, Web. 18 March 2019.

59. "sava." SanskritDictionary.com, Sanskrit Dictionary, 2019. Web. 18 March 2019.

60 "enī." SanskritDictionary.com, Sanskrit Dictionary, 2019. Web. 18 March 2019.
"enI." SpokenSanskrit.com, Spoken Sanskrit, 2019, Web. 18 March 2019.

61. "sāvinī" SanskritDictionary.com, Sanskrit Dictionary, 2019. Web. 18 March 2019.
"sAvinI." SpokenSanskrit.com, Spoken Sanskrit, 2019, Web. 18 March 2019.

3.1.10 SERCHIO (p. 27-30)

62. Wikipedia contributors. "Serchio." Wikipedia, The Free Encyclopedia. Wikipedia, The Free Encyclopedia, 2 Mar. 2018. Web. 30 Apr. 2019.

63. "sāra" SanskritDictionary.com, Sanskrit Dictionary, 2019. Web. 18 March 2019.
"sAra." SpokenSanskrit.com, Spoken Sanskrit, 2019, Web. 18 March 2019.

64. "khyā" SanskritDictionary.com, Sanskrit Dictionary, 2019. Web. 18 March 2019.
"khyAti." SpokenSanskrit.com, Spoken Sanskrit, 2019, Web. 18 March 2019.

65. "sṛ." SanskritDictionary.com, Sanskrit Dictionary, 2019. Web. 18

March 2019.
"sisarti." SpokenSanskrit.com, Spoken Sanskrit, 2019, Web. 18 March 2019.

66. "kheya." SanskritDictionary.com, Sanskrit Dictionary, 2019. Web. 18 March 2019.
"kheya." SpokenSanskrit.com, Spoken Sanskrit, 2019, Web. 18 March 2019.

67. "Serchio." *Wikipedia, L'enciclopedia libera.* 1 giu 2019, 05:10 UTC. 29 lug 2019, 14:47 <//it.wikipedia.org/w/index.php?title=Serchio&oldid=105269055>.

68. "sarga." SanskritDictionary.com, Sanskrit Dictionary, 2019. Web. 18 March 2019.
"sarga." SpokenSanskrit.com, Spoken Sanskrit, 2019, Web. 18 March 2019.

69. "ya." SanskritDictionary.com, Sanskrit Dictionary, 2019. Web. 18 March 2019.

70. "av." SanskritDictionary.com, Sanskrit Dictionary, 2019. Web. 18 March 2019.
"avati." SpokenSanskrit.com, Spoken Sanskrit, 2019, Web. 18 March 2019.

3.1.11 SIEVE (p.30-31)

71. "Sieve." Wikipedia, L'enciclopedia libera. 12 ott 2018, 20:28 UTC. 19 mar 2019, 15:16 <//it.wikipedia.org/w/index.php?title=Sieve&oldid=100291493>.

72. "va." SanskritDictionary.com, Sanskrit Dictionary, 2019. Web. 19 March 2019.
"va." SpokenSanskrit.com, Spoken Sanskrit, 2019, Web. 19 March 2019.

73. "yā." SanskritDictionary.com, Sanskrit Dictionary, 2019. Web. 19 March 2019.

74. "si." SanskritDictionary.com, Sanskrit Dictionary, 2019. Web. 19 March 2019.

75. "sū." SanskritDictionary.com, Sanskrit Dictionary, 2019. Web. 19

March 2019.
"suvati." SpokenSanskrit.com, Spoken Sanskrit, 2019, Web. 19 March 2019.

3.1.12 TORA (p.31-33)

76. "dhārā." SanskritDictionary.com, Sanskrit Dictionary, 2019. Web. 19 March 2019.
"dhArA." SpokenSanskrit.com, Spoken Sanskrit, 2019, Web. 19 March 2019.

77. "dhor." SanskritDictionary.com, Sanskrit Dictionary, 2019. Web. 19 March 2019.
"dhor." SpokenSanskrit.com, Spoken Sanskrit, 2019, Web. 19 March 2019.

78. "rantu." SanskritDictionary.com, Sanskrit Dictionary, 2019. Web. 19 March 2019.
"rantu." SpokenSanskrit.com, Spoken Sanskrit, 2019, Web. 19 March 2019.

79. "dhara." SanskritDictionary.com, Sanskrit Dictionary, 2019. Web. 19 March 2019.
"dhara." SpokenSanskrit.com, Spoken Sanskrit, 2019, Web. 19 March 2019.

80. "andha." SanskritDictionary.com, Sanskrit Dictionary, 2019. Web. 19 March 2019.
"andha." SpokenSanskrit.com, Spoken Sanskrit, 2019, Web. 19 March 2019.

3.2. MAJOR RIVERS OF THE ETRUSCAN WORLD (p.34-49)

3.2.1 ARNO (p.34-35)

81. Wikipedia contributors. "Arno." Wikipedia, The Free Encyclopedia. Wikipedia, The Free Encyclopedia, 24 Jan. 2019. Web. 19 Mar. 2019.

82. "arṇā." SanskritDictionary.com, Sanskrit Dictionary, 2019. Web. 19 March 2019.
"arNA." SpokenSanskrit.com, Spoken Sanskrit, 2019, Web. 19 March

2019.

83. "arṇa." SanskritDictionary.com, Sanskrit Dictionary, 2019. Web. 19 March 2019.
"arNa." SpokenSanskrit.com, Spoken Sanskrit, 2019, Web. 19 March 2019.

84. "ārī." SanskritDictionary.com, Sanskrit Dictionary, 2019. Web. 19 March 2019.
"ArIyate." SpokenSanskrit.com, Spoken Sanskrit, 2019, Web. 19 March 2019.

3.2.2 MARTA (p.35-38)

85. "Marta (fiume)." Wikipedia, L'enciclopedia libera. 30 nov 2018, 21:06 UTC. 19 mar 2019, 20:24 <//it.wikipedia.org/w/index.php?title=Marta_(fiume)&oldid=101301675>.

86. "ma." SanskritDictionary.com, Sanskrit Dictionary, 2019. Web. 19 March 2019.
87. "ṛta." SanskritDictionary.com, Sanskrit Dictionary, 2019. Web. 19 March 2019.
"Rta." SpokenSanskrit.com, Spoken Sanskrit, 2019, Web. 19 March 2019.

88. "mā." SanskritDictionary.com, Sanskrit Dictionary, 2019. Web. 19 March 2019.
"mAyate." SpokenSanskrit.com, Spoken Sanskrit, 2019, Web. 19 March 2019.

89. "ṛdh." SanskritDictionary.com, Sanskrit Dictionary, 2019. Web. 19 March 2019.
"Rdh." SpokenSanskrit.com, Spoken Sanskrit, 2019, Web. 19 March 2019.

90. "lā." SanskritDictionary.com, Sanskrit Dictionary, 2019. Web. 19 March 2019.
"lA." SpokenSanskrit.com, Spoken Sanskrit, 2019, Web. 19 March 2019.

91. "uma." SanskritDictionary.com, Sanskrit Dictionary, 2019. Web. 19 March 2019.
"uma." SpokenSanskrit.com, Spoken Sanskrit, 2019, Web. 19 March 2019.

92. "anu." SanskritDictionary.com, Sanskrit Dictionary, 2019. Web. 19 March 2019.

93. "kha." SanskritDictionary.com, Sanskrit Dictionary, 2019. Web. 19 March 2019.
"kha." SpokenSanskrit.com, Spoken Sanskrit, 2019, Web. 19 March 2019.

94. "nāra." SanskritDictionary.com, Sanskrit Dictionary, 2019. Web. 19 March 2019.
"nAra." SpokenSanskrit.com, Spoken Sanskrit, 2019, Web. 19 March 2019.

3.2.3 PO (p.38-40)

95. Wikipedia contributors. "Po (river)." Wikipedia, The Free Encyclopedia. Wikipedia, The Free Encyclopedia, 16 Mar. 2019. Web. 19 Mar. 2019.

96. "pī." SanskritDictionary.com, Sanskrit Dictionary, 2019. Web. 19 March 2019.
"pI." SpokenSanskrit.com, Spoken Sanskrit, 2019, Web. 19 March 2019.

97. "pha." SanskritDictionary.com, Sanskrit Dictionary, 2019. Web. 19 March 2019.
"pha." SpokenSanskrit.com, Spoken Sanskrit, 2019, Web. 19 March 2019.

98. "pada." SanskritDictionary.com, Sanskrit Dictionary, 2019. Web. 19 March 2019.
"pada." SpokenSanskrit.com, Spoken Sanskrit, 2019, Web. 19 March 2019.

99. "ārī." SanskritDictionary.com, Sanskrit Dictionary, 2019. Web. 19 March 2019.
"ArI." SpokenSanskrit.com, Spoken Sanskrit, 2019, Web. 19 March 2019.

100. "dāna." SanskritDictionary.com, Sanskrit Dictionary, 2019. Web. 19 March 2019.
"dAna." SpokenSanskrit.com, Spoken Sanskrit, 2019, Web. 19 March 2019.

101. "bhedin." SanskritDictionary.com, Sanskrit Dictionary, 2019. Web. 19 March 2019.

"bhedin." SpokenSanskrit.com, Spoken Sanskrit, 2019, Web. 19 March 2019.

102. "ka." SanskritDictionary.com, Sanskrit Dictionary, 2019. Web. 19 March 2019.
"ka." SpokenSanskrit.com, Spoken Sanskrit, 2019, Web. 19 March 2019.

103. "viṣ." SanskritDictionary.com, Sanskrit Dictionary, 2019. Web. 19 March 2019.
"viS." SpokenSanskrit.com, Spoken Sanskrit, 2019, Web. 19 March 2019.

104. "lū." SanskritDictionary.com, Sanskrit Dictionary, 2019. Web. 19 March 2019.
"lunIte." SpokenSanskrit.com, Spoken Sanskrit, 2019, Web. 19 March 2019.

3.2.4 RENO (p.40-45)

105. Wikipedia contributors. "Reno (river)." Wikipedia, The Free Encyclopedia. Wikipedia, The Free Encyclopedia, 2 Mar. 2018. Web. 19 Mar. 2019.

106. "raṇa ." SanskritDictionary.com, Sanskrit Dictionary, 2019. Web. 19 March 2019.
"raNa." SpokenSanskrit.com, Spoken Sanskrit, 2019, Web. 19 March 2019.

107. "ṛṇa." SanskritDictionary.com, Sanskrit Dictionary, 2019. Web. 19 March 2019.
"RNa." SpokenSanskrit.com, Spoken Sanskrit, 2019, Web. 19 March 2019.

108. "ṛ." SanskritDictionary.com, Sanskrit Dictionary, 2019. Web. 19 March 2019.
(note that Hrvard-Kyoto capital R was used in the body of the book, the same sound is presented in IAST as ṛ)

109. "anna." SanskritDictionary.com, Sanskrit Dictionary, 2019. Web. 19 March 2019.
"anna." SpokenSanskrit.com, Spoken Sanskrit, 2019, Web. 19 March 2019.

110. "ṛ." SanskritDictionary.com, Sanskrit Dictionary, 2019. Web. 19

March 2019.
"Rcchati." SpokenSanskrit.com, Spoken Sanskrit, 2019, Web. 19 March 2019.

111. "enī." SanskritDictionary.com, Sanskrit Dictionary, 2019. Web. 19 March 2019.
"enI." SpokenSanskrit.com, Spoken Sanskrit, 2019, Web. 19 March 2019.

112. Wikipedia contributors. "Rhine." Wikipedia, The Free Encyclopedia. Wikipedia, The Free Encyclopedia, 8 Mar. 2019. Web. 20 Mar. 2019.

113. "raya." SanskritDictionary.com, Sanskrit Dictionary, 2019. Web. 19 March 2019.
"raya." SpokenSanskrit.com, Spoken Sanskrit, 2019, Web. 19 March 2019

114. "na." SanskritDictionary.com, Sanskrit Dictionary, 2019. Web. 19 March 2019.

115. Wikipedia contributors. "Oder." Wikipedia, The Free Encyclopedia. Wikipedia, The Free Encyclopedia, 14 Jan. 2019. Web. 20 Mar. 2019.

116. "udra." SanskritDictionary.com, Sanskrit Dictionary, 2019. Web. 19 March 2019.
"udra." SpokenSanskrit.com, Spoken Sanskrit, 2019, Web. 19 March 2019

117. "uda." SanskritDictionary.com, Sanskrit Dictionary, 2019. Web. 19 March 2019.
"uda." SpokenSanskrit.com, Spoken Sanskrit, 2019, Web. 19 March 2019

118. "drā." SanskritDictionary.com, Sanskrit Dictionary, 2019. Web. 19 March 2019.
"drA." SpokenSanskrit.com, Spoken Sanskrit, 2019, Web. 19 March 2019

119. "dara." SanskritDictionary.com, Sanskrit Dictionary, 2019. Web. 19 March 2019.
"dara." SpokenSanskrit.com, Spoken Sanskrit, 2019, Web. 19 March 2019

120. "rī." SanskritDictionary.com, Sanskrit Dictionary, 2019. Web. 19 March 2019.
"rI." SpokenSanskrit.com, Spoken Sanskrit, 2019, Web. 19 March 2019

121. "vār." SanskritDictionary.com, Sanskrit Dictionary, 2019. Web. 19

March 2019.
"vAr." SpokenSanskrit.com, Spoken Sanskrit, 2019, Web. 19 March 2019

122. "ka." SanskritDictionary.com, Sanskrit Dictionary, 2019. Web. 19 March 2019.
"ka." SpokenSanskrit.com, Spoken Sanskrit, 2019, Web. 19 March 2019

3.2.5 TIBER (p.45-49)

123. Wikipedia contributors. "Tiber." Wikipedia, The Free Encyclopedia. Wikipedia, The Free Encyclopedia, 4 Mar. 2019. Web. 20 Mar. 2019.

124. "devara." SpokenSanskrit.com, Spoken Sanskrit, 2019, Web. 20 March 2019

125. "devṛ." SanskritDictionary.com, Sanskrit Dictionary, 2019. Web. 20 March 2019.

126. "dhI." SpokenSanskrit.com, Spoken Sanskrit, 2019, Web. 20 March 2019.
127. "dhī." SanskritDictionary.com, Sanskrit Dictionary, 2019. Web. 20 March 2019.

128. "deva." SanskritDictionary.com, Sanskrit Dictionary, 2019. Web. 19 March 2019.
"deva." SpokenSanskrit.com, Spoken Sanskrit, 2019, Web. 19 March 2019.

129. Wikipedia contributors. "Tiber." Wikipedia, The Free Encyclopedia. Wikipedia, The Free Encyclopedia, 4 Mar. 2019. Web. 20 Mar. 2019.

130. "val." SanskritDictionary.com, Sanskrit Dictionary, 2019. Web. 20 March 2019.
"valate." SpokenSanskrit.com, Spoken Sanskrit, 2019, Web. 20 March 2019.

131. "tu." SanskritDictionary.com, Sanskrit Dictionary, 2019. Web. 19 March 2019.
"tauti." SpokenSanskrit.com, Spoken Sanskrit, 2019, Web. 19 March 2019.

132. "ṛṇa." SanskritDictionary.com, Sanskrit Dictionary, 2019. Web. 19 March 2019.

"RNa." SpokenSanskrit.com, Spoken Sanskrit, 2019, Web. 19 March 2019.

133. "dā." SanskritDictionary.com, Sanskrit Dictionary, 2019. Web. 19 March 2019.
"datte." SpokenSanskrit.com, Spoken Sanskrit, 2019, Web. 19 March 2019.

134. "dhāv." SanskritDictionary.com, Sanskrit Dictionary, 2019. Web. 19 March 2019.
"dhAvati." SpokenSanskrit.com, Spoken Sanskrit, 2019, Web. 19 March 2019.

135. "dhav." SanskritDictionary.com, Sanskrit Dictionary, 2019. Web. 19 March 2019.
"dhav." SpokenSanskrit.com, Spoken Sanskrit, 2019, Web. 19 March 2019.

136. "oṣṭha." SanskritDictionary.com, Sanskrit Dictionary, 2019. Web. 19 March 2019.
"oSTha." SpokenSanskrit.com, Spoken Sanskrit, 2019, Web. 19 March 2019

137. "auṣṭha." SanskritDictionary.com, Sanskrit Dictionary, 2019. Web. 19 March 2019.
"auSTha." SpokenSanskrit.com, Spoken Sanskrit, 2019, Web. 19 March 2019

3.3 ITALIAN CONTEXT, CONCLUSION (p.49-53)

138. "aviṣī." SanskritDictionary.com, Sanskrit Dictionary, 2019. Web. 20 March 2019.
"aviSI." SpokenSanskrit.com, Spoken Sanskrit, 2019, Web. 20 March 2019.

139. "havis." SanskritDictionary.com, Sanskrit Dictionary, 2019. Web. 20 March 2019.
"havis." SpokenSanskrit.com, Spoken Sanskrit, 2019, Web. 20 March 2019.

140. "barbura." SanskritDictionary.com, Sanskrit Dictionary, 2019. Web. 20 March 2019.
"barbura." SpokenSanskrit.com, Spoken Sanskrit, 2019, Web. 20 March

2019.

141. "kavana." SanskritDictionary.com, Sanskrit Dictionary, 2019. Web. 20 March 2019.
"kavana." SpokenSanskrit.com, Spoken Sanskrit, 2019, Web. 20 March 2019.

142. "anna." SanskritDictionary.com, Sanskrit Dictionary, 2019. Web. 20 March 2019.
"anna." SpokenSanskrit.com, Spoken Sanskrit, 2019, Web. 20 March 2019.

143. "enī." SanskritDictionary.com, Sanskrit Dictionary, 2019. Web. 20 March 2019.
"enI." SpokenSanskrit.com, Spoken Sanskrit, 2019, Web. 20 March 2019.

144. "nāra." SanskritDictionary.com, Sanskrit Dictionary, 2019. Web. 20 March 2019.
"nAra." SpokenSanskrit.com, Spoken Sanskrit, 2019, Web. 20 March 2019.

145. "nīra." SanskritDictionary.com, Sanskrit Dictionary, 2019. Web. 20 March 2019.
"nIra." SpokenSanskrit.com, Spoken Sanskrit, 2019, Web. 20 March 2019.

146. "rāmā." SanskritDictionary.com, Sanskrit Dictionary, 2019. Web. 20 March 2019.
"rAmA." SpokenSanskrit.com, Spoken Sanskrit, 2019, Web. 20 March 2019.

147. "sala." SanskritDictionary.com, Sanskrit Dictionary, 2019. Web. 21 March 2019.
"sala."SpokenSanskrit.com, Spoken Sanskrit, 2019, Web. 21 March 2019.

148. "tāmara." SanskritDictionary.com, Sanskrit Dictionary, 2019. Web. 21 March 2019.
"tAmara." SpokenSanskrit.com, Spoken Sanskrit, 2019, Web. 21 March 2019.

149. "vār." SanskritDictionary.com, Sanskrit Dictionary, 2019. Web. 21 March 2019.
"vAr." SpokenSanskrit.com, Spoken Sanskrit, 2019, Web. 21 March 2019.

150. "vārdara." SanskritDictionary.com, Sanskrit Dictionary, 2019. Web. 21 March 2019.
"vArdara." SpokenSanskrit.com, Spoken Sanskrit, 2019, Web. 21 March 2019.

151. "vṛṣa." SanskritDictionary.com, Sanskrit Dictionary, 2019. Web. 21 March 2019.
"vRSa." SpokenSanskrit.com, Spoken Sanskrit, 2019, Web. 21 March 2019.

152. "kūma." SanskritDictionary.com, Sanskrit Dictionary, 2019. Web. 21 March 2019.
"kUma." SpokenSanskrit.com, Spoken Sanskrit, 2019, Web. 21 March 2019.

153. Pallottino, Massimo - "The Etruscans", p.49, the revised and enlarged hardcover edition based on the sixth Italian edition, Edited by David Ridgway, Indiana University Press, Bloomington & London, 1975.

4. CITIES OF ETRURIA

4.1. TEST RECONSTRUCTIONS OF CITY NAMES (p.55-67)

4.1.1 STATNA (p.55-58)

154. "stha." SanskritDictionary.com, Sanskrit Dictionary, 2019. Web. 21 March 2019.
"stha." SpokenSanskrit.com, Spoken Sanskrit, 2019, Web. 21 March 2019.

155. "sthā." SanskritDictionary.com, Sanskrit Dictionary, 2019. Web. 21 March 2019.
"stha." SpokenSanskrit.com, Spoken Sanskrit, 2019, Web. 21 March 2019.

156. "sthātṛ." SanskritDictionary.com, Sanskrit Dictionary, 2019. Web. 21 March 2019.
"sthAtR." SpokenSanskrit.com, Spoken Sanskrit, 2019, Web. 21 March 2019.

157. "sthātra." SanskritDictionary.com, Sanskrit Dictionary, 2019. Web. 21 March 2019.

"sthAtra." SpokenSanskrit.com, Spoken Sanskrit, 2019, Web. 21 March 2019.

158. "sthāna." SanskritDictionary.com, Sanskrit Dictionary, 2019. Web. 21 March 2019.
"sthAna." SpokenSanskrit.com, Spoken Sanskrit, 2019, Web. 21 March 2019.

159. "oṇi." SanskritDictionary.com, Sanskrit Dictionary, 2019. Web. 21 March 2019.
"oNi." SpokenSanskrit.com, Spoken Sanskrit, 2019, Web. 21 March 2019.

160. "pālana." SanskritDictionary.com, Sanskrit Dictionary, 2019. Web. 21 March 2019.
"pAlana" SpokenSanskrit.com, Spoken Sanskrit, 2019, Web. 21 March 2019.

161. "kha." SanskritDictionary.com, Sanskrit Dictionary, 2019. Web. 21 March 2019.
"kha." SpokenSanskrit.com, Spoken Sanskrit, 2019, Web. 21 March 2019.

162. "pallī." SanskritDictionary.com, Sanskrit Dictionary, 2019. Web. 21 March 2019.
"pallI." SpokenSanskrit.com, Spoken Sanskrit, 2019, Web. 21 March 2019.

163. "aṇaka." SanskritDictionary.com, Sanskrit Dictionary, 2019. Web. 21 March 2019.
"aNaka." SpokenSanskrit.com, Spoken Sanskrit, 2019, Web. 21 March 2019.

164. "vāra." SanskritDictionary.com, Sanskrit Dictionary, 2019. Web. 21 March 2019.
"vAra." SpokenSanskrit.com, Spoken Sanskrit, 2019, Web. 21 March 2019.

165. "vara." SanskritDictionary.com, Sanskrit Dictionary, 2019. Web. 21 March 2019.

4.1.2 CAPEVA (p.58-59)

166. Pallottino, Massimo - "The Etruscans", p.122, the revised and

enlarged hardcover edition based on the sixth Italian edition, Edited by David Ridgway, Indiana University Press, Bloomington & London, 1975.

167. Wikipedia contributors. "Capua." Wikipedia, The Free Encyclopedia. Wikipedia, The Free Encyclopedia, 18 Mar. 2019. Web. 21 Mar. 2019.

168. "kha." SanskritDictionary.com, Sanskrit Dictionary, 2019. Web. 21 March 2019.
"kha." SpokenSanskrit.com, Spoken Sanskrit, 2019, Web. 21 March 2019.

169. "pava." SanskritDictionary.com, Sanskrit Dictionary, 2019. Web. 21 March 2019.
"pava." SpokenSanskrit.com, Spoken Sanskrit, 2019, Web. 21 March 2019.

4.1.3 CAPENA OR CAPNA (p.59)

170. http://www.casacapena.com/about-capena/capena-history/. 2019. Web. 27 June. 2012.

171. "kha." SanskritDictionary.com, Sanskrit Dictionary, 2019. Web. 21 March 2019.

172. "paṇa." SanskritDictionary.com, Sanskrit Dictionary, 2019. Web. 21 March 2019.
"paNa." SpokenSanskrit.com, Spoken Sanskrit, 2019, Web. 21 March 2019.

173. "pāna." SanskritDictionary.com, Sanskrit Dictionary, 2019. Web. 21 March 2019.
"pAna." SpokenSanskrit.com, Spoken Sanskrit, 2019, Web. 21 March 2019.

4.1.4 NEPETE (p.60)

174. Wikipedia contributors. "Nepi." Wikipedia, The Free Encyclopedia. Wikipedia, The Free Encyclopedia, 12 Jul. 2018. Web. 21 Mar. 2019.

175. "nepa." SanskritDictionary.com, Sanskrit Dictionary, 2019. Web. 21 March 2019.
"nepa." SpokenSanskrit.com, Spoken Sanskrit, 2019, Web. 21 March

2019.

176. "edh." SanskritDictionary.com, Sanskrit Dictionary, 2019. Web. 21 March 2019.
"edhate." SpokenSanskrit.com, Spoken Sanskrit, 2019, Web. 21 March 2019.

4.1.5 SATURNIA (p.60-61)

177. Wikipedia contributors. "Saturnia." Wikipedia, The Free Encyclopedia. Wikipedia, The Free Encyclopedia, 7 Feb. 2019. Web. 21 Mar. 2019.

178. "sāta." SanskritDictionary.com, Sanskrit Dictionary, 2019. Web. 21 March 2019.
"sAta." SpokenSanskrit.com, Spoken Sanskrit, 2019, Web. 21 March 2019.

179. "ṛṇa." SanskritDictionary.com, Sanskrit Dictionary, 2019. Web. 21 March 2019.
RNa." SpokenSanskrit.com, Spoken Sanskrit, 2019, Web. 21 March 2019.

180. "sādhu." SanskritDictionary.com, Sanskrit Dictionary, 2019. Web. 21 March 2019.
"sAdhu.", SpokenSanskrit.com, Spoken Sanskrit, 2019, Web. 21 March 2019.

4.1.6 GRAVISCA (p.61-62)

181. "graha." SanskritDictionary.com, Sanskrit Dictionary, 2019. Web. 21 March 2019.
"graha." SpokenSanskrit.com, Spoken Sanskrit, 2019, Web. 21 March 2019.

182. "vāsa." SanskritDictionary.com, Sanskrit Dictionary, 2019. Web. 21 March 2019.
"vAsa." SpokenSanskrit.com, Spoken Sanskrit, 2019, Web. 21 March 2019.

183. "ka." SanskritDictionary.com, Sanskrit Dictionary, 2019. Web. 21 March 2019.

184. Wikipedia contributors. "Tarquinia." Wikipedia, The Free Encyclopedia. Wikipedia, The Free Encyclopedia, 15 Oct. 2018. Web. 21 Mar. 2019.

185. ghrā." SanskritDictionary.com, Sanskrit Dictionary, 2019. Web. 21 March 2019.
"jighrati., SpokenSanskrit.com, Spoken Sanskrit, 2019, Web. 21 March 2019.

186. "viṣa." SanskritDictionary.com, Sanskrit Dictionary, 2019. Web. 21 March 2019.
"viSa." SpokenSanskrit.com, Spoken Sanskrit, 2019, Web. 21 March 2019.

4.1.7 MUTINA (p.62-63)

187. Wikipedia contributors. "Modena." Wikipedia, The Free Encyclopedia. Wikipedia, The Free Encyclopedia, 15 Mar. 2019. Web. 21 Mar. 2019.

188. "mud." SanskritDictionary.com, Sanskrit Dictionary, 2019. Web. 21 March 2019.
"mud." SpokenSanskrit.com, Spoken Sanskrit, 2019, Web. 21 March 2019.

189. "moda." SanskritDictionary.com, Sanskrit Dictionary, 2019. Web. 21 March 2019.
"moda.", SpokenSanskrit.com, Spoken Sanskrit, 2019, Web. 21 March 2019.

190. "ina." SanskritDictionary.com, Sanskrit Dictionary, 2019. Web. 21 March 2019.
"ina." SpokenSanskrit.com, Spoken Sanskrit, 2019, Web. 21 March 2019.

191. "mūta." SanskritDictionary.com, Sanskrit Dictionary, 2019. Web. 21 March 2019.
"mUta." SpokenSanskrit.com, Spoken Sanskrit, 2019, Web. 21 March 2019.

4.1.8 NARCE (p.64-65)

192. "nāra." SanskritDictionary.com, Sanskrit Dictionary, 2019. Web. 21

March 2019.
"nAra." SpokenSanskrit.com, Spoken Sanskrit, 2019, Web. 21 March 2019.

193. "kha." SanskritDictionary.com, Sanskrit Dictionary, 2019. Web. 21 March 2019.

194. "nRNati." SanskritDictionary.com, Sanskrit Dictionary, 2019. Web. 21 March 2019.
195. "nṛ." SpokenSanskrit.com, Spoken Sanskrit, 2019, Web. 21 March 2019.

4.1.9 PARMA (p.66-67)

196. Wikipedia contributors. "Parma." Wikipedia, The Free Encyclopedia. Wikipedia, The Free Encyclopedia, 27 Feb. 2019. Web. 21 Mar. 2019.

197. "phara." SanskritDictionary.com, Sanskrit Dictionary, 2019. Web. 21 March 2019.
"phara." SpokenSanskrit.com, Spoken Sanskrit, 2019, Web. 21 March 2019.

198. "ma." SanskritDictionary.com, Sanskrit Dictionary, 2019. Web. 21 March 2019.
"ma." SpokenSanskrit.com, Spoken Sanskrit, 2019, Web. 21 March 2019.

199. "parama." SanskritDictionary.com, Sanskrit Dictionary, 2019. Web. 21 March 2019.
"parama." SpokenSanskrit.com, Spoken Sanskrit, 2019, Web. 21 March 2019.

200. "pāra." SanskritDictionary.com, Sanskrit Dictionary, 2019. Web. 21 March 2019.
"pAra." SpokenSanskrit.com, Spoken Sanskrit, 2019, Web. 21 March 2019.

201. "para." SanskritDictionary.com, Sanskrit Dictionary, 2019. Web. 21 March 2019.
"para." SpokenSanskrit.com, Spoken Sanskrit, 2019, Web. 21 March 2019.

ARYAN ITALY OF THE ETRUSCANS

4.2 THE DODECAPOLI CITIES (p.70-91)

4.2.1 ARRETIUM (p.70)

202. "arh." SanskritDictionary.com, Sanskrit Dictionary, 2019. Web. 21 March 2019.
"arhati.", SpokenSanskrit.com, Spoken Sanskrit, 2019, Web. 21 March 2019.

203. "rāṭi." SanskritDictionary.com, Sanskrit Dictionary, 2019. Web. 21 March 2019.
"rATi." SpokenSanskrit.com, Spoken Sanskrit, 2019, Web. 21 March 2019.

204. "uma." SanskritDictionary.com, Sanskrit Dictionary, 2019. Web. 21 March 2019.

4.2.2 CAERE (p.70-73)

205. Pallottino, Massimo - "The Etruscans", p.110, the revised and enlarged hardcover edition based on the sixth Italian edition, Edited by David Ridgway, Indiana University Press, Bloomington & London, 1975

206. "ka." SanskritDictionary.com, Sanskrit Dictionary, 2019. Web. 21 March 2019.

207. "kha." SanskritDictionary.com, Sanskrit Dictionary, 2019. Web. 21 March 2019.
"kha." SpokenSanskrit.com, Spoken Sanskrit, 2019, Web. 21 March 2019.

208. "irā." SanskritDictionary.com, Sanskrit Dictionary, 2019. Web. 21 March 2019.
"irA." SpokenSanskrit.com, Spoken Sanskrit, 2019, Web. 21 March 2019.

209. "kāya." SanskritDictionary.com, Sanskrit Dictionary, 2019. Web. 23 March 2019.
"kAya." SpokenSanskrit.com, Spoken Sanskrit, 2019, Web. 23 March 2019.

210. "irya." SanskritDictionary.com, Sanskrit Dictionary, 2019. Web. 23 March 2019.
"irya." SpokenSanskrit.com, Spoken Sanskrit, 2019, Web. 23 March 2019.

211. Bonfante, Giuliano/Bonfante, Larissa - "The Etruscan Language: An Introduction", p.75, Manchester University Press and Room 400, Second Edition, Manchester and New York, 2002.

212. "śrī." SanskritDictionary.com, Sanskrit Dictionary, 2019. Web. 23 March 2019.
"zrI." SpokenSanskrit.com, Spoken Sanskrit, 2019, Web. 23 March 2019.

What spokensanskrit.de presents as zrI in Harvard-Kyoto, sanskritdictionary.com shows in IAST as

śrī f. prosperity, welfare, good fortune, success, auspiciousness, wealth, treasure, riches (śriyā-,"according to fortune or wealth"), high rank, power, might, majesty, royal dignity (or"Royal dignity" personified; śriyo bhājaḥ-,"possessors of dignity","people of high rank") etc.

213."zrIyate." SpokenSanskrit.com, Spoken Sanskrit, 2019, Web. 23 March 2019.

214. "karvata." SanskritDictionary.com, Sanskrit Dictionary, 2019. Web. 23 March 2019.
"karvata." SpokenSanskrit.com, Spoken Sanskrit, 2019, Web. 23 March 2019.

215. "kharvaṭa." SanskritDictionary.com, Sanskrit Dictionary, 2019. Web. 23 March 2019.
"kharvaTa." SpokenSanskrit.com, Spoken Sanskrit, 2019, Web. 23 March 2019.

4.2.3 CLEVSIN (p.73-77)

216. Bonfante, Giuliano/Bonfante, Larissa - "The Etruscan Language: An Introduction", p.215, Manchester University Press and Room 400, Second Edition, Manchester and New York, 2002.

217. "glevate." SpokenSanskrit.com, Spoken Sanskrit, 2019, Web. 23 March 2019.

218. "glev." SpokenSanskrit.com, Spoken Sanskrit, 2019, Web. 23 March 2019.

219. "si.", SanskritDictionary.com, Sanskrit Dictionary, 2019. Web. 23

March 2019.
"sinite." SpokenSanskrit.com, Spoken Sanskrit, 2019, Web. 23 March 2019.

220. "ina." SanskritDictionary.com, Sanskrit Dictionary, 2019. Web. 23 March 2019.
"ina." SpokenSanskrit.com, Spoken Sanskrit, 2019, Web. 23 March 2019.

221. "cludo." http://www.latin-dictionary.net/definition/10449/cludo-cludere-clusi-clusus, LatDict, 2019. Web. 24 March 2019.

222. "uma." SanskritDictionary.com, Sanskrit Dictionary, 2019. Web. 23 March 2019.

223. "oni.", SanskritDictionary.com, Sanskrit Dictionary, 2019. Web. 23 March 2019.
"oNi." SpokenSanskrit.com, Spoken Sanskrit, 2019, Web. 23 March 2019.

224. Coulson, Michael - "Complete Sanskrit : teach yourself"; p.XV-XVI, Contributors: Benson, James D. ; Gombrich, Richard F. (Richard Francis), softcover, McGraw-Hill; 3rd edition , 2010.

225. "kṛ.", SanskritDictionary.com, Sanskrit Dictionary, 2019. Web. 24 March 2019.
"kRR." SpokenSanskrit.com, Spoken Sanskrit, 2019, Web. 24 March 2019.

226. "avi.", SanskritDictionary.com, Sanskrit Dictionary, 2019. Web. 24 March 2019.
"avi." SpokenSanskrit.com, Spoken Sanskrit, 2019, Web. 24 March 2019.

4.2.4 CURTUN (p.77-78)

227. Bonfante, Giuliano/Bonfante, Larissa - "The Etruscan Language: An Introduction", p.25, Manchester University Press and Room 400, Second Edition, Manchester and New York, 2002.

228. "gur." SanskritDictionary.com, Sanskrit Dictionary, 2019. Web. 24 March 2019.
"gur." SpokenSanskrit.com, Spoken Sanskrit, 2019, Web. 24 March 2019.

229. "guru." SanskritDictionary.com, Sanskrit Dictionary, 2019. Web. 24

March 2019.
"guru." SpokenSanskrit.com, Spoken Sanskrit, 2019, Web. 24 March 2019.

230. "gurd." SanskritDictionary.com, Sanskrit Dictionary, 2019. Web. 24 March 2019.
"gurdayati." SpokenSanskrit.com, Spoken Sanskrit, 2019, Web. 24 March 2019.

4.2.5 PERUSIA (p.78-79)

231. "pāra." SanskritDictionary.com, Sanskrit Dictionary, 2019. Web. 28 March 2019.
"pAra." SpokenSanskrit.com, Spoken Sanskrit, 2019, Web. 28 March 2019.

232. "para." SanskritDictionary.com, Sanskrit Dictionary, 2019. Web. 28 March 2019.

233. "peru." SanskritDictionary.com, Sanskrit Dictionary, 2019. Web. 28 March 2019.
"peru." SpokenSanskrit.com, Spoken Sanskrit, 2019, Web. 28 March 2019.

234. "pā." SanskritDictionary.com, Sanskrit Dictionary, 2019. Web. 28 March 2019.

235. "rūṣ." SanskritDictionary.com, Sanskrit Dictionary, 2019. Web. 28 March 2019.
"rUSati." SpokenSanskrit.com, Spoken Sanskrit, 2019, Web. 28 March 2019.

236. "rūṣaṇa." SanskritDictionary.com, Sanskrit Dictionary, 2019. Web. 28 March 2019.
"rUSaNa." SpokenSanskrit.com, Spoken Sanskrit, 2019, Web. 28 March 2019.

4.2.6 PUPLUNA or FUFLUNA or PUPULUNA (p.79-81)

237. "populus." http://www.latin-dictionary.net/search/latin/populus, Latin Dictionary, 2019. Web. 29 March 2019.

238. "bhūpāla." SanskritDictionary.com, Sanskrit Dictionary, 2019. Web. 29 March 2019.
"bhUpAla." SpokenSanskrit.com, Spoken Sanskrit, 2019, Web. 29 March 2019.

239. "bhūpālana." SanskritDictionary.com, Sanskrit Dictionary, 2019. Web. 29 March 2019.
"bhUpAlana." SpokenSanskrit.com, Spoken Sanskrit, 2019, Web. 29 March 2019.

4.2.7. TARCHUNA (p.81-82)

240. "tāra." SanskritDictionary.com, Sanskrit Dictionary, 2019. Web. 29 March 2019.
"tAra." SpokenSanskrit.com, Spoken Sanskrit, 2019, Web. 29 March 2019.

241."ku." SanskritDictionary.com, Sanskrit Dictionary, 2019. Web. 29 March 2019.

242. Wikipedia contributors. "Tarquinia." Wikipedia, The Free Encyclopedia. Wikipedia, The Free Encyclopedia, 15 Oct. 2018. Web. 29 Mar. 2019.

243. Wikipedia contributors. "Tarquinia." Wikipedia, The Free Encyclopedia. Wikipedia, The Free Encyclopedia, 15 Oct. 2018. Web. 29 Mar. 2019.

4.2.8 VEIA (p.82)

244. "va." SanskritDictionary.com, Sanskrit Dictionary, 2019. Web. 29 March 2019.

245. "yā." SanskritDictionary.com, Sanskrit Dictionary, 2019. Web. 29 March 2019.
"yA." SpokenSanskrit.com, Spoken Sanskrit, 2019, Web. 29 March 2019.

246. "ya." SanskritDictionary.com, Sanskrit Dictionary, 2019. Web. 29 March 2019.
"ya." SpokenSanskrit.com, Spoken Sanskrit, 2019, Web. 29 March 2019.

247. "vāya." SanskritDictionary.com, Sanskrit Dictionary, 2019. Web. 29

March 2019.
"vAya." SpokenSanskrit.com, Spoken Sanskrit, 2019, Web. 29 March 2019.

248. "vayā." SanskritDictionary.com, Sanskrit Dictionary, 2019. Web. 29 March 2019.
"vayA." SpokenSanskrit.com, Spoken Sanskrit, 2019, Web. 29 March 2019.

4.2.9 VELATHRI (p.82-83)

249. "val." SanskritDictionary.com, Sanskrit Dictionary, 2019. Web. 29 March 2019.
"valate." SpokenSanskrit.com, Spoken Sanskrit, 2019, Web. 29 March 2019.

250. "vala." SanskritDictionary.com, Sanskrit Dictionary, 2019. Web. 29 March 2019.
"vala." SpokenSanskrit.com, Spoken Sanskrit, 2019, Web. 29 March 2019.

251. "adri." SanskritDictionary.com, Sanskrit Dictionary, 2019. Web. 29 March 2019.
"adri." SpokenSanskrit.com, Spoken Sanskrit, 2019, Web. 29 March 2019.

252. Wikipedia contributors. "Volterra." Wikipedia, The Free Encyclopedia. Wikipedia, The Free Encyclopedia, 21 Feb. 2019. Web. 29 Mar. 2019.

4.2.10 VELCH (p.83-84)

249. "val." SanskritDictionary.com, Sanskrit Dictionary, 2019. Web. 29 March 2019.
"valate." SpokenSanskrit.com, Spoken Sanskrit, 2019, Web. 29 March 2019.

253. Wikipedia contributors. "Vulci." Wikipedia, The Free Encyclopedia. Wikipedia, The Free Encyclopedia, 30 Jan. 2019. Web. 29 Mar. 2019.

253-B. "velā." SanskritDictionary.com, Sanskrit Dictionary, 2019. Web. 29 March 2019.

"velA." SpokenSanskrit.com, Spoken Sanskrit, 2019, Web. 29 March 2019.

4.2.11 VELZNA (p.84-90)

254. Pallottino, Massimo - "The Etruscans", p.115, the revised and enlarged hardcover edition based on the sixth Italian edition, Edited by David Ridgway, Indiana University Press, Bloomington & London, 1975.

255. Bonfante, Giuliano/Bonfante, Larissa - "The Etruscan Language: An Introduction", p.27, Manchester University Press and Room 400, Second Edition, Manchester and New York, 2002.

256. Wikipedia contributors. "Etruscan cities." Wikipedia, The Free Encyclopedia. Wikipedia, The Free Encyclopedia, 10 Mar. 2019. Web. 30 Mar. 2019.

257. Wikipedia contributors. "Volsinii." Wikipedia, The Free Encyclopedia. Wikipedia, The Free Encyclopedia, 8 Jul. 2018. Web. 30 Mar. 2019.

258. "vala." SanskritDictionary.com, Sanskrit Dictionary, 2019. Web. 29 March 2019.
"vala." SpokenSanskrit.com, Spoken Sanskrit, 2019, Web. 29 March 2019.

259. "senā." SanskritDictionary.com, Sanskrit Dictionary, 2019. Web. 29 March 2019.
"senA." SpokenSanskrit.com, Spoken Sanskrit, 2019, Web. 29 March 2019.

260. "sanna." SanskritDictionary.com, Sanskrit Dictionary, 2019. Web. 29 March 2019.
"sanna." SpokenSanskrit.com, Spoken Sanskrit, 2019, Web. 29 March 2019.

261. "sunau." SanskritDictionary.com, Sanskrit Dictionary, 2019. Web. 29 March 2019.
"sunau." SpokenSanskrit.com, Spoken Sanskrit, 2019, Web. 29 March 2019.

262. "velā." SanskritDictionary.com, Sanskrit Dictionary, 2019. Web. 29 March 2019.

"velA." SpokenSanskrit.com, Spoken Sanskrit, 2019, Web. 29 March 2019.

263. "snāna." SanskritDictionary.com, Sanskrit Dictionary, 2019. Web. 29 March 2019.
"snAna." SpokenSanskrit.com, Spoken Sanskrit, 2019, Web. 29 March 2019.

264. "vela." SanskritDictionary.com, Sanskrit Dictionary, 2019. Web. 29 March 2019.
"vela." SpokenSanskrit.com, Spoken Sanskrit, 2019, Web. 29 March 2019.

265. Livius, Titus - "The History of Rome", First Eight Books, Book IV-23 (p.276), Book IV-61 (p.321), Accessed on August 31, 2019 at https://www.gutenberg.org/files/19725/19725-h/19725-h.htm

266. Pallottino, Massimo - "The Etruscans", p.141, the revised and enlarged hardcover edition based on the sixth Italian edition, Edited by David Ridgway, Indiana University Press, Bloomington & London, 1975.

267. "valli." SanskritDictionary.com, Sanskrit Dictionary, 2019. Web. 29 March 2019.
"valli." SpokenSanskrit.com, Spoken Sanskrit, 2019, Web. 29 March 2019.

268. "uṣṇa." SanskritDictionary.com, Sanskrit Dictionary, 2019. Web. 29 March 2019.
"uSNa." SpokenSanskrit.com, Spoken Sanskrit, 2019, Web. 29 March 2019.

269. "vel." SanskritDictionary.com, Sanskrit Dictionary, 2019. Web. 29 March 2019.
"velati." SpokenSanskrit.com, Spoken Sanskrit, 2019, Web. 29 March 2019.

270. "vell." SanskritDictionary.com, Sanskrit Dictionary, 2019. Web. 29 March 2019.
"vellati." SpokenSanskrit.com, Spoken Sanskrit, 2019, Web. 29 March 2019.

271. "vel." SanskritDictionary.com, Sanskrit Dictionary, 2019. Web. 29 March 2019.
"velayati." SpokenSanskrit.com, Spoken Sanskrit, 2019, Web. 29 March

2019.

272. "bala." SanskritDictionary.com, Sanskrit Dictionary, 2019. Web. 29 March 2019.
"bala." SpokenSanskrit.com, Spoken Sanskrit, 2019, Web. 29 March 2019.

273. "sena." SanskritDictionary.com, Sanskrit Dictionary, 2019. Web. 29 March 2019.

274. "sana." SanskritDictionary.com, Sanskrit Dictionary, 2019. Web. 29 March 2019.
"sana." SpokenSanskrit.com, Spoken Sanskrit, 2019, Web. 29 March 2019.

4.2.12 VETLUNA (p.90-91)

275. Pallottino, Massimo - "The Etruscans", p.105, the revised and enlarged hardcover edition based on the sixth Italian edition, Edited by David Ridgway, Indiana University Press, Bloomington & London, 1975.

276. Bonfante, Giuliano/Bonfante, Larissa - "The Etruscan Language: An Introduction", p.21, Manchester University Press and Room 400, Second Edition, Manchester and New York, 2002.

277. "vātūla." SanskritDictionary.com, Sanskrit Dictionary, 2019. Web. 29 March 2019.
"vAtUla." SpokenSanskrit.com, Spoken Sanskrit, 2019, Web. 29 March 2019.

278. "vāṭa." SanskritDictionary.com, Sanskrit Dictionary, 2019. Web. 29 March 2019.
"vATa." SpokenSanskrit.com, Spoken Sanskrit, 2019, Web. 29 March 2019.

279. "āli." SanskritDictionary.com, Sanskrit Dictionary, 2019. Web. 29 March 2019.
"Ali." SpokenSanskrit.com, Spoken Sanskrit, 2019, Web. 29 March 2019.

280 "ālī." SanskritDictionary.com, Sanskrit Dictionary, 2019. Web. 29 March 2019.
"AlI." SpokenSanskrit.com, Spoken Sanskrit, 2019, Web. 29 March 2019.
281. "hul." SanskritDictionary.com, Sanskrit Dictionary, 2019. Web. 29

March 2019.
"holati." SpokenSanskrit.com, Spoken Sanskrit, 2019, Web. 29 March 2019.

282. Pliny (1961). "Natural History" (with an English translation in ten volumes by H. Rackham), Book III, chap. 19, paragraphs 112-113, Harvard University Press, Cambridge, 1961.

5 ETRUSCAN VOCABULARY:RECONSTRUCTIONS

5.1 TESTING THE WATERS (p.97-101)

283. Bonfante, Giuliano/Bonfante, Larissa - "The Etruscan Language: An Introduction", p.217, Manchester University Press and Room 400, Second Edition, Manchester and New York, 2002.

284. Bonfante, Giuliano/Bonfante, Larissa - "The Etruscan Language: An Introduction", p.101, Manchester University Press and Room 400, Second Edition, Manchester and New York, 2002.

285. "śikhaka." SanskritDictionary.com, Sanskrit Dictionary, 2019. Web. 30 March 2019.
"zikhaka." SpokenSanskrit.com, Spoken Sanskrit, 2019, Web. 30 March 2019.

286. "ena." SanskritDictionary.com, Sanskrit Dictionary, 2019. Web. 30 March 2019.
"ena." SpokenSanskrit.com, Spoken Sanskrit, 2019, Web. 30 March 2019.

287. "ka." SanskritDictionary.com, Sanskrit Dictionary, 2019. Web. 30 March 2019.

288. "enā." SanskritDictionary.com, Sanskrit Dictionary, 2019. Web. 30 March 2019.
"enA." SpokenSanskrit.com, Spoken Sanskrit, 2019, Web. 30 March 2019.

289. "iti." SanskritDictionary.com, Sanskrit Dictionary, 2019. Web. 30 March 2019.
"iti." SpokenSanskrit.com, Spoken Sanskrit, 2019, Web. 30 March 2019.

290. "yat." SpokenSanskrit.com, Spoken Sanskrit, 2019, Web. 30 March 2019.

291. "etat." SpokenSanskrit.com, Spoken Sanskrit, 2019, Web. 30 March 2019.

292. "id." Google Translate, https://translate.google.com/#view=home&op=translate&sl=la&tl=en&text=id, 2019, Web. 30 March 2019.

5.2 FAMILY RELATIONS AND SOCIAL TERMINOLOGY (p.102-110)

293. "mātṛ." SanskritDictionary.com, Sanskrit Dictionary, 2019. Web. 31 March 2019.
"mAtR." SpokenSanskrit.com, Spoken Sanskrit, 2019, Web. 31 March 2019.

294. "ambā." SanskritDictionary.com, Sanskrit Dictionary, 2019. Web. 31 March 2019.
"ambA." SpokenSanskrit.com, Spoken Sanskrit, 2019, Web. 31 March 2019.

295. "ambālikā." SanskritDictionary.com, Sanskrit Dictionary, 2019. Web. 31 March 2019.
"ambAlikA." SpokenSanskrit.com, Spoken Sanskrit, 2019, Web. 31 March 2019.

296. "attā." SanskritDictionary.com, Sanskrit Dictionary, 2019. Web. 31 March 2019.
"attA." SpokenSanskrit.com, Spoken Sanskrit, 2019, Web. 31 March 2019.

297. "pra." SanskritDictionary.com, Sanskrit Dictionary, 2019. Web. 31 March 2019.

298. "mAtuH." SpokenSanskrit.com, Spoken Sanskrit, 2019, Web. 31 March 2019.
(Note that mAtuH is not listed as a word on very reliable SanskritDictionary.com, but you you can find *mātuḥsvasṛ*, meaning 'sister of a mother' (where *svasṛ* means 'sister')

299. "attā." SanskritDictionary.com, Sanskrit Dictionary, 2019. Web. 31 March 2019.
"attA." SpokenSanskrit.com, Spoken Sanskrit, 2019, Web. 31 March 2019.

300. "kīlita." SanskritDictionary.com, Sanskrit Dictionary, 2019. Web. 31 March 2019.
"kIlita." SpokenSanskrit.com, Spoken Sanskrit, 2019, Web. 31 March 2019.

301. "ālāna." SanskritDictionary.com, Sanskrit Dictionary, 2019. Web. 31 March 2019.
"AlAna." SpokenSanskrit.com, Spoken Sanskrit, 2019, Web. 31 March 2019.

302. "glah." SanskritDictionary.com, Sanskrit Dictionary, 2019. Web. 31 March 2019.
"glah." SpokenSanskrit.com, Spoken Sanskrit, 2019, Web. 31 March 2019.

303. "anas." SanskritDictionary.com, Sanskrit Dictionary, 2019. Web. 31 March 2019.
"anas." SpokenSanskrit.com, Spoken Sanskrit, 2019, Web. 31 March 2019.

304. "sneha." SanskritDictionary.com, Sanskrit Dictionary, 2019. Web. 31 March 2019.
"sneha." SpokenSanskrit.com, Spoken Sanskrit, 2019, Web. 31 March 2019.

305. "nādh." SanskritDictionary.com, Sanskrit Dictionary, 2019. Web. 31 March 2019.
"nAdh." SpokenSanskrit.com, Spoken Sanskrit, 2019, Web. 31 March 2019.

306. "attā." SanskritDictionary.com, Sanskrit Dictionary, 2019. Web. 31 March 2019.
"attA." SpokenSanskrit.com, Spoken Sanskrit, 2019, Web. 31 March 2019.

307. "nah." SanskritDictionary.com, Sanskrit Dictionary, 2019. Web. 31 March 2019.
"nahyati." SpokenSanskrit.com, Spoken Sanskrit, 2019, Web. 31 March

2019.

308. "gnā." SanskritDictionary.com, Sanskrit Dictionary, 2019. Web. 31 March 2019.
"gnA." SpokenSanskrit.com, Spoken Sanskrit, 2019, Web. 31 March 2019.

309. "na." SanskritDictionary.com, Sanskrit Dictionary, 2019. Web. 31 March 2019.

310. "ṭu." SanskritDictionary.com, Sanskrit Dictionary, 2019. Web. 31 March 2019.

311. "sur." SanskritDictionary.com, Sanskrit Dictionary, 2019. Web. 31 March 2019.
"sur." SpokenSanskrit.com, Spoken Sanskrit, 2019, Web. 31 March 2019.

312. "tṝ." SanskritDictionary.com, Sanskrit Dictionary, 2019. Web. 31 March 2019.
"tRR." SpokenSanskrit.com, Spoken Sanskrit, 2019, Web. 31 March 2019.

313. "dhīra." SanskritDictionary.com, Sanskrit Dictionary, 2019. Web. 31 March 2019.
"dhIra." SpokenSanskrit.com, Spoken Sanskrit, 2019, Web. 31 March 2019.

314. "lih." SanskritDictionary.com, Sanskrit Dictionary, 2019. Web. 31 March 2019.
"lih." SpokenSanskrit.com, Spoken Sanskrit, 2019, Web. 31 March 2019.

315. "lāva." SanskritDictionary.com, Sanskrit Dictionary, 2019. Web. 1 April 2019.
"lAva." SpokenSanskrit.com, Spoken Sanskrit, 2019, Web. 1 April 2019.

316. "tan." SanskritDictionary.com, Sanskrit Dictionary, 2019. Web. 1 April 2019.
"tan." SpokenSanskrit.com, Spoken Sanskrit, 2019, Web. 1 April 2019.

317. "ūḍha." SanskritDictionary.com, Sanskrit Dictionary, 2019. Web. 1 April 2019.
"UDha." SpokenSanskrit.com, Spoken Sanskrit, 2019, Web. 1 April 2019.

5.3 SOME RANDOM ETRUSCAN WORDS (p.111-127)

318. "kal." SanskritDictionary.com, Sanskrit Dictionary, 2019. Web. 1 April 2019.
"kalayati." SpokenSanskrit.com, Spoken Sanskrit, 2019, Web. 1 April 2019.

319. "kāla." SanskritDictionary.com, Sanskrit Dictionary, 2019. Web. 1 April 2019.

320. "room." Dictionary.com, Dictionary.com, 2019. Web. 10 April 2019.

321. "keli." SanskritDictionary.com, Sanskrit Dictionary, 2019. Web. 1 April 2019.
"keli." SpokenSanskrit.com, Spoken Sanskrit, 2019, Web. 1 April 2019.

322. "kara." SanskritDictionary.com, Sanskrit Dictionary, 2019. Web. 1 April 2019.
"kara." SpokenSanskrit.com, Spoken Sanskrit, 2019, Web. 1 April 2019.

323. "karoti." SpokenSanskrit.com, Spoken Sanskrit, 2019, Web. 1 April 2019.

324. "kṛ." SanskritDictionary.com, Sanskrit Dictionary, 2019. Web. 1 April 2019.

325. "kara." SanskritDictionary.com, Sanskrit Dictionary, 2019. Web. 1 April 2019.
"kara." SpokenSanskrit.com, Spoken Sanskrit, 2019, Web. 1 April 2019.

326. "gṛhakāraka." SanskritDictionary.com, Sanskrit Dictionary, 2019. Web. 1 April 2019.
"gRhakAraka ." SpokenSanskrit.com, Spoken Sanskrit, 2019, Web. 1 April 2019.

327. "gṛhakārin." SanskritDictionary.com, Sanskrit Dictionary, 2019. Web. 1 April 2019.
" gRhakArin ." SpokenSanskrit.com, Spoken Sanskrit, 2019, Web. 1 April 2019.

328. "kūl." SanskritDictionary.com, Sanskrit Dictionary, 2019. Web. 1 April 2019.
"kUl." SpokenSanskrit.com, Spoken Sanskrit, 2019, Web. 1 April 2019.

329. "kva." SanskritDictionary.com, Sanskrit Dictionary, 2019. Web. 1 April 2019.
"kva." SpokenSanskrit.com, Spoken Sanskrit, 2019, Web. 1 April 2019.

330. "kula." SanskritDictionary.com, Sanskrit Dictionary, 2019. Web. 1 April 2019.
"kula." SpokenSanskrit.com, Spoken Sanskrit, 2019, Web. 1 April 2019.

331. "dur." SanskritDictionary.com, Sanskrit Dictionary, 2019. Web. 1 April 2019.
"dur." SpokenSanskrit.com, Spoken Sanskrit, 2019, Web. 1 April 2019.

332. "vṛtti." SanskritDictionary.com, Sanskrit Dictionary, 2019. Web. 1 April 2019.
"vRtti." SpokenSanskrit.com, Spoken Sanskrit, 2019, Web. 1 April 2019.

333. "vāra." SanskritDictionary.com, Sanskrit Dictionary, 2019. Web. 1 April 2019.
"vAra." SpokenSanskrit.com, Spoken Sanskrit, 2019, Web. 1 April 2019.

334. "ātā." SanskritDictionary.com, Sanskrit Dictionary, 2019. Web. 1 April 2019.
"AtA." SpokenSanskrit.com, Spoken Sanskrit, 2019, Web. 1 April 2019.

335. "vṛt." SanskritDictionary.com, Sanskrit Dictionary, 2019. Web. 1 April 2019.
"vRt." SpokenSanskrit.com, Spoken Sanskrit, 2019, Web. 1 April 2019.

336. "aṇu." SanskritDictionary.com, Sanskrit Dictionary, 2019. Web. 1 April 2019.

337. "vartana." SanskritDictionary.com, Sanskrit Dictionary, 2019. Web. 1 April 2019.
"vartana." SpokenSanskrit.com, Spoken Sanskrit, 2019, Web. 1 April 2019.

338. "lok." SanskritDictionary.com, Sanskrit Dictionary, 2019. Web. 1 April 2019.
"lokate." SpokenSanskrit.com, Spoken Sanskrit, 2019, Web. 1 April 2019.

339. "mal." SanskritDictionary.com, Sanskrit Dictionary, 2019. Web. 1 April 2019.
"malate." SpokenSanskrit.com, Spoken Sanskrit, 2019, Web. 1 April 2019.

340. "ena." SanskritDictionary.com, Sanskrit Dictionary, 2019. Web. 1 April 2019.
"ena." SpokenSanskrit.com, Spoken Sanskrit, 2019, Web. 1 April 2019.

341. "strī." SanskritDictionary.com, Sanskrit Dictionary, 2019. Web. 1 April 2019.
"strI." SpokenSanskrit.com, Spoken Sanskrit, 2019, Web. 1 April 2019.

342. "mā." SanskritDictionary.com, Sanskrit Dictionary, 2019. Web. 1 April 2019.
"mAyate." SpokenSanskrit.com, Spoken Sanskrit, 2019, Web. 1 April 2019.

343. "stṛ." SanskritDictionary.com, Sanskrit Dictionary, 2019. Web. 1 April 2019.
"striyate." SpokenSanskrit.com, Spoken Sanskrit, 2019, Web. 1 April 2019.

344. "avi." SanskritDictionary.com, Sanskrit Dictionary, 2019. Web. 1 April 2019.

345 "sava." SanskritDictionary.com, Sanskrit Dictionary, 2019. Web. 1 April 2019.
"sava." SpokenSanskrit.com, Spoken Sanskrit, 2019, Web. 1 April 2019.

346. "īr." SanskritDictionary.com, Sanskrit Dictionary, 2019. Web. 1 April 2019.
"Irte." SpokenSanskrit.com, Spoken Sanskrit, 2019, Web. 1 April 2019.

347. "Ar." SanskritDictionary.com, Sanskrit Dictionary, 2019. Web. 1 April 2019.
"Arpayati." SpokenSanskrit.com, Spoken Sanskrit, 2019, Web. 1 April 2019.

348. "ṛ." SanskritDictionary.com, Sanskrit Dictionary, 2019. Web. 1 April 2019.

439. "rasā." SanskritDictionary.com, Sanskrit Dictionary, 2019. Web. 1 April 2019.
"rasA." SpokenSanskrit.com, Spoken Sanskrit, 2019, Web. 1 April 2019.

440. "du." SanskritDictionary.com, Sanskrit Dictionary, 2019. Web. 1 April 2019.

"dunoti." SpokenSanskrit.com, Spoken Sanskrit, 2019, Web. 1 April 2019.

441. "dhūma." SanskritDictionary.com, Sanskrit Dictionary, 2019. Web. 1 April 2019.
"dhUma." SpokenSanskrit.com, Spoken Sanskrit, 2019, Web. 1 April 2019.

442. "dura." SanskritDictionary.com, Sanskrit Dictionary, 2019. Web. 1 April 2019.
"dura." SpokenSanskrit.com, Spoken Sanskrit, 2019, Web. 1 April 2019.

443. "bhaṇ." SanskritDictionary.com, Sanskrit Dictionary, 2019. Web. 2 April 2019.
"bhaNati." SpokenSanskrit.com, Spoken Sanskrit, 2019, Web. 2 April 2019.

444. "tūṇa." SanskritDictionary.com, Sanskrit Dictionary, 2019. Web. 2 April 2019.
"tUNa." SpokenSanskrit.com, Spoken Sanskrit, 2019, Web. 2 April 2019.

445. "dharā." SanskritDictionary.com, Sanskrit Dictionary, 2019. Web. 2 April 2019.
"dharA." SpokenSanskrit.com, Spoken Sanskrit, 2019, Web. 2 April 2019.

446. "dhāra." SanskritDictionary.com, Sanskrit Dictionary, 2019. Web. 2 April 2019.
"dhAra." SpokenSanskrit.com, Spoken Sanskrit, 2019, Web. 2 April 2019.

447. "nāra." SanskritDictionary.com, Sanskrit Dictionary, 2019. Web. 2 April 2019.
"nAra." SpokenSanskrit.com, Spoken Sanskrit, 2019, Web. 2 April 2019.

448. "nīra." SanskritDictionary.com, Sanskrit Dictionary, 2019. Web. 2 April 2019.
"nIra." SpokenSanskrit.com, Spoken Sanskrit, 2019, Web. 2 April 2019.

449. "ka." SanskritDictionary.com, Sanskrit Dictionary, 2019. Web. 2 April 2019.

450. "ṇa." SanskritDictionary.com, Sanskrit Dictionary, 2019. Web. 2 April 2019.

451. "kan." SanskritDictionary.com, Sanskrit Dictionary, 2019. Web. 2 April 2019.
"kanati." SpokenSanskrit.com, Spoken Sanskrit, 2019, Web. 2 April 2019.

452. "klaitakika." SanskritDictionary.com, Sanskrit Dictionary, 2019. Web. 2 April 2019.
"klaitakika." SpokenSanskrit.com, Spoken Sanskrit, 2019, Web. 2 April 2019.

453. "kṛkavāku." SanskritDictionary.com, Sanskrit Dictionary, 2019. Web. 2 April 2019.
"kRkavAku." SpokenSanskrit.com, Spoken Sanskrit, 2019, Web. 2 April 2019.

454. "piṭ." SanskritDictionary.com, Sanskrit Dictionary, 2019. Web. 2 April 2019.
"peTati." SpokenSanskrit.com, Spoken Sanskrit, 2019, Web. 2 April 2019.

455. "madhu." SanskritDictionary.com, Sanskrit Dictionary, 2019. Web. 2 April 2019.
"madhu." SpokenSanskrit.com, Spoken Sanskrit, 2019, Web. 2 April 2019.

456. "tallī." SanskritDictionary.com, Sanskrit Dictionary, 2019. Web. 2 April 2019.
"tallI." SpokenSanskrit.com, Spoken Sanskrit, 2019, Web. 2 April 2019.

457. "ta." SanskritDictionary.com, Sanskrit Dictionary, 2019. Web. 2 April 2019.
"ta." SpokenSanskrit.com, Spoken Sanskrit, 2019, Web. 2 April 2019.

458. "laṭ." SanskritDictionary.com, Sanskrit Dictionary, 2019. Web. 2 April 2019.
"laT." SpokenSanskrit.com, Spoken Sanskrit, 2019, Web. 2 April 2019.

459. "dī." SanskritDictionary.com, Sanskrit Dictionary, 2019. Web. 2 April 2019.
"dideti." SpokenSanskrit.com, Spoken Sanskrit, 2019, Web. 2 April 2019.

460. "uru." SanskritDictionary.com, Sanskrit Dictionary, 2019. Web. 2 April 2019.
"uru." SpokenSanskrit.com, Spoken Sanskrit, 2019, Web. 2 April 2019.

461. "vṛ." SanskritDictionary.com, Sanskrit Dictionary, 2019. Web. 2 April 2019.
"varate." SpokenSanskrit.com, Spoken Sanskrit, 2019, Web. 2 April 2019.

462. "aṣ." SanskritDictionary.com, Sanskrit Dictionary, 2019. Web. 2 April 2019.
"aSati." SpokenSanskrit.com, Spoken Sanskrit, 2019, Web. 2 April 2019.

463. "tupi." http://www.etruskisch.de/pgs/vc.htm, Etruscology – Website by Dieter H. Steinbauer, 14 June 2002. Web. 2 April 2019.

464. "tup." SanskritDictionary.com, Sanskrit Dictionary, 2019. Web. 2 April 2019.
"tupati." SpokenSanskrit.com, Spoken Sanskrit, 2019, Web. 2 April 2019.

465. "vṛṣ." SanskritDictionary.com, Sanskrit Dictionary, 2019. Web. 2 April 2019.
"vRS." SpokenSanskrit.com, Spoken Sanskrit, 2019, Web. 2 April 2019.

466. "vṛṣa." SanskritDictionary.com, Sanskrit Dictionary, 2019. Web. 2 April 2019.
"vRSa." SpokenSanskrit.com, Spoken Sanskrit, 2019, Web. 2 April 2019.

467. "vārya." SanskritDictionary.com, Sanskrit Dictionary, 2019. Web. 2 April 2019.
"vArya." SpokenSanskrit.com, Spoken Sanskrit, 2019, Web. 2 April 2019.

468. "ca." SanskritDictionary.com, Sanskrit Dictionary, 2019. Web. 2 April 2019.

469. "vārī." SanskritDictionary.com, Sanskrit Dictionary, 2019. Web. 2 April 2019.
"vArI." SpokenSanskrit.com, Spoken Sanskrit, 2019, Web. 2 April 2019.

470. "aja." SanskritDictionary.com, Sanskrit Dictionary, 2019. Web. 2 April 2019.
"aja." SpokenSanskrit.com, Spoken Sanskrit, 2019, Web. 2 April 2019.

471. "vīra." SanskritDictionary.com, Sanskrit Dictionary, 2019. Web. 2 April 2019.
"vIra." SpokenSanskrit.com, Spoken Sanskrit, 2019, Web. 2 April 2019.

472. "sva." SanskritDictionary.com, Sanskrit Dictionary, 2019. Web. 2 April 2019.

"sva." SpokenSanskrit.com, Spoken Sanskrit, 2019, Web. 2 April 2019.

473. "lṛ." SanskritDictionary.com, Sanskrit Dictionary, 2019. Web. 2 April 2019.
"lR." SpokenSanskrit.com, Spoken Sanskrit, 2019, Web. 2 April 2019.

5.4 RELIGIOUS TERMS (p.128-138)

474. "dṛ." SanskritDictionary.com, Sanskrit Dictionary, 2019. Web. 3 April 2019.
"driyate." SpokenSanskrit.com, Spoken Sanskrit, 2019, Web. 3 April 2019.

475. "ud." SanskritDictionary.com, Sanskrit Dictionary, 2019. Web. 3 April 2019.
"undate." SpokenSanskrit.com, Spoken Sanskrit, 2019, Web. 3 April 2019.

476. "uda." SanskritDictionary.com, Sanskrit Dictionary, 2019. Web. 3 April 2019.
"uda." SpokenSanskrit.com, Spoken Sanskrit, 2019, Web. 3 April 2019.

477. "nāśa." SanskritDictionary.com, Sanskrit Dictionary, 2019. Web. 3 April 2019.
"nAza." SpokenSanskrit.com, Spoken Sanskrit, 2019, Web. 3 April 2019.

478. "anāśa." SanskritDictionary.com, Sanskrit Dictionary, 2019. Web. 3 April 2019.
"anAza." SpokenSanskrit.com, Spoken Sanskrit, 2019, Web. 3 April 2019.

479. "ṭā." SanskritDictionary.com, Sanskrit Dictionary, 2019. Web. 3 April 2019.

480. "dā." SanskritDictionary.com, Sanskrit Dictionary, 2019. Web. 3 April 2019.

481. "kag." SanskritDictionary.com, Sanskrit Dictionary, 2019. Web. 3 April 2019.
"kagati." SpokenSanskrit.com, Spoken Sanskrit, 2019, Web. 3 April 2019.

482. "khaga." SanskritDictionary.com, Sanskrit Dictionary, 2019. Web. 3

April 2019.
"khaga." SpokenSanskrit.com, Spoken Sanskrit, 2019, Web. 3 April 2019.

483. "kha." SanskritDictionary.com, Sanskrit Dictionary, 2019. Web. 3 April 2019.

484. "nṛ." SanskritDictionary.com, Sanskrit Dictionary, 2019. Web. 3 April 2019.

485. "nara." SanskritDictionary.com, Sanskrit Dictionary, 2019. Web. 3 April 2019.
"nara." SpokenSanskrit.com, Spoken Sanskrit, 2019, Web. 3 April 2019.

486. "nāra." SanskritDictionary.com, Sanskrit Dictionary, 2019. Web. 3 April 2019.
"nAra." SpokenSanskrit.com, Spoken Sanskrit, 2019, Web. 3 April 2019.

487. "ga." SanskritDictionary.com, Sanskrit Dictionary, 2019. Web. 3 April 2019.

488. "glev." SanskritDictionary.com, Sanskrit Dictionary, 2019. Web. 3 April 2019.
"glevate." SpokenSanskrit.com, Spoken Sanskrit, 2019, Web. 3 April 2019.

489. "gṝ." SanskritDictionary.com, Sanskrit Dictionary, 2019. Web. 3 April 2019.
"gRNati." SpokenSanskrit.com, Spoken Sanskrit, 2019, Web. 3 April 2019.

490. "avi." SanskritDictionary.com, Sanskrit Dictionary, 2019. Web. 3 April 2019.

491. "av." SanskritDictionary.com, Sanskrit Dictionary, 2019. Web. 3 April 2019.
"avati." SpokenSanskrit.com, Spoken Sanskrit, 2019, Web. 3 April 2019.

492. "ṣa." SanskritDictionary.com, Sanskrit Dictionary, 2019. Web. 3 April 2019.

493. "kha." SanskritDictionary.com, Sanskrit Dictionary, 2019. Web. 3 April 2019.

494. "sacro" http://www.latin-dictionary.net/search/latin/sacer,

LatDict, 2019. Web. 4 April 2019.

495 "sacer" http://www.latin-dictionary.net/search/latin/sacer, LatDict, 2019. Web. 4 April 2019.

496. "kṛ." SanskritDictionary.com, Sanskrit Dictionary, 2019. Web. 4 April 2019.
"karoti." SpokenSanskrit.com, Spoken Sanskrit, 2019, Web. 4 April 2019.

497. "cleri." http://www.latin-dictionary.net/search/latin/cleri, LatDict, 2019. Web. 4 April 2019.

498. "gṝ." SanskritDictionary.com, Sanskrit Dictionary, 2019. Web. 3 April 2019.
"gRNati." SpokenSanskrit.com, Spoken Sanskrit, 2019, Web. 3 April 2019.

499. "va." SanskritDictionary.com, Sanskrit Dictionary, 2019. Web. 4 April 2019.

500. "ari." SanskritDictionary.com, Sanskrit Dictionary, 2019. Web. 3 April 2019.
"ari." SpokenSanskrit.com, Spoken Sanskrit, 2019, Web. 3 April 2019.

501. "va." SanskritDictionary.com, Sanskrit Dictionary, 2019. Web. 3 April 2019.

502. "kal." SanskritDictionary.com, Sanskrit Dictionary, 2019. Web. 4 April 2019.
"kAlayati." SpokenSanskrit.com, Spoken Sanskrit, 2019, Web. 4 April 2019.

503. "khala." SanskritDictionary.com, Sanskrit Dictionary, 2019. Web. 4 April 2019.
"khala." SpokenSanskrit.com, Spoken Sanskrit, 2019, Web. 4 April 2019.

504. "du." SanskritDictionary.com, Sanskrit Dictionary, 2019. Web. 4 April 2019.
"dunoti." SpokenSanskrit.com, Spoken Sanskrit, 2019, Web. 4 April 2019.

505. "tu." SanskritDictionary.com, Sanskrit Dictionary, 2019. Web. 4 April 2019.

506. "ra." SanskritDictionary.com, Sanskrit Dictionary, 2019. Web. 4 April 2019.

507. dhur." SanskritDictionary.com, Sanskrit Dictionary, 2019. Web. 4 April 2019.

5.5 POLITICAL TERMS (p.139-162)

507. Wikisource contributors. "From the Founding of the City/Book 1.The Earliest Legends of Rome, 34 " Wikisource . Wikisource , 21 Jan. 2019. Web. 5 Apr. 2019.

508. "laukya." SanskritDictionary.com, Sanskrit Dictionary, 2019. Web. 5 April 2019.
"laukya." SpokenSanskrit.com, Spoken Sanskrit, 2019, Web. 5 April 2019.

509. "lokya." SanskritDictionary.com, Sanskrit Dictionary, 2019. Web. 5 April 2019.
"lokya." SpokenSanskrit.com, Spoken Sanskrit, 2019, Web. 5 April 2019.

510. "uma." SanskritDictionary.com, Sanskrit Dictionary, 2019. Web. 5 April 2019.
"uma." SpokenSanskrit.com, Spoken Sanskrit, 2019, Web. 5 April 2019.

511. "ūma." SanskritDictionary.com, Sanskrit Dictionary, 2019. Web. 5 April 2019.
"Uma." SpokenSanskrit.com, Spoken Sanskrit, 2019, Web. 5 April 2019.

512. "loka." SanskritDictionary.com, Sanskrit Dictionary, 2019. Web. 5 April 2019.
"loka." SpokenSanskrit.com, Spoken Sanskrit, 2019, Web. 5 April 2019.

513. "oma." SanskritDictionary.com, Sanskrit Dictionary, 2019. Web. 5 April 2019.
"oma." SpokenSanskrit.com, Spoken Sanskrit, 2019, Web. 5 April 2019.

514. "laukika." SanskritDictionary.com, Sanskrit Dictionary, 2019. Web. 5 April 2019.
"laukika." SpokenSanskrit.com, Spoken Sanskrit, 2019, Web. 5 April 2019.

515. "lokanātha." SanskritDictionary.com, Sanskrit Dictionary, 2019.

Web. 5 April 2019.
"lokanAtha." SpokenSanskrit.com, Spoken Sanskrit, 2019, Web. 5 April 2019.

516. "lokapāla." SanskritDictionary.com, Sanskrit Dictionary, 2019. Web. 5 April 2019.
"lokapAla." SpokenSanskrit.com, Spoken Sanskrit, 2019, Web. 5 April 2019.

517. "lokapālaka." SanskritDictionary.com, Sanskrit Dictionary, 2019. Web. 5 April 2019.
"lokapAlaka." SpokenSanskrit.com, Spoken Sanskrit, 2019, Web. 5 April 2019.

518. "nātha." SanskritDictionary.com, Sanskrit Dictionary, 2019. Web. 5 April 2019.
"nAtha." SpokenSanskrit.com, Spoken Sanskrit, 2019, Web. 5 April 2019.

519. "pāla." SanskritDictionary.com, Sanskrit Dictionary, 2019. Web. 5 April 2019.
"pAla." SpokenSanskrit.com, Spoken Sanskrit, 2019, Web. 5 April 2019.

520. "pālaka." SanskritDictionary.com, Sanskrit Dictionary, 2019. Web. 5 April 2019.
"pAlaka." SpokenSanskrit.com, Spoken Sanskrit, 2019, Web. 5 April 2019.

521. Wikipedia contributors. "Alexander." Wikipedia, The Free Encyclopedia. Wikipedia, The Free Encyclopedia, 4 Apr. 2019. Web. 6 Apr. 2019.

522. Wikipedia contributors. "Dictator." Wikipedia, The Free Encyclopedia. Wikipedia, The Free Encyclopedia, 26 Mar. 2019. Web. 6 Apr. 2019.

523. "pṛth." SanskritDictionary.com, Sanskrit Dictionary, 2019. Web. 6 April 2019.
"pRth." SpokenSanskrit.com, Spoken Sanskrit, 2019, Web. 5 April 2019.

524. "pūrti." SanskritDictionary.com, Sanskrit Dictionary, 2019. Web. 6 April 2019.
"pUrti." SpokenSanskrit.com, Spoken Sanskrit, 2019, Web. 5 April 2019.

525. "tha." SanskritDictionary.com, Sanskrit Dictionary, 2019. Web. 6 April 2019.
"tha." SpokenSanskrit.com, Spoken Sanskrit, 2019, Web. 6 April 2019.

526. "pūrta." SanskritDictionary.com, Sanskrit Dictionary, 2019. Web. 6 April 2019.
"pūrta." SpokenSanskrit.com, Spoken Sanskrit, 2019, Web. 6 April 2019.

527. Macnamara, Ellen - Everyday Life of the Etruscans, p. 166, Dorset Press, New York, USA, 1987.

528. "pur." SanskritDictionary.com, Sanskrit Dictionary, 2019. Web. 6 April 2019.
"pur." SpokenSanskrit.com, Spoken Sanskrit, 2019, Web. 6 April 2019.

529. "si." SanskritDictionary.com, Sanskrit Dictionary, 2019. Web. 6 April 2019.

530. "lā." SanskritDictionary.com, Sanskrit Dictionary, 2019. Web. 6 April 2019.

531. "ka." SanskritDictionary.com, Sanskrit Dictionary, 2019. Web. 6 April 2019.

532. "sil." SanskritDictionary.com, Sanskrit Dictionary, 2019. Web. 6 April 2019.

533. "śila." SanskritDictionary.com, Sanskrit Dictionary, 2019. Web. 7 April 2019.
"zila." SpokenSanskrit.com, Spoken Sanskrit, 2019, Web. 7 April 2019.

534. Wikipedia contributors. "Roman censor." Wikipedia, The Free Encyclopedia. Wikipedia, The Free Encyclopedia, 16 Mar. 2019. Web. 7 Apr. 2019.

535. "gam." SanskritDictionary.com, Sanskrit Dictionary, 2019. Web. 7 April 2019.
"gamati." SpokenSanskrit.com, Spoken Sanskrit, 2019, Web. 7 April 2019.

536. "dhī." SanskritDictionary.com, Sanskrit Dictionary, 2019. Web. 7 April 2019.

537. "uma." SanskritDictionary.com, Sanskrit Dictionary, 2019. Web. 7

April 2019.

538. "maṭha." SanskritDictionary.com, Sanskrit Dictionary, 2019. Web. 7 April 2019.
"maTha." SpokenSanskrit.com, Spoken Sanskrit, 2019, Web. 7 April 2019.

539. Wikipedia contributors. "Pomerium." Wikipedia, The Free Encyclopedia. Wikipedia, The Free Encyclopedia, 19 Oct. 2018. Web. 7 Apr. 2019.

540. Scullard, Howard Heyes - The Etruscan Cities & Rome, p. 75-76, The Johns Hopkins University Press, Baltimore, 1998.

541. Krishna, Nanditha -"The book of Demons : including a dictionary of Demons in Sanskrit literature", p.117, Penguin Books India, New Delhi, 2007.

542. "māḍ." SanskritDictionary.com, Sanskrit Dictionary, 2019. Web. 8 April 2019.
"mADate." SpokenSanskrit.com, Spoken Sanskrit, 2019, Web. 8 April 2019.

543. "ālī." SanskritDictionary.com, Sanskrit Dictionary, 2019. Web. 8 April 2019.
"AlI." SpokenSanskrit.com, Spoken Sanskrit, 2019, Web. 8 April 2019.

544. "hali." SanskritDictionary.com, Sanskrit Dictionary, 2019. Web. 8 April 2019.
"hali." SpokenSanskrit.com, Spoken Sanskrit, 2019, Web. 8 April 2019.

545. "bhūmi." SanskritDictionary.com, Sanskrit Dictionary, 2019. Web. 8 April 2019.
"bhUmi." SpokenSanskrit.com, Spoken Sanskrit, 2019, Web. 8 April 2019.

546. "arya." SanskritDictionary.com, Sanskrit Dictionary, 2019. Web. 8 April 2019.
"arya." SpokenSanskrit.com, Spoken Sanskrit, 2019, Web. 8 April 2019.

547. "bhū." SanskritDictionary.com, Sanskrit Dictionary, 2019. Web. 8 April 2019.
"bhU." SpokenSanskrit.com, Spoken Sanskrit, 2019, Web. 8 April 2019.

548. "maryā." SanskritDictionary.com, Sanskrit Dictionary, 2019. Web. 8 April 2019.
"maryA." SpokenSanskrit.com, Spoken Sanskrit, 2019, Web. 8 April 2019.

549. "halā." SanskritDictionary.com, Sanskrit Dictionary, 2019. Web. 8 April 2019.
"halA." SpokenSanskrit.com, Spoken Sanskrit, 2019, Web. 8 April 2019.

550. Becker Wills, Hilary - "Political System and Law", contributing article in the book "The Etruscan World", edited by Jean MacIntosh Turfa, p. 361, Routledge Taylor & Francis Group, London and New York, 2013.

551. "dvi." SanskritDictionary.com, Sanskrit Dictionary, 2019. Web. 8 April 2019.

552. "magha." SanskritDictionary.com, Sanskrit Dictionary, 2019. Web. 8 April 2019.
"magha." SpokenSanskrit.com, Spoken Sanskrit, 2019, Web. 8 April 2019.

553. "trā." SanskritDictionary.com, Sanskrit Dictionary, 2019. Web. 8 April 2019.
"trA." SpokenSanskrit.com, Spoken Sanskrit, 2019, Web. 8 April 2019.

554. "av." SanskritDictionary.com, Sanskrit Dictionary, 2019. Web. 8 April 2019.
"avati." SpokenSanskrit.com, Spoken Sanskrit, 2019, Web. 8 April 2019.

555. "tṝ." SanskritDictionary.com, Sanskrit Dictionary, 2019. Web. 8 April 2019.
"tarati." SpokenSanskrit.com, Spoken Sanskrit, 2019, Web. 8 April 2019.

556. "mākha." SanskritDictionary.com, Sanskrit Dictionary, 2019. Web. 10 April 2019.
"mAkha." SpokenSanskrit.com, Spoken Sanskrit, 2019, Web. 10 April 2019.

557. "megha." SanskritDictionary.com, Sanskrit Dictionary, 2019. Web. 10 April 2019.
"megha." SpokenSanskrit.com, Spoken Sanskrit, 2019, Web. 10 April 2019.

558. "parṇa." SanskritDictionary.com, Sanskrit Dictionary, 2019. Web. 10 April 2019.
"parNa." SpokenSanskrit.com, Spoken Sanskrit, 2019, Web. 10 April 2019.

559. Wikipedia contributors. "Tribune." Wikipedia, The Free Encyclopedia. Wikipedia, The Free Encyclopedia, 30 Mar. 2019. Web. 10 Apr. 2019.

560. "tribune." Dictionary.com, Dictionary.com, 2019. Web. 10 April 2019.

561. "attā." SanskritDictionary.com, Sanskrit Dictionary, 2019. Web. 10 April 2019.
"attA." SpokenSanskrit.com, Spoken Sanskrit, 2019, Web. 10 April 2019.

562. "oma." SanskritDictionary.com, Sanskrit Dictionary, 2019. Web. 10 April 2019.
"oma." SpokenSanskrit.com, Spoken Sanskrit, 2019, Web. 10 April 2019.

563. "raṭh." SanskritDictionary.com, Sanskrit Dictionary, 2019. Web. 10 April 2019.
"raThati." SpokenSanskrit.com, Spoken Sanskrit, 2019, Web. 10 April 2019.

564. "ūma." SanskritDictionary.com, Sanskrit Dictionary, 2019. Web. 10 April 2019.
"Uma." SpokenSanskrit.com, Spoken Sanskrit, 2019, Web. 10 April 2019.

565. "rādh." SanskritDictionary.com, Sanskrit Dictionary, 2019. Web. 10 April 2019.
"rAdhayati." SpokenSanskrit.com, Spoken Sanskrit, 2019, Web. 10 April 2019.

566. "ṛta." SanskritDictionary.com, Sanskrit Dictionary, 2019. Web. 10 April 2019.
"Rta." SpokenSanskrit.com, Spoken Sanskrit, 2019, Web. 10 April 2019.

5.6 CULTURE AND ENTERTAINMENT (p.163-169)

567. "hasitṛ." SanskritDictionary.com, Sanskrit Dictionary, 2019. Web. 10 April 2019.
"hasitR." SpokenSanskrit.com, Spoken Sanskrit, 2019, Web. 10 April

2019.

568. "has." SanskritDictionary.com, Sanskrit Dictionary, 2019. Web. 10 April 2019.
"hasati." SpokenSanskrit.com, Spoken Sanskrit, 2019, Web. 10 April 2019.

569. "tṝ." SanskritDictionary.com, Sanskrit Dictionary, 2019. Web. 10 April 2019.
"tarati." SpokenSanskrit.com, Spoken Sanskrit, 2019, Web. 10 April 2019.

570. "puruṣa." SanskritDictionary.com, Sanskrit Dictionary, 2019. Web. 10 April 2019.
"puruSa." SpokenSanskrit.com, Spoken Sanskrit, 2019, Web. 10 April 2019.

571. "āna." SanskritDictionary.com, Sanskrit Dictionary, 2019. Web. 10 April 2019.
"Ana." SpokenSanskrit.com, Spoken Sanskrit, 2019, Web. 10 April 2019.

572. "puras." SanskritDictionary.com, Sanskrit Dictionary, 2019. Web. 10 April 2019.
"puras." SpokenSanskrit.com, Spoken Sanskrit, 2019, Web. 10 April 2019.

573 "oṇi." SanskritDictionary.com, Sanskrit Dictionary, 2019. Web. 21 March 2019.
"oNi." SpokenSanskrit.com, Spoken Sanskrit, 2019, Web. 21 March 2019.

574. "para." SanskritDictionary.com, Sanskrit Dictionary, 2019. Web. 10 April 2019.
"para." SpokenSanskrit.com, Spoken Sanskrit, 2019, Web. 10 April 2019.

575. "pāra." SanskritDictionary.com, Sanskrit Dictionary, 2019. Web. 10 April 2019.
"pAra." SpokenSanskrit.com, Spoken Sanskrit, 2019, Web. 10 April 2019.

576. "sū." SanskritDictionary.com, Sanskrit Dictionary, 2019. Web. 10 April 2019.

577. "bhārati." SanskritDictionary.com, Sanskrit Dictionary, 2019. Web.

10 April 2019.
"bhArati." SpokenSanskrit.com, Spoken Sanskrit, 2019, Web. 10 April 2019.

578. "bhara." SanskritDictionary.com, Sanskrit Dictionary, 2019. Web. 10 April 2019.
"bhara." SpokenSanskrit.com, Spoken Sanskrit, 2019, Web. 10 April 2019.

579. "bharata." SanskritDictionary.com, Sanskrit Dictionary, 2019. Web. 10 April 2019.
"bharata." SpokenSanskrit.com, Spoken Sanskrit, 2019, Web. 10 April 2019.

580. "su." SanskritDictionary.com, Sanskrit Dictionary, 2019. Web. 10 April 2019.
"sunoti." SpokenSanskrit.com, Spoken Sanskrit, 2019, Web. 10 April 2019.

581. "su." SanskritDictionary.com, Sanskrit Dictionary, 2019. Web. 10 April 2019.
"savati." SpokenSanskrit.com, Spoken Sanskrit, 2019, Web. 10 April 2019.

582. "plu." SanskritDictionary.com, Sanskrit Dictionary, 2019. Web. 10 April 2019.
"plavate." SpokenSanskrit.com, Spoken Sanskrit, 2019, Web. 10 April 2019.

583. "likh." SanskritDictionary.com, Sanskrit Dictionary, 2019. Web. 11 April 2019.
"likhati." SpokenSanskrit.com, Spoken Sanskrit, 2019, Web. 11 April 2019.

584. "saha." SanskritDictionary.com, Sanskrit Dictionary, 2019. Web. 11 April 2019.

585. "sa." SanskritDictionary.com, Sanskrit Dictionary, 2019. Web. 11 April 2019.

586. "sama." SanskritDictionary.com, Sanskrit Dictionary, 2019. Web. 11 April 2019.

587. "grābha." SanskritDictionary.com, Sanskrit Dictionary, 2019. Web.

11 April 2019.
"grAbha." SpokenSanskrit.com, Spoken Sanskrit, 2019, Web. 11 April 2019.

5.7 FUNERARY CUSTOMS (p.170-183)

589. "ṭā." SanskritDictionary.com, Sanskrit Dictionary, 2019. Web. 11 April 2019.

590. "uru." SanskritDictionary.com, Sanskrit Dictionary, 2019. Web. 11 April 2019.
"uru." SpokenSanskrit.com, Spoken Sanskrit, 2019, Web. 11 April 2019.

591. "dā." SanskritDictionary.com, Sanskrit Dictionary, 2019. Web. 11 April 2019.

592. "vṛ." SanskritDictionary.com, Sanskrit Dictionary, 2019. Web. 11 April 2019.

593. "hīna." SanskritDictionary.com, Sanskrit Dictionary, 2019. Web. 11 April 2019.
"hIna." SpokenSanskrit.com, Spoken Sanskrit, 2019, Web. 11 April 2019.

594. "dha." SpokenSanskrit.com, Spoken Sanskrit, 2019. Web. 11 April 2019.

595. "dha." SanskritDictionary.com, Sanskrit Dictionary, 2019. Web. 11 April 2019.

596. Pallottino, Massimo – The Etruscans, p. 217-218, the revised and enlarged hardcover edition based on the sixth Italian edition, Edited by David Ridgway, Indiana University Press, Bloomington & London, 1975.

597. "lupta." SanskritDictionary.com, Sanskrit Dictionary, 2019. Web. 11 April 2019.
"lupta." SpokenSanskrit.com, Spoken Sanskrit, 2019, Web. 11 April 2019.

598. "luptatā." SanskritDictionary.com, Sanskrit Dictionary, 2019. Web. 11 April 2019.
"luptatA." SpokenSanskrit.com, Spoken Sanskrit, 2019, Web. 11 April 2019.

599. "lup." SanskritDictionary.com, Sanskrit Dictionary, 2019. Web. 11

April 2019.
"lumpate." SpokenSanskrit.com, Spoken Sanskrit, 2019, Web. 11 April 2019.

600. "śava." SanskritDictionary.com, Sanskrit Dictionary, 2019. Web. 11 April 2019.
"zava." SpokenSanskrit.com, Spoken Sanskrit, 2019, Web. 11 April 2019.

601. "śavas." SanskritDictionary.com, Sanskrit Dictionary, 2019. Web. 11 April 2019.
"zavas." SpokenSanskrit.com, Spoken Sanskrit, 2019, Web. 11 April 2019.

602. "jīvā." SanskritDictionary.com, Sanskrit Dictionary, 2019. Web. 11 April 2019.
"jIvA." SpokenSanskrit.com, Spoken Sanskrit, 2019, Web. 11 April 2019.

603. "jīva." SanskritDictionary.com, Sanskrit Dictionary, 2019. Web. 11 April 2019.
"jIva." SpokenSanskrit.com, Spoken Sanskrit, 2019, Web. 11 April 2019.

604. "jīvat." SanskritDictionary.com, Sanskrit Dictionary, 2019. Web. 11 April 2019.
"jIvat." SpokenSanskrit.com, Spoken Sanskrit, 2019, Web. 11 April 2019.

605. Bonfante, Giuliano/Bonfante, Larissa - "The Etruscan Language: An Introduction", p.77, Manchester University Press and Room 400, Second Edition, Manchester and New York, 2002.

606. "mara." SanskritDictionary.com, Sanskrit Dictionary, 2019. Web. 11 April 2019.
"mara." SpokenSanskrit.com, Spoken Sanskrit, 2019, Web. 11 April 2019.

607. "mṛ." SanskritDictionary.com, Sanskrit Dictionary, 2019. Web. 12 April 2019.
"mrayati." SpokenSanskrit.com, Spoken Sanskrit, 2019, Web. 12 April 2019.

608. "mṛ." SanskritDictionary.com, Sanskrit Dictionary, 2019. Web. 12 April 2019.
"mriyate." SpokenSanskrit.com, Spoken Sanskrit, 2019, Web. 12 April 2019.

609. "mṛ." SanskritDictionary.com, Sanskrit Dictionary, 2019. Web. 12

April 2019.
"mAryate." SpokenSanskrit.com, Spoken Sanskrit, 2019, Web. 12 April 2019.

610. "mṛ." SanskritDictionary.com, Sanskrit Dictionary, 2019. Web. 12 April 2019.
"mArayati." SpokenSanskrit.com, Spoken Sanskrit, 2019, Web. 12 April 2019.

611. "marta." SanskritDictionary.com, Sanskrit Dictionary, 2019. Web. 12 April 2019.
"marta." SpokenSanskrit.com, Spoken Sanskrit, 2019, Web. 12 April 2019.

612. "mṛta." SanskritDictionary.com, Sanskrit Dictionary, 2019. Web. 12 April 2019.
"mRta." SpokenSanskrit.com, Spoken Sanskrit, 2019, Web. 12 April 2019.

613. "mṛti." SanskritDictionary.com, Sanskrit Dictionary, 2019. Web. 12 April 2019.
"mRti." SpokenSanskrit.com, Spoken Sanskrit, 2019, Web. 12 April 2019.

614. "pā." SanskritDictionary.com, Sanskrit Dictionary, 2019. Web. 12 April 2019.
"pAti." SpokenSanskrit.com, Spoken Sanskrit, 2019, Web. 12 April 2019.

615. "vī." SanskritDictionary.com, Sanskrit Dictionary, 2019. Web. 12 April 2019.
"vyeti." SpokenSanskrit.com, Spoken Sanskrit, 2019, Web. 12 April 2019.

616. "ape." SanskritDictionary.com, Sanskrit Dictionary, 2019. Web. 12 April 2019.
"apaiti." SpokenSanskrit.com, Spoken Sanskrit, 2019, Web. 12 April 2019.

617. "khapura." SanskritDictionary.com, Sanskrit Dictionary, 2019. Web. 12 April 2019.
"khapura." SpokenSanskrit.com, Spoken Sanskrit, 2019, Web. 12 April 2019.

618. "sad." SanskritDictionary.com, Sanskrit Dictionary, 2019. Web. 12 April 2019.
"sIdati." SpokenSanskrit.com, Spoken Sanskrit, 2019, Web. 12 April

2019.

619. "set." Merriam-Webster.com. Merriam-Webster, 2019. Web. 12 April 2019.

620. "sūti." SanskritDictionary.com, Sanskrit Dictionary, 2019. Web. 14 April 2019.
"sUti." SpokenSanskrit.com, Spoken Sanskrit, 2019, Web. 14 April 2019.

621. "na." SanskritDictionary.com, Sanskrit Dictionary, 2019. Web. 14 April 2019.

622. "shuti." http://www.etruskisch.de/pgs/vc.htm, Etruscology – Website by Dieter H. Steinbauer, 14. June 2002. Web. 14 April 2019.

623. "sudhā." SanskritDictionary.com, Sanskrit Dictionary, 2019. Web. 14 April 2019.
"sudhA." SpokenSanskrit.com, Spoken Sanskrit, 2019, Web. 14 April 2019.

624. "saudha." SanskritDictionary.com, Sanskrit Dictionary, 2019. Web. 14 April 2019.
"saudha." SpokenSanskrit.com, Spoken Sanskrit, 2019, Web. 14 April 2019.

625. "sudhī." SanskritDictionary.com, Sanskrit Dictionary, 2019. Web. 14 April 2019.
"sudhI." SpokenSanskrit.com, Spoken Sanskrit, 2019, Web. 14 April 2019.

626. "yu." SanskritDictionary.com, Sanskrit Dictionary, 2019. Web. 14 April 2019.
"yauti." SpokenSanskrit.com, Spoken Sanskrit, 2019, Web. 14 April 2019.

627. "sva." SanskritDictionary.com, Sanskrit Dictionary, 2019. Web. 14 April 2019.

628. "vana." SanskritDictionary.com, Sanskrit Dictionary, 2019. Web. 14 April 2019.
"vana." SpokenSanskrit.com, Spoken Sanskrit, 2019, Web. 14 April 2019.

629. "mūta." SanskritDictionary.com, Sanskrit Dictionary, 2019. Web. 14 April 2019.
"mUta." SpokenSanskrit.com, Spoken Sanskrit, 2019, Web. 14 April

2019.

630. "anna." SanskritDictionary.com, Sanskrit Dictionary, 2019. Web. 14 April 2019.
"anna." SpokenSanskrit.com, Spoken Sanskrit, 2019, Web. 14 April 2019.

631. "mū." SanskritDictionary.com, Sanskrit Dictionary, 2019. Web. 14 April 2019.

632. "mu." SanskritDictionary.com, Sanskrit Dictionary, 2019. Web. 14 April 2019.

633. "tha." SanskritDictionary.com, Sanskrit Dictionary, 2019. Web. 14 April 2019.

634. "ṇa." SanskritDictionary.com, Sanskrit Dictionary, 2019. Web. 14 April 2019.

635. "dhāna." SanskritDictionary.com, Sanskrit Dictionary, 2019. Web. 14 April 2019.
"dhAna." SpokenSanskrit.com, Spoken Sanskrit, 2019, Web. 14 April 2019.

636. "tamera." http://www.etruskisch.de/pgs/vc.htm, Etruscology – Website by Dieter H. Steinbauer, 14. June 2002. Web. 14 April 2019.

637. "ḍāmara." SanskritDictionary.com, Sanskrit Dictionary, 2019. Web. 14 April 2019.
"DAmara." SpokenSanskrit.com, Spoken Sanskrit, 2019, Web. 14 April 2019.

638. "ṭā." SanskritDictionary.com, Sanskrit Dictionary, 2019. Web. 14 April 2019.

639. "tha." SanskritDictionary.com, Sanskrit Dictionary, 2019. Web. 14 April 2019.

640. "mara." SanskritDictionary.com, Sanskrit Dictionary, 2019. Web. 14 April 2019.
"mara." SpokenSanskrit.com, Spoken Sanskrit, 2019, Web. 14 April 2019.

641. "dama." SanskritDictionary.com, Sanskrit Dictionary, 2019. Web. 14 April 2019.
"dama." SpokenSanskrit.com, Spoken Sanskrit, 2019, Web. 14 April

2019.

642. "manes." Online-Latin-Dictionary.com. Latin Dictionary, 2019. Web. 14 April 2019.

643. "manas." SanskritDictionary.com, Sanskrit Dictionary, 2019. Web. 14 April 2019.

644. "manyu." SanskritDictionary.com, Sanskrit Dictionary, 2019. Web. 14 April 2019.

645. "laya." SanskritDictionary.com, Sanskrit Dictionary, 2019. Web. 14 April 2019.
"laya." SpokenSanskrit.com, Spoken Sanskrit, 2019, Web. 14 April 2019.

5.8. WORDS FOR ANIMALS (p.184-187)

646. "ara." SanskritDictionary.com, Sanskrit Dictionary, 2019. Web. 14 April 2019.
"ara." SpokenSanskrit.com, Spoken Sanskrit, 2019, Web. 14 April 2019.

647. "āgā." SanskritDictionary.com, Sanskrit Dictionary, 2019. Web. 14 April 2019.
"AgA." SpokenSanskrit.com, Spoken Sanskrit, 2019, Web. 14 April 2019.

648. "haraka." SanskritDictionary.com, Sanskrit Dictionary, 2019. Web. 14 April 2019.
"haraka." SpokenSanskrit.com, Spoken Sanskrit, 2019, Web. 14 April 2019.

649. "hāraka." SanskritDictionary.com, Sanskrit Dictionary, 2019. Web. 14 April 2019.
"hAraka." SpokenSanskrit.com, Spoken Sanskrit, 2019, Web. 14 April 2019.

650. "kha." SanskritDictionary.com, Sanskrit Dictionary, 2019. Web. 14 April 2019.

651. "ka." SanskritDictionary.com, Sanskrit Dictionary, 2019. Web. 14 April 2019.

652. "pā." SanskritDictionary.com, Sanskrit Dictionary, 2019. Web. 14 April 2019.

"pAti." SpokenSanskrit.com, Spoken Sanskrit, 2019, Web. 14 April 2019.

653. "krankru." http://www.etruskisch.de/pgs/vc.htm, Etruscology – Website by Dieter H. Steinbauer, 14 June 2002. Web. 14 April 2019.

654. Dennis, George - Cities and Cemeteries of Etruria, p.57; abridged two-part edition of 1883 edition, Google Books, Princetone University Press, New Jersey, 1985.

655. "krandana." SanskritDictionary.com, Sanskrit Dictionary, 2019. Web. 14 April 2019.
"krandana." SpokenSanskrit.com, Spoken Sanskrit, 2019, Web. 14 April 2019.

656. "krand." SanskritDictionary.com, Sanskrit Dictionary, 2019. Web. 14 April 2019.
"krandati." SpokenSanskrit.com, Spoken Sanskrit, 2019, Web. 14 April 2019.

657. "aNati." SpokenSanskrit.com, Spoken Sanskrit, 2019, Web. 14 April 2019.

658. "krandanaM karoti." SanskritDictionary.com, Sanskrit Dictionary, 2019. Web. 14 April 2019.

659. "aṇ." SanskritDictionary.com, Sanskrit Dictionary, 2019. Web. 14 April 2019.

660. "kāru." SanskritDictionary.com, Sanskrit Dictionary, 2019. Web. 14 April 2019.
"kAru." SpokenSanskrit.com, Spoken Sanskrit, 2019, Web. 14 April 2019.

661. "kṛ." SanskritDictionary.com, Sanskrit Dictionary, 2019. Web. 14 April 2019.
"karoti." SpokenSanskrit.com, Spoken Sanskrit, 2019, Web. 14 April 2019.

662. "ānaka." SanskritDictionary.com, Sanskrit Dictionary, 2019. Web. 14 April 2019.
"Anaka." SpokenSanskrit.com, Spoken Sanskrit, 2019, Web. 14 April 2019.

663. "ru." SanskritDictionary.com, Sanskrit Dictionary, 2019. Web. 14

April 2019.

664. "tuṣ." SanskritDictionary.com, Sanskrit Dictionary, 2019. Web. 14 April 2019.
"tuSayati." SpokenSanskrit.com, Spoken Sanskrit, 2019, Web. 14 April 2019.

5.9 VESSELS, CERAMICS (p.188-197)

665. "acilu." http://www.etruskisch.de/pgs/vc.htm, Etruscology – Website by Dieter H. Steinbauer, 14 June 2002. Web. 15 April 2019.

666. "aga." SanskritDictionary.com, Sanskrit Dictionary, 2019. Web. 15 April 2019.

667. "pātha." SanskritDictionary.com, Sanskrit Dictionary, 2019. Web. 15 April 2019.
"pAtha." SpokenSanskrit.com, Spoken Sanskrit, 2019, Web. 15 April 2019.

668. "anna." SanskritDictionary.com, Sanskrit Dictionary, 2019. Web. 15 April 2019.

669. "pat." SanskritDictionary.com, Sanskrit Dictionary, 2019. Web. 15 April 2019.
"patyate." SpokenSanskrit.com, Spoken Sanskrit, 2019, Web. 15 April 2019.

670. "ghṛṇi." SanskritDictionary.com, Sanskrit Dictionary, 2019. Web. 15 April 2019.
"ghRNi." SpokenSanskrit.com, Spoken Sanskrit, 2019, Web. 15 April 2019.

671. "caru." SanskritDictionary.com, Sanskrit Dictionary, 2019. Web. 15 April 2019.

672. "kūpa." SanskritDictionary.com, Sanskrit Dictionary, 2019. Web. 15 April 2019.
"kUpa." SpokenSanskrit.com, Spoken Sanskrit, 2019, Web. 15 April 2019.

673. "ku." SanskritDictionary.com, Sanskrit Dictionary, 2019. Web. 15 April 2019.

674. "pa." SanskritDictionary.com, Sanskrit Dictionary, 2019. Web. 15 April 2019.

675. "ma." SanskritDictionary.com, Sanskrit Dictionary, 2019. Web. 15 April 2019.

676. "TA." SanskritDictionary.com, Sanskrit Dictionary, 2019. Web. 15 April 2019.

677. "tha." SanskritDictionary.com, Sanskrit Dictionary, 2019. Web. 15 April 2019.

678. "ātta." SanskritDictionary.com, Sanskrit Dictionary, 2019. Web. 15 April 2019.
"Atta." SpokenSanskrit.com, Spoken Sanskrit, 2019, Web. 15 April 2019.

679. "pṝ." SanskritDictionary.com, Sanskrit Dictionary, 2019. Web. 16 April 2019.
"pArayati." SpokenSanskrit.com, Spoken Sanskrit, 2019, Web. 16 April 2019.

680. "ukha." SanskritDictionary.com, Sanskrit Dictionary, 2019. Web. 16 April 2019.
"ukha." SpokenSanskrit.com, Spoken Sanskrit, 2019, Web. 16 April 2019.

681. "pur." SanskritDictionary.com, Sanskrit Dictionary, 2019. Web. 16 April 2019.
"pur." SpokenSanskrit.com, Spoken Sanskrit, 2019, Web. 16 April 2019.

682. "pāna." SanskritDictionary.com, Sanskrit Dictionary, 2019. Web. 16 April 2019.
"pAna." SpokenSanskrit.com, Spoken Sanskrit, 2019, Web. 16 April 2019.

683. "lā." SanskritDictionary.com, Sanskrit Dictionary, 2019. Web. 16 April 2019.
"lAti." SpokenSanskrit.com, Spoken Sanskrit, 2019, Web. 16 April 2019.

684. "arṇas." SanskritDictionary.com, Sanskrit Dictionary, 2019. Web. 16 April 2019.
"arNas." SpokenSanskrit.com, Spoken Sanskrit, 2019, Web. 16 April 2019.

685. "kṣā." SanskritDictionary.com, Sanskrit Dictionary, 2019. Web. 16 April 2019.

"kSA." SpokenSanskrit.com, Spoken Sanskrit, 2019, Web. 16 April 2019.

686. Wikipedia contributors. "Ceramic." Wikipedia, The Free Encyclopedia. Wikipedia, The Free Encyclopedia, 15 Apr. 2019. Web. 16 Apr. 2019.

687. "ka." SanskritDictionary.com, Sanskrit Dictionary, 2019. Web. 16 April 2019.

688. "rāmā." SanskritDictionary.com, Sanskrit Dictionary, 2019. Web. 16 April 2019.
"rAmA." SpokenSanskrit.com, Spoken Sanskrit, 2019, Web. 16 April 2019.

689. Wikipedia contributors. "Bucchero." Wikipedia, The Free Encyclopedia. Wikipedia, The Free Encyclopedia, 1 Nov. 2018. Web. 16 Apr. 2019.

690. "bhū." SanskritDictionary.com, Sanskrit Dictionary, 2019. Web. 16 April 2019.
"bhU." SpokenSanskrit.com, Spoken Sanskrit, 2019, Web. 16 April 2019.

691. "ra." SanskritDictionary.com, Sanskrit Dictionary, 2019. Web. 16 April 2019.

692. "pota." SanskritDictionary.com, Sanskrit Dictionary, 2019. Web. 16 April 2019.
"pota." SpokenSanskrit.com, Spoken Sanskrit, 2019, Web. 16 April 2019.

693. "uda." SanskritDictionary.com, Sanskrit Dictionary, 2019. Web. 16 April 2019.
"uda." SpokenSanskrit.com, Spoken Sanskrit, 2019, Web. 16 April 2019.

694. "vār." SanskritDictionary.com, Sanskrit Dictionary, 2019. Web. 16 April 2019.
"vAr." SpokenSanskrit.com, Spoken Sanskrit, 2019, Web. 16 April 2019.

695. "tūṇ." SanskritDictionary.com, Sanskrit Dictionary, 2019. Web. 16 April 2019.
"tUNayate." SpokenSanskrit.com, Spoken Sanskrit, 2019, Web. 16 April 2019.

696. "sā." SanskritDictionary.com, Sanskrit Dictionary, 2019. Web. 16 April 2019.

697. "vana." SanskritDictionary.com, Sanskrit Dictionary, 2019. Web. 16 April 2019.
"vana." SpokenSanskrit.com, Spoken Sanskrit, 2019, Web. 16 April 2019.

698. "śava." SanskritDictionary.com, Sanskrit Dictionary, 2019. Web. 16 April 2019.
"zava." SpokenSanskrit.com, Spoken Sanskrit, 2019, Web. 16 April 2019.

699. "anna." SanskritDictionary.com, Sanskrit Dictionary, 2019. Web. 16 April 2019.
"anna." SpokenSanskrit.com, Spoken Sanskrit, 2019, Web. 16 April 2019.

700. "va." SanskritDictionary.com, Sanskrit Dictionary, 2019. Web. 16 April 2019.

701. "va." SanskritDictionary.com, Sanskrit Dictionary, 2019. Web. 16 April 2019.

702. "āsa." SanskritDictionary.com, Sanskrit Dictionary, 2019. Web. 16 April 2019.

703. "sphur." SanskritDictionary.com, Sanskrit Dictionary, 2019. Web. 17 April 2019.
"sphurati." SpokenSanskrit.com, Spoken Sanskrit, 2019, Web. 17 April 2019.

704. "sūnā." SanskritDictionary.com, Sanskrit Dictionary, 2019. Web. 17 April 2019.
"sUnA." SpokenSanskrit.com, Spoken Sanskrit, 2019, Web. 17 April 2019.

705. "dhāra." SanskritDictionary.com, Sanskrit Dictionary, 2019. Web. 17 April 2019.
"dhAra." SpokenSanskrit.com, Spoken Sanskrit, 2019, Web. 17 April 2019.

5.10 NAMES OF MONTHS (p.198-211)

706. "valgita." SanskritDictionary.com, Sanskrit Dictionary, 2019. Web. 17 April 2019.
"valgita." SpokenSanskrit.com, Spoken Sanskrit, 2019, Web. 17 April 2019.

708. "aṇu." SanskritDictionary.com, Sanskrit Dictionary, 2019. Web. 17 April 2019.

709. "anna." SanskritDictionary.com, Sanskrit Dictionary, 2019. Web. 17 April 2019.
"anna." SpokenSanskrit.com, Spoken Sanskrit, 2019, Web. 17 April 2019.

710. "velā." SanskritDictionary.com, Sanskrit Dictionary, 2019. Web. 17 April 2019.
"velA." SpokenSanskrit.com, Spoken Sanskrit, 2019, Web. 17 April 2019.

711. "gīta." SanskritDictionary.com, Sanskrit Dictionary, 2019. Web. 17 April 2019.
"gIta." SpokenSanskrit.com, Spoken Sanskrit, 2019, Web. 17 April 2019.

712. "valg." SanskritDictionary.com, Sanskrit Dictionary, 2019. Web. 17 April 2019.
"valgati." SpokenSanskrit.com, Spoken Sanskrit, 2019, Web. 17 April 2019.

713. "idāni." SanskritDictionary.com, Sanskrit Dictionary, 2019. Web. 17 April 2019.
"idAni." SpokenSanskrit.com, Spoken Sanskrit, 2019, Web. 17 April 2019.

714. "ka." SanskritDictionary.com, Sanskrit Dictionary, 2019. Web. 17 April 2019.

715. "khā." SanskritDictionary.com, Sanskrit Dictionary, 2019. Web. 17 April 2019.

716. "pṛ." SanskritDictionary.com, Sanskrit Dictionary, 2019. Web. 17 April 2019.
"piparti." SpokenSanskrit.com, Spoken Sanskrit, 2019, Web. 17 April 2019.

717. At Home In Tuscany, writer - Gloria. "Tuscany in April" http://www.athomeintuscany.org/2012/04/26/tuscany-in-april/. At Home In Tuscany, 26 Apr. 2012. Web. 16 Dec. 2015.

718. "āmpa." SanskritDictionary.com, Sanskrit Dictionary, 2019. Web. 18 April 2019.
"Ampa." SpokenSanskrit.com, Spoken Sanskrit, 2019, Web. 18 April 2019.

719. "il." SanskritDictionary.com, Sanskrit Dictionary, 2019. Web. 18 April 2019.
"ilati." SpokenSanskrit.com, Spoken Sanskrit, 2019, Web. 18 April 2019.

720. Weather In Tuscany Month By Month, http://unseentuscany.com/weather-in-tuscany-month-by-mont, 2019. Web. 18. April 2019.

721. "aga." SanskritDictionary.com, Sanskrit Dictionary, 2019. Web. 18 April 2019.

722. "ākāla." SanskritDictionary.com, Sanskrit Dictionary, 2019. Web. 18 April 2019.
"AkAla." SpokenSanskrit.com, Spoken Sanskrit, 2019, Web. 18 April 2019.

723. "āgā." SanskritDictionary.com, Sanskrit Dictionary, 2019. Web. 18 April 2019.
"AjigAti." SpokenSanskrit.com, Spoken Sanskrit, 2019, Web. 18 April 2019.

724. "lū." SanskritDictionary.com, Sanskrit Dictionary, 2019. Web. 18 April 2019.
"lunAti." SpokenSanskrit.com, Spoken Sanskrit, 2019, Web. 18 April 2019.

725. "dhṛ." SanskritDictionary.com, Sanskrit Dictionary, 2019. Web. 18 April 2019.
"dhArayati." SpokenSanskrit.com, Spoken Sanskrit, 2019, Web. 18 April 2019.

726. "anna." SanskritDictionary.com, Sanskrit Dictionary, 2019. Web. 18 April 2019.
"anna." SpokenSanskrit.com, Spoken Sanskrit, 2019, Web. 18 April 2019.

727. "tṝ." SanskritDictionary.com, Sanskrit Dictionary, 2019. Web. 18 April 2019.
"tarati." SpokenSanskrit.com, Spoken Sanskrit, 2019, Web. 18 April 2019.

728. "drāh." SanskritDictionary.com, Sanskrit Dictionary, 2019. Web. 18 April 2019.
"drAhate." SpokenSanskrit.com, Spoken Sanskrit, 2019, Web. 18 April 2019.

729. "nava." SanskritDictionary.com, Sanskrit Dictionary, 2019. Web. 18 April 2019.
"nava." SpokenSanskrit.com, Spoken Sanskrit, 2019, Web. 18 April 2019.

730. "dū." SanskritDictionary.com, Sanskrit Dictionary, 2019. Web. 18 April 2019.
"dUyate." SpokenSanskrit.com, Spoken Sanskrit, 2019, Web. 18 April 2019.

731. "gad." SanskritDictionary.com, Sanskrit Dictionary, 2019. Web. 18 April 2019.
"gadayati." SpokenSanskrit.com, Spoken Sanskrit, 2019, Web. 18 April 2019.

732. At Home In Tuscany, writer - Gloria. "Tuscany in August" http://www.athomeintuscany.org/2012/08/17/tuscany-in-august/. At Home In Tuscany, 17 Aug. 2012. Web. 16 Dec. 2015.

733. "duh." SanskritDictionary.com, Sanskrit Dictionary, 2019. Web. 18 April 2019.

734. "duh." SanskritDictionary.com, Sanskrit Dictionary, 2019. Web. 18 April 2019.
"dogdhi." SpokenSanskrit.com, Spoken Sanskrit, 2019, Web. 18 April 2019.

735. "gātu." SanskritDictionary.com, Sanskrit Dictionary, 2019. Web. 18 April 2019.
"gAtu." SpokenSanskrit.com, Spoken Sanskrit, 2019, Web. 18 April 2019.

736. "dugdha." SanskritDictionary.com, Sanskrit Dictionary, 2019. Web. 18 April 2019.
"dugdha." SpokenSanskrit.com, Spoken Sanskrit, 2019, Web. 18 April 2019.

737. "duḥkha." SanskritDictionary.com, Sanskrit Dictionary, 2019. Web. 18 April 2019.
"duHkha." SpokenSanskrit.com, Spoken Sanskrit, 2019, Web. 18 April 2019.

738. "duḥkhatā." SanskritDictionary.com, Sanskrit Dictionary, 2019. Web. 18 April 2019.
"duHkhatA." SpokenSanskrit.com, Spoken Sanskrit, 2019, Web. 18 April 2019.

739. "er." SanskritDictionary.com, Sanskrit Dictionary, 2019. Web. 18 April 2019.
"Irayati." SpokenSanskrit.com, Spoken Sanskrit, 2019, Web. 18 April 2019.

740. "ma." SanskritDictionary.com, Sanskrit Dictionary, 2019. Web. 18 April 2019.

741. "āhṛ." SanskritDictionary.com, Sanskrit Dictionary, 2019. Web. 18 April 2019.
"Aharati." SpokenSanskrit.com, Spoken Sanskrit, 2019, Web. 18 April 2019.

742. "hṛ." SanskritDictionary.com, Sanskrit Dictionary, 2019. Web. 18 April 2019.
"harati." SpokenSanskrit.com, Spoken Sanskrit, 2019, Web. 18 April 2019.

743. "īrma." SanskritDictionary.com, Sanskrit Dictionary, 2019. Web. 18 April 2019.
"Irma." SpokenSanskrit.com, Spoken Sanskrit, 2019, Web. 18 April 2019.

744. "yu." SanskritDictionary.com, Sanskrit Dictionary, 2019. Web. 18 April 2019.
"yauti." SpokenSanskrit.com, Spoken Sanskrit, 2019, Web. 18 April 2019.

745. "yu." SanskritDictionary.com, Sanskrit Dictionary, 2019. Web. 18 April 2019.
"yAvayati." SpokenSanskrit.com, Spoken Sanskrit, 2019, Web. 18 April 2019.

746. "keli." SanskritDictionary.com, Sanskrit Dictionary, 2019. Web. 18 April 2019.

747. "kāla." SanskritDictionary.com, Sanskrit Dictionary, 2019. Web. 18 April 2019.
"kAla." SpokenSanskrit.com, Spoken Sanskrit, 2019, Web. 18 April 2019.

748. "ku." SanskritDictionary.com, Sanskrit Dictionary, 2019. Web. 18 April 2019.

748. "sphāra." SanskritDictionary.com, Sanskrit Dictionary, 2019. Web. 18 April 2019.
"sphAra." SpokenSanskrit.com, Spoken Sanskrit, 2019, Web. 18 April

2019.

749. "kuṣ." SanskritDictionary.com, Sanskrit Dictionary, 2019. Web. 18 April 2019.
"kUSNAti." SpokenSanskrit.com, Spoken Sanskrit, 2019, Web. 18 April 2019.

750. "peru." SanskritDictionary.com, Sanskrit Dictionary, 2019. Web. 18 April 2019.
"peru." SpokenSanskrit.com, Spoken Sanskrit, 2019, Web. 18 April 2019.

751. "māsa." SanskritDictionary.com, Sanskrit Dictionary, 2019. Web. 18 April 2019.
"mAsa." SpokenSanskrit.com, Spoken Sanskrit, 2019, Web. 18 April 2019.

752. "vadhyā." SanskritDictionary.com, Sanskrit Dictionary, 2019. Web. 18 April 2019.
"vadhyA." SpokenSanskrit.com, Spoken Sanskrit, 2019, Web. 18 April 2019.

753. "aga." SanskritDictionary.com, Sanskrit Dictionary, 2019. Web. 18 April 2019.
"aga." SpokenSanskrit.com, Spoken Sanskrit, 2019, Web. 18 April 2019.

754. "maṣ." SanskritDictionary.com, Sanskrit Dictionary, 2019. Web. 18 April 2019.
"maSati." SpokenSanskrit.com, Spoken Sanskrit, 2019, Web. 18 April 2019.

755. "masana." SanskritDictionary.com, Sanskrit Dictionary, 2019. Web. 18 April 2019.

756. "lūna." SanskritDictionary.com, Sanskrit Dictionary, 2019. Web. 18 April 2019.
"lUna." SpokenSanskrit.com, Spoken Sanskrit, 2019, Web. 18 April 2019.

757. "sṛpa." SanskritDictionary.com, Sanskrit Dictionary, 2019. Web. 18 April 2019.
"sRpa." SpokenSanskrit.com, Spoken Sanskrit, 2019, Web. 18 April 2019.

5.11 WORDS BELIEVED TO BE ADOPTED BY ETRUSCANS FROM OTHER LANGUAGES (p.212-217)

758. "kūṭa." SanskritDictionary.com, Sanskrit Dictionary, 2019. Web. 18 April 2019.
"kUTa." SpokenSanskrit.com, Spoken Sanskrit, 2019, Web. 18 April 2019.

759. "kulīnasa." SanskritDictionary.com, Sanskrit Dictionary, 2019. Web. 19 April 2019.
"kulInasa." SpokenSanskrit.com, Spoken Sanskrit, 2019, Web. 19 April 2019.

760. "kulija." SanskritDictionary.com, Sanskrit Dictionary, 2019. Web. 19 April 2019.
"kulija." SpokenSanskrit.com, Spoken Sanskrit, 2019, Web. 19 April 2019.

761. "golaka." SanskritDictionary.com, Sanskrit Dictionary, 2019. Web. 19 April 2019.
"golaka." SpokenSanskrit.com, Spoken Sanskrit, 2019, Web. 19 April 2019.

762. "gu." SanskritDictionary.com, Sanskrit Dictionary, 2019. Web. 19 April 2019.

763. "lagna." SanskritDictionary.com, Sanskrit Dictionary, 2019. Web. 19 April 2019.
"lagna." SpokenSanskrit.com, Spoken Sanskrit, 2019, Web. 19 April 2019.

764. "ās." SanskritDictionary.com, Sanskrit Dictionary, 2019. Web. 19 April 2019.
"Asyate." SpokenSanskrit.com, Spoken Sanskrit, 2019, Web. 19 April 2019.

765. "go." SanskritDictionary.com, Sanskrit Dictionary, 2019. Web. 19 April 2019.
766. "ka." SanskritDictionary.com, Sanskrit Dictionary, 2019. Web. 19 April 2019.

767. "val." SanskritDictionary.com, Sanskrit Dictionary, 2019. Web. 19 April 2019.
"valate." SpokenSanskrit.com, Spoken Sanskrit, 2019, Web. 19 April

2019.

768. "peya." SanskritDictionary.com, Sanskrit Dictionary, 2019. Web. 19 April 2019.
"peya." SpokenSanskrit.com, Spoken Sanskrit, 2019, Web. 19 April 2019.

769. "pāyya." SanskritDictionary.com, Sanskrit Dictionary, 2019. Web. 19 April 2019.
"pAyya." SpokenSanskrit.com, Spoken Sanskrit, 2019, Web. 19 April 2019.

770. "pā." SanskritDictionary.com, Sanskrit Dictionary, 2019. Web. 19 April 2019.

771. "dharā." SanskritDictionary.com, Sanskrit Dictionary, 2019. Web. 19 April 2019.
"dharA." SpokenSanskrit.com, Spoken Sanskrit, 2019, Web. 19 April 2019.

772. "ātara." SanskritDictionary.com, Sanskrit Dictionary, 2019. Web. 19 April 2019.
"Atara." SpokenSanskrit.com, Spoken Sanskrit, 2019, Web. 19 April 2019.

773. "ādara." SanskritDictionary.com, Sanskrit Dictionary, 2019. Web. 19 April 2019.
"Adara." SpokenSanskrit.com, Spoken Sanskrit, 2019, Web. 19 April 2019.

774. "panū." SanskritDictionary.com, Sanskrit Dictionary, 2019. Web. 20 April 2019.
"panU." SpokenSanskrit.com, Spoken Sanskrit, 2019, Web. 20 April 2019.

775. "pāṇa." SanskritDictionary.com, Sanskrit Dictionary, 2019. Web. 20 April 2019.
"pANa." SpokenSanskrit.com, Spoken Sanskrit, 2019, Web. 20 April 2019.

776. "pāna." SanskritDictionary.com, Sanskrit Dictionary, 2019. Web. 20 April 2019.
"pAna." SpokenSanskrit.com, Spoken Sanskrit, 2019, Web. 20 April 2019.

777. "paṇa." SanskritDictionary.com, Sanskrit Dictionary, 2019. Web. 20 April 2019.
"paNa." SpokenSanskrit.com, Spoken Sanskrit, 2019, Web. 20 April 2019.

778. "ūma." SanskritDictionary.com, Sanskrit Dictionary, 2019. Web. 20 April 2019.
"Uma." SpokenSanskrit.com, Spoken Sanskrit, 2019, Web. 20 April 2019.

779. "umā." SanskritDictionary.com, Sanskrit Dictionary, 2019. Web. 20 April 2019.
"umA." SpokenSanskrit.com, Spoken Sanskrit, 2019, Web. 20 April 2019.

5.12 WORDS IN OTHER LANGUAGES THAT MIGHT BE OF ETRUSCAN ORIGIN (p.218-229)

780. "arena." Dictionary.com. Dictionary, 2019. Web. 1 January 2019.

781. Wikipedia contributors. "List of English words of Etruscan origin." Wikipedia, The Free Encyclopedia. Wikipedia, The Free Encyclopedia, 30 May. 2018. Web. 20 Apr. 2019.

782 "hāra." SanskritDictionary.com, Sanskrit Dictionary, 2019. Web. 20 April 2019.
"hAra." SpokenSanskrit.com, Spoken Sanskrit, 2019, Web. 20 April 2019.

783. "anna." SanskritDictionary.com, Sanskrit Dictionary, 2019. Web. 20 April 2019.

784. "pauṣa." SanskritDictionary.com, Sanskrit Dictionary, 2019. Web. 20 April 2019.
"pauSa." SpokenSanskrit.com, Spoken Sanskrit, 2019, Web. 20 April 2019.

785. "reṇu." SanskritDictionary.com, Sanskrit Dictionary, 2019. Web. 20 April 2019.
"reNu." SpokenSanskrit.com, Spoken Sanskrit, 2019, Web. 20 April 2019.

786. "ha." SanskritDictionary.com, Sanskrit Dictionary, 2019. Web. 20 April 2019.

787 "Wikipedia contributors. "Curia." Wikipedia, The Free Encyclopedia. Wikipedia, The Free Encyclopedia, 27 Dec. 2018. Web. 21 Apr. 2019.

788. "vīra." SanskritDictionary.com, Sanskrit Dictionary, 2019. Web. 20 April 2019.
"vIra." SpokenSanskrit.com, Spoken Sanskrit, 2019, Web. 20 April 2019.

789. "go." SanskritDictionary.com, Sanskrit Dictionary, 2019. Web. 20 April 2019.

790. "gṛhya." SanskritDictionary.com, Sanskrit Dictionary, 2019. Web. 20 April 2019.
"gRhya." SpokenSanskrit.com, Spoken Sanskrit, 2019, Web. 20 April 2019.

791. Wikipedia contributors. "Fasces." Wikipedia, The Free Encyclopedia. Wikipedia, The Free Encyclopedia, 26 Jul. 2019. Web. 2 Aug. 2019.

792. "pas." SanskritDictionary.com, Sanskrit Dictionary, 2019. Web. 20 April 2019.
"pasati." SpokenSanskrit.com, Spoken Sanskrit, 2019, Web. 20 April 2019.

793. "sku." SanskritDictionary.com, Sanskrit Dictionary, 2019. Web. 20 April 2019.
"coskoti." SpokenSanskrit.com, Spoken Sanskrit, 2019, Web. 20 April 2019.

794. "ku." SanskritDictionary.com, Sanskrit Dictionary, 2019. Web. 20 April 2019.

795 Wikipedia contributors. "Military." Wikipedia, The Free Encyclopedia. Wikipedia, The Free Encyclopedia, 19 Apr. 2019. Web. 21 Apr. 2019.

796. "mīl." SanskritDictionary.com, Sanskrit Dictionary, 2019. Web. 20 April 2019.
"mIlati." SpokenSanskrit.com, Spoken Sanskrit, 2019, Web. 20 April 2019.

797. "iṭ." SanskritDictionary.com, Sanskrit Dictionary, 2019. Web. 20 April 2019.

798. "hāra." SanskritDictionary.com, Sanskrit Dictionary, 2019. Web. 20 April 2019.
"hAra." SpokenSanskrit.com, Spoken Sanskrit, 2019, Web. 20 April 2019.

799. "mela." SanskritDictionary.com, Sanskrit Dictionary, 2019. Web. 20 April 2019.
"mela." SpokenSanskrit.com, Spoken Sanskrit, 2019, Web. 20 April 2019.

800. "ta." SanskritDictionary.com, Sanskrit Dictionary, 2019. Web. 20 April 2019.

801. "arha." SanskritDictionary.com, Sanskrit Dictionary, 2019. Web. 20 April 2019.
"arha." SpokenSanskrit.com, Spoken Sanskrit, 2019, Web. 20 April 2019.

802. "column." Dictionary.com, Dictionary.com, 2019. Web. 21 April 2019.

803. "gola." SanskritDictionary.com, Sanskrit Dictionary, 2019. Web. 21 April 2019.
"gola." SpokenSanskrit.com, Spoken Sanskrit, 2019, Web. 21 April 2019.

804. "ūma." SanskritDictionary.com, Sanskrit Dictionary, 2019. Web. 21 April 2019.
"Uma." SpokenSanskrit.com, Spoken Sanskrit, 2019, Web. 21 April 2019.

805. "ṇa." SanskritDictionary.com, Sanskrit Dictionary, 2019. Web. 21 April 2019.

806. "nah." SanskritDictionary.com, Sanskrit Dictionary, 2019. Web. 21 April 2019.
"nahyate." SpokenSanskrit.com, Spoken Sanskrit, 2019, Web. 21 April 2019.

807. "nah." SanskritDictionary.com, Sanskrit Dictionary, 2019. Web. 21 April 2019.
"nahyati." SpokenSanskrit.com, Spoken Sanskrit, 2019, Web. 21 April 2019.

808. "palace." Wiktionary, The Free Dictionary. 20 Feb 2019, 05:45 UTC. 22 Apr 2019, 02:31 <https://en.wiktionary.org/w/index.php?title=palace&oldid=51554277>.

809. "pāla." SanskritDictionary.com, Sanskrit Dictionary, 2019. Web. 21 April 2019.
"pAla." SpokenSanskrit.com, Spoken Sanskrit, 2019, Web. 21 April 2019.

810. "pāl." SanskritDictionary.com, Sanskrit Dictionary, 2019. Web. 21 April 2019.
"pAlayati." SpokenSanskrit.com, Spoken Sanskrit, 2019, Web. 21 April 2019.

811. "palenque." Wiktionary, The Free Dictionary. 6 Apr 2019, 16:33 UTC. 22 Apr 2019, 02:36 <https://en.wiktionary.org/w/index.php?title=palenque&oldid=52271802>.

812. "palisade." Dictionary.com, Dictionary.com, 2019. Web. 10 April 2019.

813. "pāli." SanskritDictionary.com, Sanskrit Dictionary, 2019. Web. 21 April 2019.
"pAlayati." SpokenSanskrit.com, Spoken Sanskrit, 2019, Web. 21 April 2019.

814. "as." SanskritDictionary.com, Sanskrit Dictionary, 2019. Web. 21 April 2019.

815. "palli." SanskritDictionary.com, Sanskrit Dictionary, 2019. Web. 21 April 2019.
"palli." SpokenSanskrit.com, Spoken Sanskrit, 2019, Web. 21 April 2019.

816. Wikipedia contributors. "List of English words of Etruscan origin." Wikipedia, The Free Encyclopedia. Wikipedia, The Free Encyclopedia, 30 May. 2018. Web. 22 Apr. 2019.

817. "varṇa." SanskritDictionary.com, Sanskrit Dictionary, 2019. Web. 21 April 2019.
"varNa." SpokenSanskrit.com, Spoken Sanskrit, 2019, Web. 21 April 2019.

818. "kula." SanskritDictionary.com, Sanskrit Dictionary, 2019. Web. 21 April 2019.

819. Wikipedia contributors. "List of English words of Etruscan origin." Wikipedia, The Free Encyclopedia. Wikipedia, The Free Encyclopedia, 30 May. 2018. Web. 22 Apr. 2019.

820. "alam." SanskritDictionary.com, Sanskrit Dictionary, 2019. Web. 21 April 2019.
"alam." SpokenSanskrit.com, Spoken Sanskrit, 2019, Web. 21 April 2019.

821. "antu." SanskritDictionary.com, Sanskrit Dictionary, 2019. Web. 21 April 2019.
"antu." SpokenSanskrit.com, Spoken Sanskrit, 2019, Web. 21 April 2019.

822. "anta." SanskritDictionary.com, Sanskrit Dictionary, 2019. Web. 21 April 2019.
"anta." SpokenSanskrit.com, Spoken Sanskrit, 2019, Web. 21 April 2019.

823. "um." SanskritDictionary.com, Sanskrit Dictionary, 2019. Web. 21 April 2019.

5.13 NAMES OF FAMOUS PERSONS (p.230-240)

824. Wikipedia contributors. "Lars Porsena." Wikipedia, The Free Encyclopedia. Wikipedia, The Free Encyclopedia, 9 Apr. 2019. Web. 22 Apr. 2019.

825. "aruṇa." SanskritDictionary.com, Sanskrit Dictionary, 2019. Web. 22 April 2019.
"aruNa." SpokenSanskrit.com, Spoken Sanskrit, 2019, Web. 22 April 2019.

826. "lṛ." SanskritDictionary.com, Sanskrit Dictionary, 2019. Web. 22 April 2019.
"lR." SpokenSanskrit.com, Spoken Sanskrit, 2019, Web. 22 April 2019.

827. "gaya." SanskritDictionary.com, Sanskrit Dictionary, 2019. Web. 22 April 2019.
"gaya." SpokenSanskrit.com, Spoken Sanskrit, 2019, Web. 22 April 2019.

828. "gu." SanskritDictionary.com, Sanskrit Dictionary, 2019. Web. 22 April 2019.

829. "go." SanskritDictionary.com, Sanskrit Dictionary, 2019. Web. 22 April 2019.

830. "ya." SanskritDictionary.com, Sanskrit Dictionary, 2019. Web. 22 April 2019.

831. "para." SanskritDictionary.com, Sanskrit Dictionary, 2019. Web. 22 April 2019.
"para." SpokenSanskrit.com, Spoken Sanskrit, 2019, Web. 22 April 2019.

832. "sana." SanskritDictionary.com, Sanskrit Dictionary, 2019. Web. 22 April 2019.
"sana." SpokenSanskrit.com, Spoken Sanskrit, 2019, Web. 22 April 2019.

833. "pur." SanskritDictionary.com, Sanskrit Dictionary, 2019. Web. 22 April 2019.
"pur." SpokenSanskrit.com, Spoken Sanskrit, 2019, Web. 22 April 2019.

834. "pur." SanskritDictionary.com, Sanskrit Dictionary, 2019. Web. 22 April 2019.
"purati." SpokenSanskrit.com, Spoken Sanskrit, 2019, Web. 22 April 2019.

835. "senā." SanskritDictionary.com, Sanskrit Dictionary, 2019. Web. 22 April 2019.
"senA." SpokenSanskrit.com, Spoken Sanskrit, 2019, Web. 22 April 2019.

836. "sphura." SanskritDictionary.com, Sanskrit Dictionary, 2019. Web. 22 April 2019.
"sphura." SpokenSanskrit.com, Spoken Sanskrit, 2019, Web. 22 April 2019.

837. "spṛ." SanskritDictionary.com, Sanskrit Dictionary, 2019. Web. 22 April 2019.

838. "deva." SanskritDictionary.com, Sanskrit Dictionary, 2019. Web. 22 April 2019.
"deva." SpokenSanskrit.com, Spoken Sanskrit, 2019, Web. 22 April 2019.

839. "ār." SanskritDictionary.com, Sanskrit Dictionary, 2019. Web. 22 April 2019.
"Aryanti." SpokenSanskrit.com, Spoken Sanskrit, 2019, Web. 22 April 2019.

840. "ārya." SanskritDictionary.com, Sanskrit Dictionary, 2019. Web. 22 April 2019.
"Arya." SpokenSanskrit.com, Spoken Sanskrit, 2019, Web. 22 April 2019.

841. "devārha." SanskritDictionary.com, Sanskrit Dictionary, 2019. Web.

22 April 2019.
"devArha." SpokenSanskrit.com, Spoken Sanskrit, 2019, Web. 22 April 2019.

842. "velā." SanskritDictionary.com, Sanskrit Dictionary, 2019. Web. 22 April 2019.
"velA." SpokenSanskrit.com, Spoken Sanskrit, 2019, Web. 22 April 2019.

843. "anna." SanskritDictionary.com, Sanskrit Dictionary, 2019. Web. 22 April 2019.

844. "valī." SanskritDictionary.com, Sanskrit Dictionary, 2019. Web. 22 April 2019.
"valI." SpokenSanskrit.com, Spoken Sanskrit, 2019, Web. 22 April 2019.

845. "val." SanskritDictionary.com, Sanskrit Dictionary, 2019. Web. 22 April 2019.
"vAlayati." SpokenSanskrit.com, Spoken Sanskrit, 2019, Web. 22 April 2019.

846. "yāna." SanskritDictionary.com, Sanskrit Dictionary, 2019. Web. 22 April 2019.
"yAna." SpokenSanskrit.com, Spoken Sanskrit, 2019, Web. 22 April 2019.

847. Wikipedia contributors. "Servius Tullius." Wikipedia, The Free Encyclopedia. Wikipedia, The Free Encyclopedia, 18 Mar. 2019. Web. 23 Apr. 2019.

848. "sarva." SanskritDictionary.com, Sanskrit Dictionary, 2019. Web. 23 April 2019.
"sarva." SpokenSanskrit.com, Spoken Sanskrit, 2019, Web. 23 April 2019.

849. "sārva." SanskritDictionary.com, Sanskrit Dictionary, 2019. Web. 23 April 2019.
"sArva." SpokenSanskrit.com, Spoken Sanskrit, 2019, Web. 23 April 2019.

850. "tulā." SanskritDictionary.com, Sanskrit Dictionary, 2019. Web. 23 April 2019.
"tulA." SpokenSanskrit.com, Spoken Sanskrit, 2019, Web. 23 April 2019.

851. "yu." SanskritDictionary.com, Sanskrit Dictionary, 2019. Web. 23

April 2019.
"yu." SpokenSanskrit.com, Spoken Sanskrit, 2019, Web. 23 April 2019.

852. "glev." SanskritDictionary.com, Sanskrit Dictionary, 2019. Web. 23 April 2019.
"glevate." SpokenSanskrit.com, Spoken Sanskrit, 2019, Web. 23 April 2019.

853. "sev." SanskritDictionary.com, Sanskrit Dictionary, 2019. Web. 23 April 2019.
"sevate." SpokenSanskrit.com, Spoken Sanskrit, 2019, Web. 23 April 2019.

854. "śīl." SanskritDictionary.com, Sanskrit Dictionary, 2019. Web. 23 April 2019.
"zIlati." SpokenSanskrit.com, Spoken Sanskrit, 2019, Web. 23 April 2019.

855. "niSev." SanskritDictionary.com, Sanskrit Dictionary, 2019. Web. 23 April 2019.
"niSevate." SpokenSanskrit.com, Spoken Sanskrit, 2019, Web. 23 April 2019.

856. "pratibhūṣ." SanskritDictionary.com, Sanskrit Dictionary, 2019. Web. 23 April 2019.
"pratibhUSati." SpokenSanskrit.com, Spoken Sanskrit, 2019, Web. 23 April 2019.

857. "mīl." SanskritDictionary.com, Sanskrit Dictionary, 2019. Web. 20 April 2019.
"mIlati." SpokenSanskrit.com, Spoken Sanskrit, 2019, Web. 20 April 2019.

858. "mela." SanskritDictionary.com, Sanskrit Dictionary, 2019. Web. 23 April 2019.
"mela" SpokenSanskrit.com, Spoken Sanskrit, 2019, Web. 23 April 2019.

859. "ta." SanskritDictionary.com, Sanskrit Dictionary, 2019. Web. 20 April 2019.

860. "arha." SanskritDictionary.com, Sanskrit Dictionary, 2019. Web. 23 April 2019.
"arha" SpokenSanskrit.com, Spoken Sanskrit, 2019, Web. 23 April 2019.

861. "makṣ." SanskritDictionary.com, Sanskrit Dictionary, 2019. Web. 23 April 2019.
"makSati." SpokenSanskrit.com, Spoken Sanskrit, 2019, Web. 23 April 2019.

862. "ṛṇa." SanskritDictionary.com, Sanskrit Dictionary, 2019. Web. 23 April 2019.
"RNa." SpokenSanskrit.com, Spoken Sanskrit, 2019, Web. 23 April 2019.

863 Pallottino, Massimo - "The Etruscans", p.96, the revised and enlarged hardcover edition based on the sixth Italian edition, Edited by David Ridgway, Indiana University Press, Bloomington & London, 1975.

864. "masta." SanskritDictionary.com, Sanskrit Dictionary, 2019. Web. 23 April 2019.
"masta." SpokenSanskrit.com, Spoken Sanskrit, 2019, Web. 23 April 2019.

865. "tāra." SanskritDictionary.com, Sanskrit Dictionary, 2019. Web. 23 April 2019.
"tAra." SpokenSanskrit.com, Spoken Sanskrit, 2019, Web. 23 April 2019.

5.14 THE NAME OF THE ETRUSCANS (p.241-250)

867. "ras." SanskritDictionary.com, Sanskrit Dictionary, 2019. Web. 23 April 2019.
"rasati." SpokenSanskrit.com, Spoken Sanskrit, 2019, Web. 23 April 2019.

868. "anna." SanskritDictionary.com, Sanskrit Dictionary, 2019. Web. 23 April 2019.

869. "rāṣṭra." SanskritDictionary.com, Sanskrit Dictionary, 2019. Web. 23 April 2019.
"rASTra." SpokenSanskrit.com, Spoken Sanskrit, 2019, Web. 23 April 2019.

870. "rāśi." SanskritDictionary.com, Sanskrit Dictionary, 2019. Web. 23 April 2019.
"rAzi." SpokenSanskrit.com, Spoken Sanskrit, 2019, Web. 23 April 2019.

871. "rasya." SanskritDictionary.com, Sanskrit Dictionary, 2019. Web. 23 April 2019.

"rasya." SpokenSanskrit.com, Spoken Sanskrit, 2019, Web. 23 April 2019.

872. "rasā." SanskritDictionary.com, Sanskrit Dictionary, 2019. Web. 23 April 2019.
"rasA." SpokenSanskrit.com, Spoken Sanskrit, 2019, Web. 23 April 2019.

873. "anas." SanskritDictionary.com, Sanskrit Dictionary, 2019. Web. 23 April 2019.
"anas." SpokenSanskrit.com, Spoken Sanskrit, 2019, Web. 23 April 2019.

874. Pešić, Radivoje - "Vincansko pismo i drugi gramatoloski ogledi", p.40-41, Pesic i sinovi, Beograd, 1995

875. "rasana." SanskritDictionary.com, Sanskrit Dictionary, 2019. Web. 23 April 2019.
"rasana." SpokenSanskrit.com, Spoken Sanskrit, 2019, Web. 23 April 2019.

876. "rasnā." SanskritDictionary.com, Sanskrit Dictionary, 2019. Web. 23 April 2019.
"rasnA." SpokenSanskrit.com, Spoken Sanskrit, 2019, Web. 23 April 2019.

877. "laṇḍ." SanskritDictionary.com, Sanskrit Dictionary, 2019. Web. 23 April 2019.
"laNDayati." SpokenSanskrit.com, Spoken Sanskrit, 2019, Web. 23 April 2019.

878. "raṭh." SanskritDictionary.com, Sanskrit Dictionary, 2019. Web. 23 April 2019.
"raThati." SpokenSanskrit.com, Spoken Sanskrit, 2019, Web. 23 April 2019.

879. "reṭ." SanskritDictionary.com, Sanskrit Dictionary, 2019. Web. 23 April 2019.
"reTati." SpokenSanskrit.com, Spoken Sanskrit, 2019, Web. 23 April 2019.

880. "sara." SanskritDictionary.com, Sanskrit Dictionary, 2019. Web. 23 April 2019.
"sara." SpokenSanskrit.com, Spoken Sanskrit, 2019, Web. 23 April 2019.

881. "dā." SanskritDictionary.com, Sanskrit Dictionary, 2019. Web. 23

April 2019.
"datte." SpokenSanskrit.com, Spoken Sanskrit, 2019, Web. 23 April 2019.

882. "balh." SanskritDictionary.com, Sanskrit Dictionary, 2019. Web. 23 April 2019.
"valhate." SpokenSanskrit.com, Spoken Sanskrit, 2019, Web. 23 April 2019.

883. "ārī." SanskritDictionary.com, Sanskrit Dictionary, 2019. Web. 23 April 2019.
"AriNanti." SpokenSanskrit.com, Spoken Sanskrit, 2019, Web. 23 April 2019.

884. "om." SanskritDictionary.com, Sanskrit Dictionary, 2019. Web. 23 April 2019.

885. "brū." SanskritDictionary.com, Sanskrit Dictionary, 2019. Web. 23 April 2019.
"bravIti." SpokenSanskrit.com, Spoken Sanskrit, 2019, Web. 23 April 2019.

886. "ūma." SanskritDictionary.com, Sanskrit Dictionary, 2019. Web. 23 April 2019.

887. "brū." SanskritDictionary.com, Sanskrit Dictionary, 2019. Web. 23 April 2019.
"brUte." SpokenSanskrit.com, Spoken Sanskrit, 2019, Web. 23 April 2019.

888. "vāṇi." SanskritDictionary.com, Sanskrit Dictionary, 2019. Web. 23 April 2019.
"vANi." SpokenSanskrit.com, Spoken Sanskrit, 2019, Web. 23 April 2019.

889. "veṇī." SanskritDictionary.com, Sanskrit Dictionary, 2019. Web. 23 April 2019.
"veNI." SpokenSanskrit.com, Spoken Sanskrit, 2019, Web. 23 April 2019.

890. "lap." SanskritDictionary.com, Sanskrit Dictionary, 2019. Web. 23 April 2019.

891. "anta." SanskritDictionary.com, Sanskrit Dictionary, 2019. Web. 23 April 2019.

"anta." SpokenSanskrit.com, Spoken Sanskrit, 2019, Web. 23 April 2019.

892. "lapana." SanskritDictionary.com, Sanskrit Dictionary, 2019. Web. 23 April 2019.
"lapana." SpokenSanskrit.com, Spoken Sanskrit, 2019, Web. 23 April 2019.

893. "ṭā." SanskritDictionary.com, Sanskrit Dictionary, 2019. Web. 23 April 2019.

894. "lāṭī." SanskritDictionary.com, Sanskrit Dictionary, 2019. Web. 23 April 2019.
"lATI." SpokenSanskrit.com, Spoken Sanskrit, 2019, Web. 23 April 2019.

895. "ina." SanskritDictionary.com, Sanskrit Dictionary, 2019. Web. 23 April 2019.

896. "kath." SanskritDictionary.com, Sanskrit Dictionary, 2019. Web. 23 April 2019.
"kathayati." SpokenSanskrit.com, Spoken Sanskrit, 2019, Web. 23 April 2019.

897. "ilā." SanskritDictionary.com, Sanskrit Dictionary, 2019. Web. 23 April 2019.
"ilA." SpokenSanskrit.com, Spoken Sanskrit, 2019, Web. 23 April 2019.

898. "irā." SanskritDictionary.com, Sanskrit Dictionary, 2019. Web. 23 April 2019.

899. "dhīra." SanskritDictionary.com, Sanskrit Dictionary, 2019. Web. 23 April 2019.
"dhIra." SpokenSanskrit.com, Spoken Sanskrit, 2019, Web. 23 April 2019.

900. "raṇa." SanskritDictionary.com, Sanskrit Dictionary, 2019. Web. 23 April 2019.
"raNa." SpokenSanskrit.com, Spoken Sanskrit, 2019, Web. 23 April 2019.

901. "yāna." SanskritDictionary.com, Sanskrit Dictionary, 2019. Web. 23 April 2019.
"yAna." SpokenSanskrit.com, Spoken Sanskrit, 2019, Web. 23 April 2019.

902. "raṇya." SanskritDictionary.com, Sanskrit Dictionary, 2019. Web. 23

April 2019.
"raNya." SpokenSanskrit.com, Spoken Sanskrit, 2019, Web. 23 April 2019.

903. "senā." SanskritDictionary.com, Sanskrit Dictionary, 2019. Web. 23 April 2019.
"senA." SpokenSanskrit.com, Spoken Sanskrit, 2019, Web. 23 April 2019.

5.14 THE CONCLUSION (p.252-260)

904. Wikipedia contributors. "Old European hydronymy." Wikipedia, The Free Encyclopedia. Wikipedia, The Free Encyclopedia, 28 Feb. 2019. Web. 24 Apr. 2019.

905. Snoj, Marko - "Etimološki slovar slovenskih zemljepisnih imen", p.124, Modrijan, Ljubljana, 2009.

906. "drava." SanskritDictionary.com, Sanskrit Dictionary, 2019. Web. 24 April 2019.
"drava." SpokenSanskrit.com, Spoken Sanskrit, 2019, Web. 24 April 2019.

907. "dravantī." SanskritDictionary.com, Sanskrit Dictionary, 2019. Web. 24 April 2019.
"dravantI." SpokenSanskrit.com, Spoken Sanskrit, 2019, Web. 24 April 2019.

908. "dravaya." SanskritDictionary.com, Sanskrit Dictionary, 2019. Web. 24 April 2019.
"dravayate." SpokenSanskrit.com, Spoken Sanskrit, 2019, Web. 24 April 2019.

909. "drā." SanskritDictionary.com, Sanskrit Dictionary, 2019. Web. 24 April 2019.
"drAti." SpokenSanskrit.com, Spoken Sanskrit, 2019, Web. 24 April 2019.

910. "vā." SanskritDictionary.com, Sanskrit Dictionary, 2019. Web. 24 April 2019.

911. Wikipedia contributors. "Old European hydronymy." Wikipedia, The Free Encyclopedia. Wikipedia, The Free Encyclopedia, 28 Feb.

2019. Web. 24 Apr. 2019.

912. "sirā." SanskritDictionary.com, Sanskrit Dictionary, 2019. Web. 24 April 2019.
"sirA." SpokenSanskrit.com, Spoken Sanskrit, 2019, Web. 24 April 2019.

913. Pallottinno, Massimo – "The Etruscans", p. 234, First Italian Edition 1942, Published by Penguin Books 1955, reprinted 1956, Bloomington & London, 1975.

914. Hempl, Goerge - Early Etruscan Inscriptions (Fabretti 2343-2346),p. 5-6, The University Press, Stanford University California, 1911. https://archive.org/details/cu31924029769316 (accessed on April 25, 2017)

915. Bonfante, Giuliano/Bonfante, Larissa - "The Etruscan Language: An Introduction", p.94-98, Manchester University Press and Room 400, Second Edition, Manchester and New York, 2002.

7 NON-SCIENTIFIC CONCLUSION: IT ALL ENDS WITH PROSCIUTTO (p.261-263)

916. Wikipedia contributors. "Prosciutto." Wikipedia, The Free Encyclopedia. Wikipedia, The Free Encyclopedia, 14 Mar. 2019. Web. 25 Apr. 2019.

917. "prasut." SanskritDictionary.com, Sanskrit Dictionary, 2019. Web. 24 April 2019.
"prasut." SpokenSanskrit.com, Spoken Sanskrit, 2019, Web. 24 April 2019.

918. "preṣ." SanskritDictionary.com, Sanskrit Dictionary, 2019. Web. 24 April 2019.
"preS." SpokenSanskrit.com, Spoken Sanskrit, 2019, Web. 24 April 2019.

919. "sut." SanskritDictionary.com, Sanskrit Dictionary, 2019. Web. 24 April 2019.
"sut." SpokenSanskrit.com, Spoken Sanskrit, 2019, Web. 24 April 2019.

920. "pṛ." SanskritDictionary.com, Sanskrit Dictionary, 2019. Web. 24 April 2019.
"pArayati." SpokenSanskrit.com, Spoken Sanskrit, 2019, Web. 24 April 2019

INDEX

ZORAN MASLIĆ

A

Adriatic Sea   16, 23, 247
Alba Longa   47
Albula River   47
Alps   4, 243
Apennine Mountains   21, 23, 45, 54
Arath (Etruscan personal name)   97, 98
Arretium (Etruscan city)   69, 70
Arezzo (city)   23, 70
Ariminos (Greek name of Marecchia River)   24, 25
Arno (River in Italy)   15, 18, 20, 30, 31, 34, 51, 54, 96, 254
Arnus (Roman name of Arno)   34
Aruns (Etruscan name)   230, 231
Athena (Greek Goddess)   225
Auro (river in Italy)   25, 26
Auser (old name of Serchio River)   27, 29, 30, 52
Avisio River   50

B

Balares (one of ancient peoples of Sardinia)   244
Barker, Graeme   7
Benares (holy city in India)   9
Bileća (city in Bosnia-Herzegovina)   2
Boii (Celtic tribe)   40, 63
Bolsena (lake in Italy)   36, 37, 84, 85, 86, 87, 89, 90, 155
Bodincus (old Ligurian name of Po River)   38, 39, 40
Bonfante, Giuliano (Italian Linguist)   5, 6, 9, 72, 77, 94, 96, 180, 208, 212, 257 (also see under the Bonfantes)
Bonfante, Larissa (Italian-American classicist)   5, 6, 9, 72, 77,

94, 96, 180, 208, 212, 257 (see also under the Bonfantes)
Bonfantes   36, 73, 78, 83, 85, 90, 95, 96, 97, 98, 99, 100, 102, 103, 104, 105, 108, 109, 110, 111, 112, 113, 114, 115, 117, 118, 119, 120, 123, 124, 125, 126, 127, 128, 129, 130, 131, 134, 135, 137, 139, 143, 145, 147, 148, 149, 150, 157, 159, 160, 161, 162, 163, 164, 167, 170, 171, 172, 173, 174, 175, 176, 177, 178, 179, 182, 183, 184, 188, 189, 190, 191, 192, 194, 195, 197, 198, 200, 201, 202, 203, 205, 206, 207, 208, 209, 212, 213, 214, 215, 216, 221, 230, 233, 258, 259
Borbera River   50
Bosnia-Herzegovina   7, 11, 50, 225
Brutti (one of ancient peoples of Italy)   245
Budimir, Milan (Serbian philologist)   258
Bulgarian   210, 258
Bure (torrent in Italy)   16, 17

C

Caelius Vibenna (an Etruscan noble)   237
Caere (Roman name of Chaire)   70, 71, 233
Capena (town in Lazio, Italy)   59
Capeva (ancient name of Capua)   58
Capua (city in Italy)   58
Carroll, Lewis   11
Catari (ancient Italic people)   247
Cavone River   50
Celts   12, 40, 87, 111, 253, 258
Cerveteri (Italian name of Chaire)   70, 73
Chaire (Etruscan city)   69, 70, 73
Chaisrie (another name of Chaire)   72
Cherniack, David (Canadian documentary film producer) and director)   8
Chiana (river in Italy)   16, 18, 19, 28, 52
Cisra (another name of Chaire)   71, 73

Clanis (Roman name of Chiana river) 18, 52
Clara (personal name) 137
Claudius (Roman emperor) 236, 237, 240
Clevsin (Etruscan city) 69, 73, 74, 76, 132, 230
Clusium (Roman name of Clevsin) 74
Como (Lake) 51, 86
Corssen, Wilhelm Paul (German philologist) 257, 258
Cortona (Italian name of Curtun) 77
Croatian 210, 254
Curtun (Etruscan city) 69, 77
Czech 17, 43, 210

D

Deecke, Wilhelm (German philologist) 257
Dennis, George (British explorer and historian) 11, 185
Dionysius of Halicarnassus 60
Dionysus 81
Drava (river in Italy, Slovenia, Austria, Hungary and Croatia) 254, 255, 256
Dravus (Roman name of Drava) 255

E

Emilia-Romagna 45
English 8, 20, 32, 43, 44, 45, 55, 74, 97, 98, 102, 103, 104, 109, 113, 121, 122, 132, 156, 157, 167, 168, 169, 172, 173, 174, 177, 185, 189, 190, 191, 194, 198, 206, 215, 216, 222, 225, 226, 227, 228, 242, 243, 259
Enna River 50
Eridanus (old name of Po River) 38, 39

F

Faliscans (one of ancient peoples of Italy)   64, 65
Falisci (version of ethnonym Faliscans)   65
Fellini, Federico (Italian film director)   23
Fufluna (version of Pupuluna)   79, 81, 185
Fufluns (God, Etruscan Dionyssus)   81

G

Gaius (Roman name)   224, 231
German   10, 11, 42, 43, 44, 185, 254, 255, 256, 258
Georgiev, Vladimir (Bulgarian linguist)   258

H

Hanipaluscle   230
Hannibal   63, 230
Hempl, Georg (German-American linguist)   259, 260
Herodotus (ancient Greek historian)   4
Hittite   54, 258

I

Idice (river in Italy)   16, 20
Illyria   254
Illyrian   12, 209, 247, 255
Illyrians   247, 248, 253, 255, 256
Ivanov, Vyacheslav Vsevolodovich (philologist)   318

J

Jupiter (Roman chief god)   47, 87

K

Krahe, Hans (German linguist)   34
Krishna, Nanditha (Indian historian)   151

L

La Cannara (ancient Etruscan settlement)   38, 64
Lars Porsena (king of Etruscan city Clevsin)   230, 231, 232
Larthe (old name of Marta River)   35, 37
Latin   3, 4, 10, 18, 19, 25, 26, 28, 30, 34, 37, 38, 39, 40, 43, 45, 46, 54, 55, 56, 62, 64, 65, 66, 71, 74, 77, 79, 80, 83, 92, 93, 100, 102, 104, 111, 113, 134, 135, 136, 137, 139, 141, 149, 153, 154, 156, 159, 160, 161, 162, 163, 164, 165, 166, 167, 174, 176, 183, 188, 189, 193, 198, 200, 209, 210, 216, 218, 219, 220, 221, 222, 223, 224, 225, 228, 230, 236, 238, 239, 240, 255, 258, 259, 260, 261
Latins   105, 225, 247
Lawrence, D.H (English writer)   8
Lazio   4, 45, 60
Lepontii (one of ancient peoples of Italy)   246
Ligurian (ancient people in Italy)   38, 40, 63
Limentra (river in Italy)   16, 21, 22
Livy (historian)   87, 139, 143, 151, 153, 236, 237, 238
Lucius Tarquinius Priscus (Etruscan king of Rome)   139, 236
Lydia (ancient state in Asia Minor)   4

M

Macnamara, Ellen (historian)   6, 145
Macstarna (Etruscan "name" of Servius Tullius)   239, 240
Magra (river in Italy)   16, 22, 23
Marecchia (river in Italy)   16, 23, 24, 25
Maslić, Dragoljub (journalist in former Yugoslavia)   12
Mastarna (Etruscan "name" of Servius Tullius according to emperor Claudius)   235, 237, 239, 240
Maremma (region in Tuscany)   7
Marta (river in Italy)   15, 34, 35, 36, 37, 38
Martanum (ancient Etruscan settlement)   35, 37, 38
Meta (river in Italy)   25
Metauro (river in Italy)   16, 25
Mihalkov, Nikita (Russian film director)   5
Modena (city in Italy)   62
Mutina (Etruscan name of Modena)   62, 63
Mutna (version of Mutina)   62, 63

N

Narce (Faliscan city)   64
Nepete (Etruscan city)   60, 92, 96
Nera River   50

O

Oder River   43, 44
Odra River   43
Orvieto (city in Italy)   84
Ostia (ancient port of Rome)   49

P

Padus (old name of Po River)   38, 39, 52
Pallas Athena (Gr.)   225
Pale (a city in Serbian Republic, Bosnia-Herzegovina)   225
Pallottino   (last name)   225
Pallottino, Massimo   4, 52, 58, 71, 72, 78, 83, 84, 87, 145,
                          226, 257, 258
Parma (city in Italy)   66, 67, 233
Pelasgi (version of the name of Pelasgians)   60, 65
Pelasgians (pre-Greek people of Greece)   60, 64, 65, 68, 93,
133, 173, 174
Perusna (Etruscan city)   69, 78, 79
Perusia (version or Perusna)   78, 79
Perugia (Italian name of Perusna)   78, 79
Pešić, Radivoje (Serbian scholar)   242, 259
Pliny (Roman historian)   34, 93
Po (river in Italy)   4, 34, 38, 39, 52, 95
Populonia (Latin version of Pupluna)   79, 80
Pupluna (Etruscan city)   69, 79, 81, 82, 175
Pupuluna (version of Pupluna)   79, 80, 81
Pyrgi (port of Etruscan city Chaire)   208, 209, 233

R

Rasenna (name of the Etruscan land)   118, 241, 242, 243, 248
Rasmussen, Tom   7
Rasna (version of Rasenna)   118, 241, 242
Ram River (also Rom)   50
Rama (river in Bosnia)   50
Rayna River   42
Reno River   21, 34, 40, 41, 42
Rhaeti (ancient people)   243, 247

Rhein River   42
Rhenus (Latin name of Reno River)   40, 41
Rheti (variant spelling of Rhaeti)   243
Rhine River   40, 42
Rom (river, also Ram)   50
Russia   243

S

Šamac (city in Serbian Republic, Bosnia-Herzegovina)   7
Sardinia   244
Saturnia (town in Tuscany)   60, 68
Sava, Savo (personal names)   13
Sava Bohinjka (river in Slovenia)   14
Sava Dolinka (river in Slovenia)   14
Sava River   11, 12, 13, 14, 15, 26, 94, 196
Savena (river in Italy)   16, 26, 27
Scandinavians   258
Scullard, H.H. (British historian)   151, 156
Sele River   50
Serbia   11, 50
Serbian   3, 10, 16, 17, 44, 45, 49, 55, 56, 57, 58, 76, 97, 98, 99, 100, 102, 103, 104, 106, 107, 109, 110, 113, 114, 115, 116, 117, 121, 122, 123, 124, 125, 126, 127, 129, 132, 156, 167, 168, 169, 172, 173, 174, 175, 177, 180, 189, 196, 204, 211, 225, 226, 235, 242, 258, 259, 262
Serbian Republic   225
Serchio (river in Italy)   27, 28, 29, 52
Seretos (apparent Thracian name of Siret River)   256
Servius Tullius (king of Rome)   146, 235, 236, 237, 238, 239
Shakespeare, William   11
Sharma, Vipin (Indian actor and film-maker)   7, 8, 9
Sherden (believed to be rendering of Sardinians)   244

Shiva (Hindu deity)   9
Sieve (river)   16, 30, 31
Singidunum (Roman rendition of Singidun, old name of Belgrade)   149
Siret (river in Ukraine and Romania)   256
Slavs   87, 258
Slavic   2, 12, 16, 17, 42, 43, 55, 71, 104, 123, 132, 156, 197, 202, 203, 210, 234, 246, 258, 262
Sleeping Giant Productions (Canadian TV company)   8
Slovenian   17
Statna (Etrusacn name of Statonia)   55, 56, 68
Statonia (Roman name of Statna)   56
Steinbauer, Dieter H.(German etruscologist   96, 124, 178, 182, 185, 187, 188

T

Tabaković, Risto   2, 262, 263
Tamar River (Walles)   50
Tammaro River   50
Tarchna (version of Tarchuna)   56
Tarchuna (Etruscan city)   56, 61, 74, 81
Tarquinia (Italian name of Tarchuna)   35
Tarquinii (Roman name of Tarchuna)   74, 139
Tevere (local name of Tiber)   45, 46, 47, 48, 49, 233
Thefarie (Etruscan name)   46, 208, 233, 234
Thefarie Velianas (Etruscan ruler of Caere)   208, 233
Thracian   255, 256
Thracians   253, 255, 256
Tiber River   15, 34, 45, 46, 47, 48, 49, 54, 233
Tiberinus Silvius   47
Tin (Etruscan God)   124, 185
Tinia (version of Tin)   87, 185
Tora (river in Italy)   31, 32, 33
Tyrrhenian language   173

Tyrrhenian Sea   35, 45, 54, 250, 251
Tyrrhenians   249, 250, 251
Tyrsenian language   173
Tyrsenoi   250

U

Umbri or Umbrians (one of ancient peoples of Italy)   4, 93, 244, 245
Umbria   4, 45
Umbrian   31, 54, 93, 215

V

Vara (tributary of Magra River) 23, 50
Vardar (river in Macedonia) 51, 195
Vatluna (version of Vetluna, Etruscan city)   69, 90, 91
Veia (Etruscan city)   69, 82
Veii (Latin version of Veia)   237
Velathri (Etruscan city)   69, 82, 83
Velch (Etruscan city)   69, 83, 84
Velsna (variant of Velzna)   85, 86, 90
Velsnana (version of Velzna)   86
Velsu (version of Velsna)   85
Velusna (Etruscan city)   85, 88, 89
Velzna   69, 84, 85, 86, 87, 89, 90
Velznani (version of Velsna)   85, 86
Veneti (ancient people of Northern Italy)   245, 247
Verdura River   51, 195
Vetluna (version of Vatluna)   90
Vetulonia (Italian name of Vetluna)   90
Villanovan Culture   4, 5
Vincha culture   5

Volosko (a place in Croatia)   317
Volssini (Roman name of Velusna)   313
Volterra (Roman name of Velathri)   82, 83
Voltumna (Etruscan God)   87
Volturnus (Roman God)   47, 48
Vulci (Roman name of Velch)   83, 145, 239

W

Wisła (river in Poland)   40

Y

Yugoslavia   3, 7, 11, 247, 254, 261, 262

Z

Zeus (Greek God)   185

ZORAN MASLIĆ

INDEX
OF DISCUSSED WORDS

ZORAN MASLIĆ

A

acale, aclus (Etr.)   201
acil (Etr.)   188
am (Etr.)   98
ampiles (Etr.)   200, 201
an (Etr.)   99
apa (Etr.)   102, 103
ar-, er- (Etr.)   117, 118
arac (Etr.)   184
arena (Eng.)   218, 219, 220
arm (English)   206
aska (Etr.)   213, 214
aterś, aturs, atrs, atrus (Etr.)   105
athumi (Etr.)   161
ati (Etr.)   102. 103, 105
ati nacna (Etr.)   107, 108
avil (Etr.)   117

B

bura (Serb. and Slavic)   16
bucchero (Italian type of black ceramics)   193, 194
boreas (Gr.)   17
boundary (Engl.)   119, 120

C

camthi (Etr.)   147, 148
capre (Etr.)   200
capu (Etr.)   184, 185
car-, cer- (Etr.)   112
cecha (Etr.)   129, 130

cechaneri (Etr.) 130
cehen (Etr.) 99, 100
cel (Etr.) 111, 206
cela (Etr.) 111
celi, caelius, celius (Etr.) 206
ceramics (English) 95, 188, 190, 192, 193, 195
cheat (Eng. verb) 20
chosfer (Etr.) 207
cilt (Etr.) 105, 106
clan (Etr.) 102, 103, 106
cleos (Gr.) 131, 132, 133
clergy (Eng.) 135, 136, 137
cleri (Lat) 135, 136, 137
clerical (Eng.) 135
cleva (Etr.?; Illyrian?) 73, 131, 132, 133, 135, 136, 230
column (Eng.) 215
columna (Lat.) 223, 224
culichna (Etr.) 212, 213
culscva (Etr.) 112, 113
cup (Eng.) 189, 190
cupe (Etr.) 189
curiae (Lat.) 220

D

dever (Serb.) 45
door (Engl.) 112, 113

E

elementum (Lat.) 228
ermius (Etr.) 203, 205, 206
etera (Etr.) 215, 216

eth, et (Etr.)   100

F

fanu (Etr.)   216
farthan, fartn- (Etr.)   114, 115
fasces (Lat.)   221, 222
fasena (Sabine word for 'arena')   219
favi (Etr.)   175, 176
flute (Eng.)   167

G

grab (Eng. verb)   169
grabiti (Serb. verb)   169
grnčarija (Serb. noun)   189

H

harena (Lat.)   218, 219
hinth, hinthi, hinthis (Etr.)   171
histrio (Lat.)   163, 167, 218

I

ister (Etr.)   163, 167
ita (Etr.)   100. 101

K

kana, kanna (Etr.)   120

keramikos (greek) 192
keramos (Greek) 192. 193
kleva 73, 133
krankru (Etr.) 185, 186, 187
kukuriku (Serb.) 121
kylix (Greek) 212, 213

L

laive (Etr.) 122
larnas (Etr.) 192
larnax (Gr.) 192
lauchume (Etr.) 139, 140, 141, 142
lautn (Etr.) 109, 110
lein- (Etr.) 183
luna (Lat.) 210
lupu, lupuce (Etr.) 171, 172

M

macstrev (Etr.) 157, 158, 159
mal (Etr.) 115, 116, 117
malena (Etr.) 115, 116, 117
malstria (Etr.) 115, 116, 117
man, mani (Etr.) 183
masan, masn (Etr.) 198, 208, 209, 210
mata (Etr.) 190
math (Etr.) 122
mech (Etr.) 159, 160
melicraticce (Etr.) 121
mes (Portuguese) 210
mesec (Serbian, Slav.) 210
mi (Etr.) 97, 98

militarie (Lat.) 222
military (Eng.) 222, 223, 239
muškarac (Serb.) 123
mutana, mutna (Etr.) 180, 181
murs (Etr.) 174, 175

N

nefts´ (Etr.) 103

O

olpe (Greek) 214
ona (Serb.) 99

P

palace (Eng.) 225, 226
palanka (Serb.) 57, 58, 226
palenque (Span.) 226
palisade (Eng.) 226
papa (Etr.) 102, 103
parnich (Etr.) 160
patane (Greek) 188
patna (Etr.) 188, 190
penthuna, penthna (Etr.) 119
persona (Lat.) 164, 165, 166, 167
petao (Serb.) 122
phersu (Etr.) 164, 165, 166, 167, 218
polis (Gr.) 226
pot (Eng.) 194

prosciutto (Italian)   1, 2 ,3, 4, 261, 262
pršut (Serb.)   2 ,3, 262
pruch, pruchum (Etr.)   191
prumathś, prumts (Etr.)   103, 104
purth (Etr.)   143, 144, 145
put-, puth- (Etr.)   194

Q

qutun, qutum (Etr.)   212

R

ratum, ratm (Etr.)   161, 162
reka (Serb word for 'river')   44
restm, rastum (Etr.)   118
river (Eng.)   44

S

sac (Etr.)   134
sacni (Etr.)   135, 136
sacnicleri (Etr.)   135, 136
sacred (Eng.)   134
sath-, śat- (Etr.)   177, 178
sech, sec (Etr.)   103
seka (Serb.)   103
slica (Etr.)   167, 168, 169
slika (Serb.)   167, 168, 169
slikati (Serb.)   168
snaha (Serb.)   107

snenath (Etr.)   106, 107
span-, spanthi (Etr.)   191
spur (Etr.)   232, 233
srp (Serb.)   211
strije (Serb., pronounced 'struye')   116, 117
suntheruza (Etr.)   196, 197
suplu (Etr.)   167
śuth-, sut- (Etr.)   178
śuthi (Etr.)   178, 179
śuthina (Etr.)   178
suthiu (Etr.)   178, 179
suthiusve (Etr.)   179
sveleri (Etr.)   127

T

talitha (Etr.)   123
tamera (Etr.)   181, 182
thaure, thaura (Etr.)   171
teta (Etr.)   103
thucte (Etr.)   203, 204, 205
thval (Etr.)   155, 156, 157
tiur (Etr.)   123, 124
torrent (Eng.)   32, 33
torrente (Ital.)   32, 33
traneus (Etr.)   202
trut, truth (Etr.)   128
trutanaśa (Etr.)   128, 129
tupi (Etr.)   124, 125
tur- (Etr.)   119
tura (Etr.)   138
tusna (Etr.)   187
tusurthir (Etr.)   108, 109

U

udati (Serb.) 110
ulpaia (Etr.) 214, 215
umbilical (Eng.,Lat.) 102
useti (Etr.) 124

V

vacal, vacil, vacl (Etr.) 137
varjača (Serb.) 125
vase (Eng.) 196
vatieke (Etr.) 208
vaza (Serb.) 196
velcitanus, velcitna (Etr.) 198, 199
vernacular (Eng.) 227
vernaculus (Lat.) 227
vers (Etr.) 125, 126
vertun (Etr.) 195
vetar (Serb.) 17
vrata (Serb.) 113, 114
vrt (Serb.) 11**4, 115**

Z

zavena (Etr.) 195, 196
zic, zich (Etr.) 98
zichuche (Etr.) 97, 98
zilath (Etr.) 145, 145, 147
zilch cechaneri (Etr.) 130
ziva (Etr.) 172, 173

ARYAN ITALY OF THE ETRUSCANS

ABOUT THE AUTHOR

Zoran Maslic is an award-winning film-maker from Canada known for his underground documentary trilogy In the City of Exile Kings (When You Die as a Cat, Nobody Knows My Songs, Annoying).
He also makes music videos (Zoran Maslic's YouTube channel), wrote a dystopian sci-fi novel Northern Guard and produced a folk-punk CD album Duct Tape Rose by Chad Fontaine.

www.ingramcontent.com/pod-product-compliance
Lightning Source LLC
Chambersburg PA
CBHW050428240426
43661CB00055B/2310